LINCOLN CHRISTIAN COLLEGE AND SEMINARY

W9-CBU-481

LIBRARY
OF
WALT ZORN

COMMON ROOTS

COMMON ROOTS

A CALL TO EVANGELICAL MATURITY

Robert E. Webber

ZONDERVAN
PUBLISHING HOUSE OF THE ZONDERVAN CORPORATION
GRAND RAPIDS, MICHIGAN 49506

COMMON ROOTS: A CALL TO EVANGELICAL MATURITY

Copyright © 1978 by The Zondervan Corporation
Grand Rapids, Michigan

Library of Congress Cataloging in Publication Data

Webber, Robert.
   Common roots.

   Bibliography
      1.   Evangelicalism.   I.   Title.
   BR1640.W4   269'.2   77-26188

ISBN 0-310-36630-5

All rights reserved. No part of this publication may be
reproduced in any form or by any means without the prior
permission of the copyright owner.

Printed in the United States of America

To my mother and father

Gratis

64984

CONTENTS

PREFACE

The purpose of *Common Roots* is twofold. The primary concern is, as the title suggests, to search for the roots of evangelical Christianity. The secondary concern, and one which naturally arises out of the first, is to look critically at those beliefs and practices of contemporary evangelicalism which out of harmony with historic appear to be evangelical Christianity, thus the subtitle A Call to Evangelical Maturity.

In order to achieve these two purposes, a threefold approach has been taken. Each chapter contains a statement of the problem, an investigation of the belief and practices of the early church, and a suggested agenda for evangelical Christianity.

My argument is that the era of the early church (A.D. 100–500), and particularly the second century, contains insights which evangelicals need to recover. Obviously, the early church is not perfect. Like other periods of history, the early church needs to be judged by the apostolic norm. But the best insights of the early church, those which they struggled to maintain were, in fact, those convictions which they regarded as apostolic. Thus, to recover this era of the church is to restore the earliest expressions of Christian theology and church practice which grew out of apostolic teaching.

The reader should be aware of certain limitations which naturally arise from such an approach. Because the aim is *perspectival*, the work is not oriented toward proving a case or setting forth an apologetic. Thus broad strokes are sometimes taken at the expense of details. For the interested reader, however, a generous sprinkling of footnotes has been supplied for a more detailed treatment of subjects touched briefly in the text.

The agenda I propose for an evangelical recovery of historic Christianity is concerned with five areas:

1. The church—a recovery of the *nature* of the church, both local and universal. What does it mean to be the church?
2. Worship—a recovery of the *meaning and form* of Christian worship. How does the church become a worshiping community?
3. Theology—a recovery of the basic fundamental truth of *confessional Christianity*. How does the church think about what she believes?
4. Mission—a recovery of the *basic mission* of the church. What is the purpose of the church in the world?
5. Spirituality—a recovery of the church's *devotional response* to her Lord. How may we become a more spiritual people?

All these issues are now being addressed by evangelicals concerned about renewal. For example, a considerable amount of writing has appeared on the nature of the church, with particular emphasis given to the renewal of a local congregation. Also, a voluminous amount of material has been published on the mission of the church, especially since the Lausanne Congress in 1974. Furthermore, since the publication of Lindsell's *Battle for the Bible* (Zondervan, 1976), a new flurry of issues about theology is beginning to emerge. However, only scattered attention has been given to worship and spirituality.

I have attempted to show *why* evangelical renewal is needed and *how* the principles drawn from the early church may apply to the changes which are already taking place and those which need to occur among evangelicals today. Some will argue that a return to the principles of the early church is not the *only* way toward renewal. While that may be true, I have tried to show that no far-reaching renewal can afford to ignore the basic convictions and practices of the early Christians.

Finally, it should be noted that this work is offered as a preliminary excursus into a broad range of subjects. There are many evangelical scholars, young and old alike, who are prepared to delve into these issues at a level of greater depth. If this work will generate a scholarly exchange of views which will serve to deepen our appreciation of the Christian heritage, I will be gratified.

Finally I would like to express my debt of gratitude to a number of colleagues and friends who have provided me with advice and suggestions. In particular my thanks go to Arthur Holmes, Tom Howard, Donald Bloesch, and Jim Hedstom who gave me a generous portion of their time and their valuable insights, which have served to strengthen this work considerably.

SECTION I
INTRODUCTION

Chapter 1

A Call to Historic Christianity

INTRODUCTION

This book is about evangelical Christianity. It is written to evangelicals by an evangelical who speaks from inside the movement.

This book has been written because evangelical Christianity faces an uncertain future. Certain forces have moved evangelicalism away from a traditional biblical and historical foundation. Because many evangelicals are unaware of the ways in which their beliefs and practices are not consistent with historic Christianity, I intend to state where they diverge and to set forth the historic practices of the church as an alternative.

Not everyone will agree with what I have to say. The scholarly leaders of evangelical Christianity will be the most supportive, for some of them have already aired similar concerns. People who have been raised in what I will call "popular evangelicalism" may be the least acquainted with historic Christianity and therefore may be most resistant to my proposals. Nevertheless, it should be remembered that just showing the common roots of evangelicalism does not solve all the problems. Therefore I want to outline the subjects for discussion, point to the problem, attempt to define it, and call for action. The purpose of this book is to raise the central issues which evangelicals must face in the near future, to put them into focus, and to call for action.

To begin with, let's look briefly at the situation of today's church.

13

The situation of today's church

In general, Christians around the world are longing for strong leadership in the church. With the demise of liberalism, the floundering of historic denominations, the ecumenical movement at a standstill, and the world in crisis, the evangelical church has not only the opportunity but also the responsibility to offer leadership. If this is true, Martin Marty, recognized chronicler of American religion, was correct when he stated that evangelicals must find a way to "replenish and revitalize their theological tradition."[1]

My conviction, and the subject of this writing, is that evangelicalism must mature into a truly biblical and historic faith, and that through this maturation, the replenishment of its tradition and the revitalization of its message will occur. This will not take place, however, without both a chastening and a renewing. The process necessitates a purging of our modernity and a return to Christianity in its historic form.

The situation of the evangelical church today is similar to that of more than one hundred years ago in America, when Philip Schaff wrote in *The Principle of Protestantism*, "the significance of the church has been forgotten in favor of personal piety; the sacraments, in favor of faith; sanctification, in favor of justification; and tradition in its right sense, in favor of the Holy Scriptures."[2] What is needed is a thoroughgoing reform which will restore the historic balance of Christianity to the evangelical church. As Donald Bloesch observed in *The Evangelical Renaissance*, "the hope of the church certainly does not lie in new strategies, programs and techniques. Instead it lies in a rediscovery of the catholic and evangelical roots of the faith."[3] In 1947, Carl F. H. Henry made a similar appeal in *The Uneasy Conscience of Modern Fundamentalism:*

> The time has come now for Fundamentalism to speak with an ecumenical outlook and voice; if it speaks in terms of the historic Biblical tradition, rather than in the name of secondary accretions or of eschatological biases on which evangelicals divide, it can refashion the modern mind. But a double-minded fundamentalism—which veers between essentials and inessentials—will receive little of the Lord and not much of a hearing from the perishing multitudes.[4]

I believe that evangelicals have come a long way toward reaching the goal set by Henry, but we cannot be satisfied with our progress since 1947, nor can we retreat from the challenge at hand. Instead, we must accept the challenge and prospects of the future by overcoming our modernity and recapturing historic Christian orthodoxy and orthopraxis. Only then, as chastened and newly informed evangelicals, will we be able to offer a healing and reconciling leadership to the church.

WHAT IS THE ISSUE?

The major issue facing evangelical Christianity, the one from which all other problems flow, is a kind of evangelical amnesia. Evangelicals have forgotten the past. There is a need to change what Bernard Ramm calls our "sadly deficient" state of historical knowledge.

In *The Evangelicals*, edited by Wells and Woodbridge, the contributors write of the evangelical search for historic roots. In the introduction, the editors refer to primitive biblical Christianity and imply that evangelicalism "seeks to reaffirm these truths." Kenneth Kantzer suggests that evangelicals stand "in line of direct descent from Luther, Melanchthon, Calvin, Zwingli, Knox, Cranmer, Hooker, Chemnitz, Arminius, Menno Simons, and all but the most radical Anabaptists."[5] William Pannell sees the origins of black Christianity going back to Africa with Tertullian and Augustine.[6] Bill Bentley argues "the black evangelical is an integral part of the black community. As such, he is shaped, affected, and interpreted by the collective experience which all blacks historically share."[7] Martin E. Marty sees early evangelicalism shaped by "the first and second Great Awakenings, with their accent on revivalism and personal conversion."[8] And Sydney E. Ahlstrom looks for the origins of evangelicalism "in that revolution in Christendom which the English Puritan movement intended to accomplish."[9]

While these writers are to be commended for their concern to find evangelical roots, they must nevertheless be faulted for tracing the origins of evangelicalism as a movement to no earlier than the sixteenth-century Protestant Reformation, except for an occasional reference to Augustine. This strange silence toward the ancient and medieval church could lead one to believe that the history of God's *real* people began in the sixteenth century. Another conclusion may be that modern evangelicalism is a phenomenon of the last four centuries—that twentieth-century evangelicalism is, as a matter of fact, a reflection of modern culture, shaped by the Renaissance, the

Enlightenment, the romantic era, the industrial age, and modern technology.

However, these thoughts seldom cross the minds of those who unreservedly and unquestionably identify evangelicalism with primitive or apostolic Christianity. It is this naive notion of history that concerns Ernest Sandeen in *The Origins of Fundamentalism*, "The fundamentalist's assertion of his own orthodoxy and conservatism cannot be accepted uncritically. Both dispensationalism and the Princeton theology were marked by doctrinal innovations and emphases which must not be confused with Apostolic belief, Reformation theology, or nineteenth century evangelism."[10]

Scholarship, for example, agrees that the intellectual and technological revolutions of the last half of the nineteenth century deeply influenced American thought and action and led to a variety of efforts to reconstruct the Christian message. There are some Christian groups which intentionally broke from the Christian heritage while others who had no intention of reshaping the faith did so unknowingly by allowing a particular aspect of the faith to become devisive. The immediate objective of one or more of these groups was to preserve the principle of authority.

For example, while Roman Catholicism resisted change through its overemphasis on the authority of the church, protestant conservatism resisted change by emphasizing scholastic theology, pietism, and apocalypticism. It was an overemphasis on these points of controversy that had the effect of shaping popular American evangelicalism into an expression of Christianity different from the shape of historic Christianity. *Consequently, popular evangelicalism not only represents a movement away from the reformational heritage, but even more, a digression from the historic Christian faith. Therefore, if evangelicalism as a movement is going to be more representative of the historic faith it must become more conscious not only of the cultural shape of its own faith, but also by way of contrast, to the aspects of the historic Christian faith which it has forgotten.*

It is the return to a full affirmation of historic Christianity which should be the agenda for evangelical Christianity.

AN AGENDA FOR EVANGELICALS

The agenda for evangelicals must go in two directions simultaneously. On the one hand, we need to face the negative task of overcoming our modernity, while on the other hand we need to grow into a more mature and historic expression of the faith. Both will occur without the loss of "evangelical distinctives" if we are successful in bringing together the "evangelical spirit" with the "historic substance" of Christianity. I will not describe the "evangelical spirit," but in doing so will only point to where the "historic substance" of Christianity may be found, since the latter occupies the major emphasis of the entire book.

The evangelical spirit

The evangelical spirit is the inward, passionate, and zealous personal commitment to the Christian faith which is born out of a deep conviction that faith in Jesus Christ, who died and was raised from the dead, produces life-changing effects in man and his culture. Evangelicals believe that this is the central message of Christianity, that it is the good news which gives meaning to life, that it has the power to heal the broken relationship that exists between man and God, man and his neighbor, man and nature, and man's separation from himself. This is grasped, not merely as an objective fact, but also as a personal reality, changing persons from the inside, filling the believer with a sense of overwhelming joy, providing peace within the heart, offering a new moral purposefulness and a sense of the fulfillment of life.

It is the personal apprehension of this message which has produced the three traits of a strong religion, as suggested by Dean M. Kelley in *Why Conservative Churches are Growing:* commitment, discipline, and missionary zeal. Commitment is the "willingness to sacrifice status, possessions, safety, life itself, for the cause or the company of the faithful." It is a "total response to a total demand" that arises out of a "group solidarity" which is defined as the total identification of the individual's goals with that of the group. Discipline is the "willingness to obey the commands of charismatic leadership without question" and a missionary zeal is the eagerness to tell the "good news" of one's experience of salvation to others.[11]

This evangelical spirit has always been at the forefront of renewal and reform in the church throughout her history. It was as the spirit that motivated the earliest missionaries, Stephen, Philip, Peter, Paul, Barnabas. It moved Martin of Tours to go to southern Gaul, Patrick to evangelize Ireland, and Columba to Spain. It characterized the founders of monasticism—Anthony, Pachomius, Basil, and Benedict. It is implicit in the great medieval movements of reform—the Clunaic, the Cistercian, the Franciscan, and the Dominican, which produced spiritual leaders like Bernard, St. Francis, and Meister Eckhart. It is the spirit of the great forerunners of the Reformation—Wycliffe, Huss, and Savonarola, as well as the mystics John Tauler, John of Ruysbroeck, and Thomas a Kempis. The Reformers, Luther, Calvin, Zwingli, Menno Simons, Tyndale, and Cranmer; the Pietists, Francke, Spener, and Law; the Revivalists, Wesley, Whitefield, and Edwards; and the leaders of the nineteenth-century missionary movement, William Carey, Hudson Taylor, and David Livingstone, were all men of vision born of the evangelical spirit.

An increasing number of Catholics and main-line Protestants are showing an interest in recapturing the evangelical spirit. For example, Dean Kelley, after documenting the decline of main-line Protestant churches, presents the contents of a typical discussion in a local church board, where the leaders of the church are dismayed over declining attendance, and are proposing gimmicks and other irrelevant methods to improve church attendance and commitment. In this context a woman finally gets to the heart of the problem:

> We've done all those things before, and none of them helped. We don't need more sales, more social events, more entertainments. People can get those somewhere else if they want them. They come to church for religion, and if they don't get it, why should they come for anything else? Maybe we ought to ask whether we're giving people the religious help they need.[12]

Perhaps this is the kind of sentiment that drove almost one-third of the delegates at the 1976 World Council of Christian Churches in Nairobi to enroll in the study encounter "Confessing Christ Today."[13] The report called for the proclamation of the whole gospel to the whole world by the whole church. "We are called to preach Christ crucified" and risen again, it said. Proclamation includes "the announcement of God's Kingdom and love through Jesus Christ, the offer of grace and forgiveness of sins, the invitation to repentance and faith in Him, the summons to fellowship in God's church."

In March, 1976, the National Council of Churches, which has constantly been criticized for its lack of attention to evangelism, produced a policy statement on evangelism to effect a "corrective to the recent dichotomy between 'personal' evangelism and 'social action.'" It chides member churches for their "reluctance to name the name of Jesus as Lord and Saviour" and urges them toward a "commitment to Jesus Christ" which is "not a once-for-all event" but the beginning of one's "spiritual pilgrimage of discipleship."

Catholics, as well, because of their studies in the early church fathers, are questioning some of their own practices and theology and looking with favor at evangelicals, particularly their grasp of the gospel. Paul W. Witte, a Catholic, wrote, "I have learned that there is only one truth that can motivate man simply through life: Christ. Before we can consider ourselves Christians we must have believed in Christ and accepted all the consequences of a radically altered life. Without this first basic commitment, growth in Christ through any church structure is impossible."[14]

Harry Winter, a Catholic theologian, also writes approvingly of the evangelical principle of faith. "The basic reality for an Evangelical Christian," Winter writes, "is the fact that he has been born again in water and the Holy Spirit, he has experienced Christ. The evangelical grasps one of the central characteristics of the New Testament: the disciples of Christ experienced Him; the language of the Scriptures is conviction language."[15]

Father Killian McDonnell writes favorably of the evangelical sense of inwardness and interiority, the sense of God's real presence in his life. "God is perceived as present not in terms of a philosophical imminence but present as force, power, meaning, reality, summons. . . . However simplistic their theological formulations, they have retained the ultimate reality: presence in power, presence in meaning. For this reason they endure and prosper."[16]

The main thrust of evangelical Christianity has always been and still is today a passionate zeal to follow Christ and call others into repentance and faith. In 1974, at the International Congress on World Evangelization, Billy Graham gave voice to this central concern: "we stand on the threshold of a new era . . . never before have the opportunities been so great. I believe that God will . . . direct our strategy toward total world evangelization in our time."

Because the "evangelical spirit" is at the heart of the Christian faith, there can be no movement toward "historic substance" without it. The substance of Christianity is made real through the personal appropriation of Christ's death and resurrection. Without the "evangelical spirit" historic substance is lifeless and dead.

The historic substance

My concern about evangelical Christianity is directed toward its ahistorical character. Ignoring God's work in the history of the church, it leaps from the New Testament to the present. Certainly the substance of Christian teaching is found in the New Testament, but to ignore the development of Christian truth in history is a grave mistake.

A major concern is that our ahistorical approach to Christianity has cut us off from the great heritage of thought which has grown up in the church and which has been passed down through the centuries. In the history of the church lies untold treasures of theological thought, devotional literature, and guidelines for nearly every issue which Christians face today.

My interest is to help us recapture this history, and to be so judged by it and challenged because of it that we will turn from our modernizations to the practice of the historic faith.

What would Clement, Ignatius, Irenaeus, Cyprian, Hippolytus, Athanasius, or others think of evangelicalism as the successor to their understanding of the faith? Would they look on us with favor? Would they approve of our view of the church, worship, theology, mission, and spirituality? These persons who stood so close to the apostles, who fought so valiantly to defend and preserve apostolic Christianity—what would they say to us today?

It would be impossible under the limitation of this volume to tap all the resources available. For this reason we will concentrate mainly on the substance of the early church, particularly the fathers of the second century. These fathers of the church are the direct descendants of the apostles themselves and claim to hold the faith as it was held by the apostles. We will also refer to some of the fathers of the third, fourth, and fifth centuries whose thought gave shape to the creeds of the early church. These confessions have stood as testimonies to the heart of biblical Christianity and, although accepted by evangelical Christians, have not always been understood.

In particular, we will probe the self-understanding of the early Christians of the nature of the church, worship, theology, mission, and spirituality. Hopefully their biblical understanding of the Christian faith will provide an agenda for evangelicals which will help us overcome our modernity and recapture the historic substance of the Christian faith. The special significance of their theology for evangelicals today is underscored by T. F. Torrance in *Theology in Reconciliation*. He speaks of the relevance of classical theology to the present dynamic conception of the universe. As a result of the theory of relativity and quantum mechanics our perception of the world has shifted from a dualistic and mechanistic conception to a more dynamic and fluid understanding. While our picture of the world was at one time that of a vast collection of individualized particles, externally related but essentially independent, the new revolution in physics has been transformed into one of a "single, continuous, unbroken space-time whole, constituted by a web of interrelated events themselves determined by the geometrical properties of the field in which they occur and from which they and the physical properties of the entities participating in them are inseparable."[17]

Furthermore, quantum theory has demonstrated that the substance-quantity nature of the particle, a basic feature of Newtonian physics, has been replaced by a concept which is essentially dynamic, involving both space and time. This new perception of the universe, instead of necessitating a *new* theology, makes the historic and traditional theology of the ancient church relevant once again. As Torrance observes:

> From the perspective of the new orientation in science, it is classical Greek theology, especially as expounded by Athanasius and Cyril in Alexandria, that appears most relevant to the modern scene, for it was a theology forged through a basic rejection of dualist structures of thought, whether of a "Platonic" or of an "Aristotelian" kind, and developing onto-relational concepts both, though differently, in its doctrine of the Being-and-Act of the Triune God and in its understanding of inter-personal human existence. . . . The very relevance of that classical theology for our own scientific world reinforces its claim to constitute the ground upon which ancient and modern thought, Eastern and Western, Orthodox, Roman Catholic and Evangelical theology, can come together and work out fundamental agreement, as they seek together to rethink and reformulate the essential dogmas of the Christian Church in the mode and idiom of our own day and yet in basic continuity with the foundations of theology in the ancient undivided Church.[18]

We should remember that the Reformers, Luther and Calvin, did not wish to break from the early church, but to reform the church of their day to make it truly evangelical and historic. Both agreed that the church of the first five hundred years had succeeded in maintaining the essential substance of New Testament Christianity. Calvin, for example, in the dedication of his *Institutes* to Francis I, developed at length his attitude toward the early church fathers, arguing that if the divisions between Catholicism and Protestantism were to be determined on the authority of the church fathers, "the victory in most parts of the controversy . . . to speak in the most modern terms . . . would be on our side."[19]

This picture of Calvin as a doctor of the Catholic Church is vividly portrayed in the recent biography of Calvin by T. H. C. Parker:

> So far as hard facts go, the present book adds little or nothing to what is already known. But in one or two respects it may claim to be a bit different . . . what is important is the Interpretation of Calvin. As I have been writing the book he has more and more taken on the character and stature of a doctor of the Catholic Church. A 'Reformer'? Yes, certainly, for it is the office of the doctors of the Church to reform the Church—and *ecclesia semper reformanda*. But not just 'Reformer' in its historical sense, not just the first of the Calvinists or the Calvinians or the 'Reformed' or the Presbyterians. Rather, at a time when the Western Church had become provincial, he was a doctor of the Catholic Church. Perhaps this will come through to the reader as strongly as I, myself, have felt it.[20]

In modern times the break from the historic Christian substance came when the church began to interpret its faith through modern categories of thought.[21] The shape, then, of dominant Protestant theology, both liberal and conservative as it developed through the eighteenth, nineteenth, and twentieth centuries, was neither reformational nor historic, but modern. Consequently the return to historic Christianity is also a return to reformational Christianity. Since it is in understanding the early church that evangelical Christians are most deficient, we will draw mainly from the early church fathers in this work.

CONCLUSION

In short, what is being urged is that a return to the historic church, to the great fathers of the first five centuries, is a return to evangelical foundations. Without a knowledge of these fathers, evangelicals are bound to spend years working through problems the fathers worked through, and perhaps not as well. With a knowledge of the fathers there is access to solid theological thinking as well as a direction and a source for the revitalization and replenishment of the evangelical church.

My concern is for the future of the evangelical church—to know where it is going, what path it is taking in the final years of the twentieth century. This branch of Christianity is waiting for direction, longing for a leadership that will help it become a potent world influence for the historic faith. My hope is that our subcultural evangelicalism in the next two decades will succeed in breaking loose from ideas, attitudes, practices, associations, and values which have held it back from being a full and mature expression of historic Christianity.

My desire is not to modernize, not to secularize, not to water down or in any way dilute evangelical Christianity, but to challenge it to develop into biblically and historically informed adulthood. If we can overcome our modernity, retain our evangelical spirit, and recapture the historic substance of Christianity, we will have found a way to replenish and revitalize our tradition and, as a consequence, offer significant leadership to the church and to the world.

But before we look at this task more closely, we must define who the evangelicals are.

Notes

[1]See Wells and Woodbridge, *The Evangelicals* (New York: Abingdon, 1975), p. 187

[2](Boston: United Church Press, 1964), p. 118

[3](Grand Rapids: Eerdmans, 1973), p. 29

[4](Grand Rapids: Eerdmans, 1947), p. 63

[5]Wells and Woodbridge, *The Evangelicals*, pp. 38-39

[6]Ibid., p. 97

[7]Ibid., p. 109

[8]Ibid., p. 171

[9]Ibid., p. 271

[10](Philadelphia: Fortress, 1968), p. 25

[11](New York: Harper & Row, 1972), p. 58

[12]Ibid., p. 12

[13]See David M. Paton (ed.), *Breaking Barriers: The Report of the Fifth Assembly of World Council of Churches, Nairobi, 1975* (Grand Rapids: Eerdmans, 1976), pp. 41ff.

[14]"Can Catholics Learn Anything from Evangelical Protestants," *Christianity Today, 15: 12-14, D 18 '70. See also T. Mockus with K. Anderson, I'm Learning from Protestants How to Be a Better Catholic* (Waco: Word, 1976)

[15]"Evangelical and Catholic,"*America*, 127, 8, Aug. 5, 1972

[16]"A Catholic Looks at Evangelical Protestantism,"*Commonweal XCII*, 17, Aug. 21, 1970

[17]Harris, E. E., *The Foundations of Metaphysics in Science* (New York: Humanities Press, 1965), p. 37. See also T. S. Kuhn, *The Structure of Scientific Revolutions* (Chicago: U. of Chicago Press, 1957)

[18]*Theology in Reconciliation* (Grand Rapids: Eerdmans, 1975), p. 12

[19](Grand Rapids: Eerdmans, 1949), I, p. 28

[20]*John Calvin: A Biography* (Philadelphia: Westminster Press, 1976), p. VI

[21]See Louis Bouyer, *The Spirit and Forms of Protestantism* (Westminster: Newman Press, 1961)

Chapter 2

Who Are the Evangelicals?

In the last few years several attempts have been made to define who the evangelicals are. A reading of *The Evangelical Heritage* by Bernard Ramm, *The Young Evangelicals* by Richard Quebedeaux or *The Evangelicals*, edited by Wells and Woodbridge, gives the uneasy conclusion that the phenomenon known as evangelicalism is very difficult to pinpoint. For that reason, we will try to clarify who the evangelicals are by looking first at the biblical meaning of the word; second, the theological implications; third, the historical sources; and fourth, the current sociological distinctions.

BIBLICAL MEANING OF EVANGELICAL

The word "evangelical" comes from the Greek word *evangelion*. A glance at any Greek lexicon shows that the word in its various forms is translated as good tidings, good news, or gospel.

The content of this gospel is contained particularly in the *kerygma* of the early church, which as C. H. Dodd points out in *The Apostolic Preaching and Its Development*, includes first the insistence that the age of fulfillment is shown by the life, death, and resurrection of Jesus the Messiah: that in virtue of His resurrection He is exalted as Lord; that the Holy Spirit's presence in the church is a token of God's favor toward His people; that Christ will come again as Judge and Savior; and that, on condition of repentance, forgiveness and the gift of the Holy Spirit are offered, with an assurance of salvation.[1]

This is the gospel which was preached by Paul, Mark, Barnabas, Peter, and Stephen, and was responded to with enthusiasm in Jerusalem, Antioch, Ephesus, Corinth, Rome, and many other places throughout the Roman Empire. It is the good news, the message of Christianity in its most elemental sense.

In this broad and basic sense, then, anyone who stands in the biblical tradition and preaches this gospel is evangelical no matter which denomination he belongs to—whether Catholic, Eastern Orthodox, one of the major Protestant denominations, or any of the many churches which stand in the free church tradition.

THEOLOGICAL IMPLICATIONS OF THE TERM EVANGELICAL

The term evangelical has, through its historical development, acquired specific theological connotations. It first came into prominence with the reformers whose goal was to recover the gospel. These concerns were summarized by Luther in four terms: *sola gratia, sola fide, sola scriptura, sola Christus* (grace alone, faith alone, Scripture alone, Christ alone). These theological convictions were expanded, clarified, and defined more clearly in the many confessions produced as a result of the Reformation—the most well-known being the *Lutheran Augsburg Confession of 1530,* the *Anglican Thirty-nine Articles of 1563,* and the *Westminster Confession of Faith of 1643.*

In the nineteenth century, Protestant evangelicals regrouped to preserve this faith in the nine articles of the Evangelical Alliance (1846). These terse statements of faith were adopted by more than 800 delegates, representing more than fifty churches. They asserted the divine inspiration, authority, and sufficiency of the Scriptures; the right and duty of private judgment in the interpretation of them; the unity of the godhead and the trinity of persons; the depravity of human nature; the incarnation of the Son of God and His atonement for the sins of others; the justification of sinners by faith alone; the work of the Holy Spirit as sanctifier; the immortality of the soul, the resurrection of the body, and the final judgment by Jesus Christ; and the divine institution of the Christian ministry.

A similar phenomenon occurred again with the fundamentalist-modernist debate of the early twentieth century. In order to preserve the truth, from a fundamentalist perspective, five "fundamental" doctrines were insisted upon. They included the verbal inspiration of the Bible; the virgin birth of Christ; His substitutionary atonement; His bodily resurrection; and His imminent and visible second coming. Evangelicalism, as a specific theological camp which has developed in respect to these conflicts, continues to this day to list the doctrines of Christianity which are felt to be essential to the Christian faith.

Kenneth Kantzer stands in this tradition in his contribution to *The Evangelicals*. First he summarizes both the formal and material principles of evangelical Christianity (the formal principle is "the authority of Scripture in matters of faith and practice" while the material principle is "the good news of how man can be rightly related to God"). He then suggests a number of doctrines which flow out of Scripture as essential to an evangelical understanding of the faith. These are:

(1) the eternal pre-existence of the Son as the second person of the one God; (2) the incarnation of God the Son in man as the divine-human person—two natures in one person; (3) the virgin birth, the means by which God the Son entered into the human race and, without ceasing to be fully God, became also fully man; (4) the sinless life of Christ while sharing the life and experiences of alien men apart from sin; (5) the supernatural miracles of Christ as acts of his compassion and signs of his divine nature; (6) Christ's authoritative teaching as Lord of the church; (7) the substitutionary atonement in which God did all that was needed to redeem man from sin and its consequences; (8) the bodily resurrection of Christ as the consummation of his redemptive work and the sign and seal of its validity; (9) the ascension and heavenly mission of the living Lord; (10) the bodily second coming of Christ at the end of the age; (11) the final righteous judgment of all mankind and the eternal kingdom of God; (12) the eternal punishment of the impenitent and disbelieving wicked of this world.[2]

We may conclude from this data that there is a specific body of doctrines which one ought to identify with to be an evangelical. In *Christ the Controversialist*, John Stott emphasizes that these doctrines are biblical, original, and fundamental. Thy are biblical in the sense that they affirm what the Bible teaches, original because they constitute the apostolic faith, and fundamental in that they are loyal to biblical Christianity.[3]

HISTORICAL SOURCES OF EVANGELICALISM

Although contemporary evangelicals agree with the points of doctrine outlined by Kantzer, all evangelical groups do not come from a single historical source. There are at least nine major movements in the past four and one half centuries which have produced varying shades of contemporary evangelicals. These include the Reformation; seventeenth-century orthodoxy (also known as Protestant scholasticism); Puritanism; pietism, revivalism, and the missionary movement; the pentecostal movement; dispensationalism; the fundamentalist movement; neoevangelicalism; and the charismatic movement. These nine groups include divergent strands such as the Lutheran Church; various Reformed groups, such as the Presbyterians, the Christian Reformed, the Baptists, Congregationalists, Episcopalians; Arminian bodies, particularly the Methodists, the Wesleyans, and various holiness groups; and Anabaptist groups, the more recent communal Anabaptists as well as the more traditional Brethren and Mennonite denominations.

Perhaps the most dominant force in twentieth-century evangelicalism is drawn, however, from the movements peculiar to the twentieth century.

The matrix out of which twentieth-century evangelicalism grew was the fundamentalist-modernist contoversy in the first three decades of this century. In the face of a growing denial of the validity of a biblical Christianity, certain Protestants (with what could be aptly termed an evangelical concern) regrouped, as in the past, to affirm what they believed to be the primitive gospel. A series of books, published between 1910 and 1915, called *The Fundamentals*, set forth the major issues from an evangelical point of view. Unfortunately, and to the dismay of their leaders, these "evangelicals" were dubbed "fundamentalists." By 1930 the strategy of much of this movement had shifted to a policy of retreat in the face of overwhelming opposition.

In a spirit similar to Pope Pius the X's *Oath against Modernism*, 1910, evangelicals saw the church divided into two camps: those who wanted to preserve the faith once delivered to the saints and those who wanted to reinterpret the faith in keeping with the presupposition of modern scientific conclusions. Although most evangelicals remained in their denomination, a number of extremists left their churches (considering them apostate) and began new denominations. For example, a significant split occurred in the Presbyterian Church resulting in the formation of a new Presbyterian denomination (now represented by the Orthodox, Reformed, and Bible Presbyterian churches). This particular group, especially through Westminster Seminary, represented and continues to model a scholarly tradition among the twentieth-century evangelicals who separated from their mother church.

In the meantime the effects of a parallel movement, dispensationalism, beginning in England in the nineteenth century, spread independently through America. Fanned by the popularity of the Scofield Bible and the simplicity of dispensational charts, as well as the zeal, fervor, and commitment of its Bible teachers, preachers, and evangelists, this movement took firm hold among many people who had left the historic denominations. It also gained many converts from the previously unchurched. Perhaps they grew so rapidly because they had something to offer people—an approach to Christianity packaged in an easy-to-remember and neatly systematized comprehensive view.

Soon, these two movements—what we have here termed separatist Protestant evangelicalism and dispensationalism—discovered a common allegiance against the so-called liberals, and an unofficial alliance between the two occurred. This development is difficult to trace and even more difficult to unravel. Nevertheless, it was this end result which came to be known as "fundamentalism" in the proper sense.

Meanwhile, other groups whose heritage was not rooted in the fundamentalist-modernist controversy, but whose sympathies were with a more conservative, historic, or orthodox Christian persuasion continued to model a position *in the middle,* between liberals and fundamentalists. Church groups such as the Pentecostals, the continuing Wesleyan tradition with its Arminian perspective, the blacks with their sensitivity to a biblical literalism, Southern Baptists and Missouri Synod Lutherans, as well as many Christians in the mainline Protestant churches, remained in the mainstream of Protestant Christianity.

Between 1930 and 1960 fundamentalism spread, almost unnoticed, throughout the United States and the world. Fundamentalists founded numerous Bible schools, colleges, and seminaries, a number of new denominations, mission boards, publishing houses, evangelistic associations, and other Christian enterprises.

After World War II, however, a new set of divisions and regroupings occurred as an intellectual sophistication developed within the ranks of fundamentalism. This new group of leaders headed by Edward J. Carnell, Carl F. H. Henry, Billy Graham, Harold

Lindsell, Harold Ockenga, and others, dubbed the "neoevangeli-cals," attempted to bring fundamentalism into the mainstream of the church through a genuine social concern, a renewed interest in scholarship, and dialogue with nonevangelicals. More recently, these three concerns have received further impetus by a new leader-ship emerging among the "neoevangelicals." The concerns of this movement are described by Richard Quebedeaux in his book, *The Young Evangelicals*. The result of these shifts appears to have moved many former fundamentalists closer to a mainline Protestantism. In turn, fundamentalists have disassociated themselves from this shift, making a clear distinction between themselves and the "neoevan-gelicals."

In the meantime a resurgence of evangelicalism has been growing in mainline Protestant churches. In some cases the charismatic movement is associated with this renewal, but not in all of them. This highly complex movement, which is breaking down former lines of demarcation, has been called the Evangelical Renaissance by Donald Bloesch in his book by the same title. These shifts make it clear that the identification of evangelicals is becoming increasingly complex. For this reason we will have to rely more extensively on a sociological analysis to determine exactly who the evangelicals are.

SOCIOLOGICAL USE OF THE TERM EVANGELICAL

The analysis of the historic and theological uses of the word "evangelical" demonstrates how difficult it is to identify the evangel-ical. For this reason it seems necessary to go beyond the standard definition. It is something more than a particular historical move-ment or a listing of theological beliefs. It comprises a complex variety of subcultures within the larger evangelical culture.

Webster's Unabridged Dictionary defines "subcultural" as "an ethnic, regional, economic, or social group exhibiting characteristic pat-terns of behavior sufficient to distinguish it from others within an embracing culture or society." A casual glance at the sociological make-up of evangelical Christianity readily convinces one that twentieth-century Protestant evangelicalism can be seen a a com-plex web of subcultures, tied together by common notions of faith but widely diversified in emphasis.

This subcultural approach to evangelicalism has been taken into consideration by other writers, although not identified as such.

Bernard Ramm in *The Evangelical Heritage* suggests a flexible use of the term:

> It will include the obscurantist fundamentalist and the learned Lutheran or Reformed confessional theologian. It includes the Pentecostals who, in spite of their emphasis on experience to the neglect of theology and biblical interpretation, nevertheless hold to the historic doctrines of the church. It also includes a person who might bear such a vague title as an evangelical neo-orthodox.[4]

Kenneth Kantzer in *The Evangelicals* includes conservative Lutherans, Presbyterians, Anglicans, Anabaptists, and Pentecostals but excludes Christian Science and Mormonism "which have departed from the two fundamental principles of the Reformation."[5] John Gerstner in his contribution to the same work includes Carl Henry, Jonathan Edwards, and John Wesley, but excludes Emil Brunner, Oscar Cullmann, and Karl Barth with the assertion that "if these men are evangelicals we must give it a definition so broad as to be somewhat meaningless."[6] But Donald Bloesch in *The Evangelical Renaissance* includes among many others Karl Barth, C. S. Lewis, Emil Brunner, and Dietrich Bonhoeffer as "recent figures on the theological scene who seem to be exerting an influence upon the movement."[7] Obviously there is a great deal of difference of opinion over the question "Who are the evangelicals?" In some instances the identification of an evangelical is circumscribed by membership in a particular subculture. For this reason there will always be a variety of answers to the question.

In an attempt to be more specific about these subcultural evangelical groups, however, the following list of evangelical subcultures is offered. All these groups reflect a theological unity at the center—in their confession of Christ and the doctrines which the Protestant church has always believed. But because of their various historical origins and cultural shapes they reflect a diversity of expression in theological particulars and practice in areas where differences of opinion have been tolerated. For this reason, each group has been defined by some specific denominational or attitudinal adjective which clarifies its *difference* with other subcultural groupings. To specify this more clearly, a word or phrase which captures the major emphasis of each group has been added. In this way an attempt is made to identify the group through one of its major symbols, either an institution, an organization, or a person.

Subcultural Evangelical Group	Major Emphasis	Symbols
1. Fundamentalist Evangelicalism	Personal and ecclesiastical separationism; biblicism	Bob Jones University; American Council of Christian Churches; *Sword of the Lord*
2. Dispensational Evangelicalism	Dispensational hermeneutics; pretribulationalism and premillennarianism	Dallas Theological Seminary; Moody Bible Institute; *Moody Monthly;* Moody Press
3. Conservative Evangelicalism	Cooperative evangelism; inclusive of all evangelical groups; broad theological base	Wheaton College; Trinity Seminary; Gordon-Conwell Seminary; *Christianity Today;* Billy Graham; The Zondervan Corp.; National Association of Evangelicals
4. Nondenominational Evangelicalism	Unity of the Church; restoration of N.T. Christianity	Milligan College
5. Reformed Evangelicalism	Calvinism (some with a decidedly Puritan flavor); covenant theology and hermeneutics	Calvin College and Seminary; Westminster Seminary; Covenant Seminary; Reformed Seminary; Francis Schaeffer
6. Anabaptist Evangelicalism	Discipleship; poverty; the Peace movement; pacifism	Goshen College; Reba Place Fellowship; John Howard Yoder
7. Wesleyan Evangelicalism	Arminianism; sanctification	Asbury College and Seminary; Seattle Pacific College
8. Holiness Evangelicalism	The second work of grace	Lee College; Nazarene Church
9. Pentecostal Evangelicalism	Gift of tongues	Church of God; Assembly of God
10. Charismatic Evangelicalism	Gifts of the Holy Spirit	Oral Roberts University; Melodyland School of Theology
11. Black Evangelicalism	Black consciousness	National Association of Black Evangelicals
12. Progressive Evangelicalism	Openness toward critical scholarship and ecumenical relations	Fuller Seminary
13. Radical Evangelicalism	Moral, social, and political consciousness	*Sojourners; The Other Side; Wittenburg Door*
14. Main-line Evangelicalism	Historic consciousness at least back to the Reformation	Movements in major denominations: Methodist, Lutheran, Presbyterian, Episcopal, Baptist

Although the categorization of Protestant evangelicals into these fourteen groups may be helpful, it certainly does not tell the whole story. One complicating factor is the existence of smaller groups within the various subcultures. One example may be drawn from the variety of Pentecostal or charismatic groups as described by Frederick D. Bruner in *A Theology of the Holy Spirit.*[8] Even more complicating is the existence of varying shades of ethos within a single evangelical subculture.

Richard Quebedeaux, in *The Young Evangelicals,* points to five attitudinal classifications: separatistic fundamentalism, open fundamentalism, established evangelicalism, new evangelicalism, and young evangelicals.[9] Peter Beyerhaus in his essay, "Lausanne between Geneva and Berlin," has suggested that there are six different attitudes within evangelicalism: new evangelicals; fundamentalists; confessing evangelicals; Pentecostalists; radical evangelicals; and ecumenical evangelicals.[10] Augustus Cerillo, Jr., in "A Survey of Recent Evangelical Social Thought" isolated three evangelical approaches to social problems: the conservative, the liberal, and the radical.[11]

Although we may continue to describe various shades of thought within evangelicalism, it will have to be admitted that most evangelical subcultures probably contain the whole spectrum, even though a dominant mood may be characteristic of a single institution or subculture. I think we will have to argue that the movement as a historical event is too complex and dynamic to be fully explained by neat categories, no matter how helpful they may be.

CONCLUSION

Our study of the word "evangelical" shows us that it is an extremely difficult word to pinpoint. In the broadest biblical sense it refers to anyone who believes in the message that the death and resurrection of Jesus Christ is the good news of the forgiveness of sin, the inauguration of a new humanity; in the theological sense it includes an affirmation of the doctrines about Jesus which the church has always affirmed; in the historical sense, the word points to groups of people who have focused on the biblical and theological meaning of the word in a fresh discovery of the presence and power of Jesus; and in the sociological sense the word is used of groups of Christians who are heirs of one or more of the past movements which have given fresh meaning and vitality to the word.

The evangelicals to whom this book is being written are the

fourteen evangelical cultural groups and the many subcultures within those cultures. These evangelicals are united in the common faith of the Protestant heritage, yet diversified because of the specific historic, cultural, and social movements which have given them birth. They are also united by their common participation in history, although diversified by specific geographic areas and social classes, as well as the peculiar struggles that determined their present shape. I am speaking especially to American evangelicalism, which is a product of western culture, not to be confused with British and European evangelicalism, nor with Asian, African, Latin American, Indian, or Russian evangelicalism.However, it must be remembered that it is western evangelicalism that originally gave shape to evangelicalism in these countries. For this reason, evangelicals in these countries share the problems of American evangelicalism. Interestingly, however, third-world evangelical leaders are more aware of the problems raised by American evangelicalism than the Americans are.

Because American evangelicals have recently emerged to a position of prominence and power in the United States, there is an urgent need to take a close look at ourselves, to step for a moment outside of the phenomenon, and to take time to evaluate and ponder the future of the movement. If evangelicals are to offer leadership to the church, we must stand in continuity with biblical and historic Christianity, a stance which will provide healing and reconciliation, both inwardly to the church herself and outwardly to the world.

My conviction is that evangelicalism needs revitalizing. Her strong point is her grasp of the central message of the Christian faith and the zeal with which she proclaims it. Her weakness lies in the lack of a truly historic substance of the Christian gospel. Therefore, the urgent necessity of evangelical Christianity is to become a more historic expression of the faith. It is my conviction that only through an understanding of the traditional shape of Christianity will evangelicals be able to provide a vision for the future which will bring all evangelicals together, and make Christianity a more powerful influence in the life of the world.

Notes

[1](New York: Harper, 1939), pp. 21-23

[2]Wells and Woodbridge (eds.), *The Evangelicals* (New York: Abingdon, 1975), pp. 53-54

[3](Downers Grove: InterVarsity, 1970), pp. 32-46

[4](Waco: Word, 1973), p. 14

[5]Wells and Woodbridge, *The Evangelicals* p.56.

[6]Ibid., p. 35

[7](Grand Rapids: Eerdmans, 1973), p. 33

[8](Grand Rapids: Eerdmans, 1970), chapters 1 and 2

[9](New York: Harper, 1974), chapter 2

[10]Nicholls, Bruce S., *Defending and Confirming the Gospel:* The report of the 1975 consultation of the Theological Commission of the World Evangelical Fellowship

[11]*Christian Scholars Review*, V 3, 76, pp. 272-280

Section I
Bibliography for Further Reading

Since the immediate background for twentieth-century evangelicalism is rooted in the fundamentalist movement, books on the movement both as to its origins and its theological interests should be read. Although no full and adequate treatment of the entire movement has appeared, a number of attempts have been made, although not without bias. Stewart G. Cole in *The History of Fundamentalism* (Hamden: Archon, 1937), originally published by Harper in 1931, documents the emergence of the movement from both a sociological and ecclesiastical perspective. Louis Gasper brings this study up to date in *The Fundamentalist Movement* (The Hague: Mouton & Co., 1963), bringing into focus such movements as the American Council of Churches, The National Association of Evangelicals, and the role of Billy Graham. George W. Dollar, writing from inside the fundamentalist movement, provides a rather biased presentation in *A History of Fundamentalism in America* (Greenville: Bob Jones University Press, 1973). The sources of fundamentalism are probed by Ernest Sandeen in his books, *The Roots of Fundamentalism* (Chicago: University of Chicago Press, 1970), and a smaller work *The Origins of Fundamentalism* (Philadelphia: Fortress Press, 1968).

To understand the transition from fundamentalism to evangelicalism, read Carl F. H. Henry, *Uneasy Conscience of Modern Fundamentalism* (Grand Rapids: Eerdmans, 1947), and *The Case for Orthodox Theology* (Philadelphia: Westminster Press, 1959) by E. J. Carnell. The orthodox character of this so-called new evangelicalism is defended by Ronald H. Nash, *The New Evangelicalism* (Grand Rapids: Zondervan, 1963), interpreted by Millard Erickson, *The New Evangelical Theology* (Westwood: Revell, 1968), and its impact described by Bruce Shelley, *Evangelicalism in America* (Grand Rapids: Eerdmans, 1967).

More recent books describing the changes taking place among evangelicals since 1970 include Donald G. Bloesch, *The Evangelical Renaissance* (Grand Rapids: Eerdmans, 1973); Jack Rogers, *Confessions of a Conservative Evangelical* (Philadelphia: Westminster Press, 1974); Richard Quebedeaux, *The Young Evangelicals* (New York: Harper & Row, 1974); Wells and Woodbridge, *The Evangelicals* (New York: Abingdon, 1975); and René Padilla (ed.) *The New Face of Evangelicalism* (Downers Grove: InterVarsity, 1976).

Two books which make an attempt to discover the heritage of evangelical Christianity are Bernard L. Ramm, *The Evangelical Heritage* (Waco: Word, 1973) and Don Dayton, *Discovering an Evangelical Heritage* (New York: Harper & Row, 1976). Ramm traces the evangelical heritage from the Reformation and Dayton concentrates on the nineteenth-century backgrounds, especially in revivalism. Little of critical substance has been written to show the problems of evangelical Christianity. The more recent books mentioned above contain scattered references to modernity, but no one treats the subject in any real depth. Daniel Stevick's work, *Beyond Fundamentalism* (Richmond: John Knox, 1964) is a thorough critique of legalism and deserves much wider attention than it has received. Jim Wallis in *Agenda for Biblical People* (New York: Harper & Row, 1976) points to a number of modernisms in evangelical practice. This work, as well as the publication *Sojourners* (1029 Vermont Ave. N.W., Washington, D.C. 20005) and *The Other Side* (Box 158, Savannah, Ohio 44874), deserves wide reading and careful thought, as does *The Wittenburg Door* (861 Sixth Avenue, Suite 411, San Diego, California 92101). Also, Francis Schaeffer has focused on some evangelical faults in his writings, especially *The God Who Is There* (Downers Grove: InterVarsity Press, 1968).

Even less has been written on the need to bring together the evangelical spirit and catholic substance as it relates to the evangelical subculture I have outlined. Of course, in history this has been a concern that has provoked a considerable amount of interest. The student should examine the nineteenth-century tractarian movement in England—start with Marvin R. O'Connell, *The Oxford Conspirators: A History of the Oxford Movement* (New York: The Macmillan Company, 1969). Also the Mercersburg Theology of Philip Schaff and John Nevin in America is significant. Unfortunately nothing on this movement is now in print. You should be able to find *The Principle of Protestantism* by Philip Schaff, republished by the United Church Press (Boston: 1964) in most seminary libraries. Along this line, R. H. Flew and Rupert Davies produced *The Catholicity of Protestantism* (Philadelphia: Muhlenberg Press, 1950) and more recently Bela Vassady has written *Christ's Church: Evangelical, Catholic, and Reformed* (Grand Rapids: Eerdmans, 1965). Donald Bloesch has spelled it out for evangelicals more clearly in his work, *The Reform of the Church* (Grand Rapids: Eerdmans, 1970) and T. F.

Torrance, in a very scholarly work which deserves thoughtful reading, has shown how Catholics, Orthodox, and Protestants are all evangelical at the center in *Theology in Reconciliation* (Grand Rapids: Eerdmans, 1976).

SECTION II

AN AGENDA FOR THE CHURCH

Chapter 3

Biblical Images of the Church

In recent years evangelical leaders have recognized the failure of the evangelical church to be the church. Books such as Larry Richards' *A New Face for the Church*, Francis Schaeffer's *The Church at the End of the Twentieth Century*, Ray Stedman's *Body Life*, Howard Snyder's *The Problem of Wineskins*, Donald Bloesch's *The Invaded Church*, Gene Getz's *Sharpening the Focus of the Church*, Gary Inrig's *Life in His Body*, Michael Griffeths' *God's Forgetful Pilgrims*, and John MacArthur's *The Church: The Body of Christ* are widely received and eagerly read by evangelicals in search of church renewal.

Although these books have been helpful to many people, additional help may be gained from a study of the early church. In particular, the early Christians lead us toward an understanding of the meaning of the whole church, not just the local congregation. Also, while our concern is pragmatic—making our churches *work*—the interest of the early church was theological—*what is the church?* Perhaps this suggests that a knowledge of what the church *is* should precede questions about what the church *does*. If this is true, then a knowledge of the early church's struggle to clarify the nature of the church is an indispensable prerequisite to a renewal of the church among evangelicals.

The purpose of Section II, then, is to first define the theological understanding which the early Christians had of the church and second, to apply their understanding to popular evangelicalism in hopes of finding an agenda for evangelical ecclesiology.

We will begin by looking at the biblical images of the church in the

41

New Testament. The most helpful work along this line is Paul Minear, *Images of the Church in the New Testament*.[1] Minear cites more than eighty images—including such examples as the salt of the earth, the boat, the ark, one loaf, branches of the vine, God's building, the bride of Christ, exiles, and many more. He concludes, however, that four images in particular capture the essence of the church. These are *the people of God; the new creation; the fellowship in faith;* and *the body of Christ*.

THE PEOPLE OF GOD

The most basic definition of the *ecclesia* in the New Testament is "the people of God in Christ" (1 Cor. 1:2). It is more than that, to be sure. But the church is no more than that to start with. It takes people to worship, people to do theology, people to fulfill the mission, people to be spiritual.

We first note that these people are the people of *God*. It is God who gives birth to His people. He creates, calls, sustains, and saves them. The origin of the church lies, then, in the mind of God and in His covenant-making activity. In history, God first began to create a people for Himself with Abraham, then with Moses through whom God said: "I am the LORD, and I will bring you out from under the burdens of the Egyptians, and I will deliver you from their bondage, and I will redeem you with an outstretched arm and with great acts of judgment, and I will take you for my people, and I will be your God" (Exod. 6:6-7). In the Sinai covenant Israel became God's special people. For our purposes, the most significant fact to keep in mind is the eschatological concept of the people of God which emerged in Israel, especially in the preaching of the prophets. In this sense the OT people pointed beyond the people of Israel to the people of God *in Christ*.[2]

It is apparent in the New Testament that the church understood herself to be this eschatological community of God's people. For example, consider the birth narrative of Jesus, especially the announcement to Joseph: "You shall call his name Jesus, for he shall save *his people* from their sins" (Matt. 1:21; see also Luke 1:17, 68ff., 77; 2:10,31-32). Furthermore the church throughout the New Testament is designated by words which connect it with God's people in the Old Testament. The church is "a chosen race," "a holy nation," "the true circumcision," "Abraham's sons," "heirs of David's throne," "a remnant," "the elect." Even the life of the church is often compared with the life of Israel. Christians are making their "exodus" to the "promised land." They are "aliens" in a strange land and Christ is the "bread" from heaven.

Not only is the church the eschatological community, she is also a people moving toward a goal. Like Israel, the church must be viewed in terms of the future. Michael Griffeths[3] reminds us that "the idea of traveling to a destination is common in the Bible" (see Heb. 3:1; Phil. 3:14; 1 Tim. 6:12). The image of the church as a traveling people, moving toward a destination is suggested by a variety of other images in the New Testament: The church is a pilgrim people which has not yet entered into Sabbath rest (Hebrews); an exiled people (Peter); a people who are at enmity with the world (James); a people who wrestle with diabolic powers (Eph. 6); and a bride (Rev. 19:8).

Now we must ask: In what way does an understanding of this image of the church as the people of God help set the agenda for an evangelical ecclesiology?

The answer is that it sees the church as the *historical* people of God. Thus it calls into question the ahistorical and exclusivistic attitudes characteristic of some evangelicals. Because popular evangelicalism has lost its past it has become exclusivistic, thinking itself to be the true church alone. This exclusivism was vividly brought home to me when a fundamentalist-evangelical preached a sermon titled, "The False Prophets of Lansdale." The sum of the sermon which pointed to every church in that small town was "we are right but everyone else is wrong."

The origins of this attitude in our own century, is to some extent a carryover from the fundamentalist-modernist debate. The break from historical ties which many fundamentalists made is similar to the break the Protestants made from the past in the sixteenth century. With each progressive split, these separatist evangelicals have moved further and further away from the notion of a people who are traveling toward a destination and their memory of the past has grown increasingly dim.

For example, the fundamentalist-evangelicals who separated from the main-line denominations to found new denominations or independent churches, regarded those who stayed in the historic denominations as apostate and theologically corrupt. In many cases the separatist successors, having no contact with the mother denomination, continued to perpetuate the view that everyone in the mother church was apostate or at least suspect, without taking into consideration the fact that most of those who stayed in the historic denominations were evangelicals. Nor have many separatists recognized the vast changes which have occurred within the historic denominations since the fundamentalist controversy. The result is that these fundamentalist-evangelicals have cut themselves off from their own history, and have assumed a judgmental stance toward a large portion of God's own people.

This attitude of suspicion sometimes appears within the larger evangelical camp as well. In spite of a professed spiritual unity, and cooperation in missions, evangelism, education, and publications, there are still lingering suspicions among some evangelicals toward each other. These suspicions find expression through rivalry, as well as through hostile and judgmental attitudes. These attitudes come to the foreground when evangelicals allow denominational, theological, and political differences to be divisive. Then we have to resort to labels to distinguish between fundamentalists, neoevangelicals, confessing evangelicals, radical evangelicals, and ecumenical evangelicals. Some of us have not yet learned to affirm each other, to recognize that not everyone has to be the same.

As we learn to take more seriously the broader view of the church implicit in the image "the people of God in Christ," we will gradually see the barriers of our exclusivism break down. We will learn that God's people are found in every cultural expression of His church. And, in proportion to our more inclusive appreciation of the church, we will become increasingly interested in the pilgrimage of God's people in history. An aspect of the evangelical agenda for the church, therefore, should be to affirm the whole life of the church— both in her history that stretches over the past two thousand years and in the present life of God's church in the world today. Perhaps we can begin by recognizing that the church is the people of God[4]—wherever God's people are found and by whatever name they are called—Catholic, Orthodox, Protestant, or Evangelical.

THE NEW CREATION

Throughout the New Testament the people of God are designated as the new creation.[5] The meaning of this image is that something new began in Christ, the old was done away with, and a new age began. As Paul said in 2 Corinthians 5:17, "Therefore, if any one is in Christ, he is a new creation; the old has passed away, behold, the new has come." This new creation is to be taken in both an individual and corporate sense—a new person; a new community of people.

The nature of this new creation is understood best when it is set in contrast to the old creation. An underlying motif of the New Testament is the concept of two kingdoms—the rule of Satan and the rule of Christ. The New Testament teaches that Christ is the victor over sin and death, over the rule of Satan. He "bound" Satan in the temptation; He demonstrated His victory over Satan in His resurrection; and in His return, He will completely destroy the works of Satan. Paul wrote that God "disarmed the principalities and powers and made a public example of them, triumphing over them" in Christ (Col. 2:15). For this reason, "He has delivered us from the dominion of darkness and transferred us to the kingdom of his beloved Son" (Col. 1:13). Thus, the church which is the result of Christ's victory over Satan, is a new creation, a new beginning, a new kingdom.

Although the church, as the new creation, is not to be equated with the kingdom which is still future, the church is, as George Eldon Ladd states, a *witness* to the kingdom, an *instrument* of the kingdom, and the *custodian* of the kingdom.[6] In that sense the church is the presence of the future in the midst of the old. Although the old creation is dying and will be destroyed (at the Second Coming), a new creation has been born, and is growing up in the midst of the old. A new thrust was released in the death and resurrection of Christ. It is here now, present in this life, and will be fully realized in the New Heavens and the New Earth. For this reason the major emphasis of the church as the new creation is that *the church is to be the visible presence of the new creation in the world now.*

We must now ask what implications this may have for the evangelical view of the church.

First, the biblical idea of the church as the new creation challenges the overemphasis on the church as "invisible" or "spiritual." Some of us have failed to come to grips with the biblical emphasis on the church as a visible entity within history. In our century, this failure, at least in part, may be attributed to the heavy concentration on the future through the influence of a misguided understanding of premillennialism. Because the new creation has been regarded as a future event, the church in the present is often viewed as unimportant as compared with the church in the future. Thus, the emphasis has fallen naturally on the church in the mind of God, the church which will be raised in the Rapture, the church which will return with Christ to reign in the millennium. Furthermore, among some, this view has propagated a conviction that the established church is an apostate instrument of Satan, a means by which even the elect will be led astray. This emphasis has created (especially among fundamentalist and dispensationalist evangelicals) an anti-institutional bias, and a schismatic remnant mentality. The most extreme result of this is a suspicious attitude toward any emphasis on the church as a visible and tangible society in the world.

In the second place, the motif of the new creation calls us to return to an understanding of the church as a society within the society. The church is to *be* a demonstration of the new creation in the world now. The church is the heavenly people on earth who do God's will on earth as Jesus' prayer bids, "Thy will be done, on earth as it is in heaven." There is a place where God's will is being followed perfectly—heaven. And the church is to be a kind of heaven on earth—doing the will of God. When the church is not obedient to the will of God, and when it does not stand against the will of evil, it offers no check against evil. This problem is recognized in *The Chicago Declaration:*

> We acknowledge that God requires justice. But we have not proclaimed or demonstrated his justice to an unjust American society. Although the Lord calls us to defend the social and economic rights of the poor and oppressed, we have mostly remained silent. We deplore the historic involvement of the church in America with racism and the conspicuous responsibility of the evangelical community for perpetuating the personal attitudes and institutional structures that have divided the body of Christ along color lines. Further, we have failed to condemn the exploitation of racism at home and abroad by our economic system.[7]

The Declaration then calls for a "Christian discipleship that confronts the social and political injustice of our nation." It demands evangelicals to "attack the materialism of our culture and the maldistribution of the nation's wealth and services" and challenges evangelicals to "rethink our values regarding our present standard of living and promote more just acquisition and distribution of the world's resources."

This same emphasis is picked up by the Lausanne Covenant of 1974: "The church is at the very center of God's cosmic purpose and is his appointed means of spreading the Gospel. But a church which preaches the cross must itself be marked by the cross."[8]

An agenda for the future of evangelical ecclesiology must continue to include this growing awareness of the church as the visible society of God's people who are called to act as the presence of the future, the eschatological community of the world made new through Christ. The church will begin to make an impact on society when we learn to concretize the new creation through obedience to the will of God. How this new society takes shape in the world is more clearly defined by the next image, the fellowship in faith.

THE FELLOWSHIP IN FAITH

This third biblical image, the church as a fellowship in faith,[9] emphasizes the fabric of human relationships which characterize the people of God, the new creation. This fellowship is a community—what the Nicene Creed calls "the communion of the saints."

The fellowship in faith means that the church shares a corporate life. For example, Luke describes the early Christians as being of "one heart and soul" (Acts 4:32). They even sold their possessions and lived in common, although as the rebellion of Ananias and Sapphira illustrates, this original common community was difficult to administrate. Living together was no easy thing, and the principles of being the church together had to be *learned* as each member of the community submitted to the rule of Christ. But faith in the end was to overcome the boundaries that separated people—transcending racial, economic, and sexual differences, "There is neither Jew nor Greek, there is neither slave nor free, there is neither male nor female" (Gal. 3:28). These descriptions leave no doubt that the character of this community is far different than the character of other communities.

The difference in character is rooted in a common slavery to Jesus Christ. The image of a slave, so often overlooked, is an image that Paul often used of himself in relation to other believers, "For what we preach is not ourselves, but Jesus Christ as Lord, with ourselves as your *servants* for Jesus' sake" (2 Cor. 4:5). A slavery to God immediately transforms relations on the horizontal level. No longer can one person "lord it over" another. All God's people are equal before Him and each other. For this reason the church is called the household of God (1 Peter 4:17). We all serve in His house under His authority. Thus, the church is a fellowship in faith—a corporate existence under God, a mutual slavery to each other.

We must now ask how this image of the church as the fellowship in faith is applicable to evangelicals today.

From a negative perspective, the fellowship in faith speaks against an individualistic form of Christianity—that practice of the faith which neglects the experience of the community and overemphasizes the subjective and personal dimension of the faith. It is true that the Christian faith is intensely personal. Christ died for *me*, is an article of faith. Individualism, however, is something different than a personal relationship with God in Christ. It is a form of Christianity which fails to understand the integral relationship that exists between the *members* of Christ's body. It often exhibits itself in a failure to realize the importance of involvement with other Christians in a local church; in a failure to recognize that being a Christian is not something a person does alone; in an overemphasis on personal experience; and in a devaluation of the corporate life of the church. It is what Dave Jackson calls "free-lance" Christianity.[10] This neglect of the whole body of Christ is a dangerous rejection of the body in which Christ dwells. To be cut off from the church in this way is to be put outside the means of grace for nourishment and strength received through the church. The result is a weakened and ineffective faith.

The origin of this kind of individualism lies, to some extent at least, in the failure of a misguided revivalism: a revivalism that is geared toward the personal experience of the individual with Christ to the neglect of the individual's corporate experience in the body of Christ. Because revivalism has crossed denominational boundaries, there is a tendency to tell converts to "attend the church of your choice," often without a sufficient definition and explanation of what it means to be part of the church. Thus evangelism tends to make the church less important than experience and unwittingly supports the "Christ is in" but the "church is out" syndrome. Of course, this notion is contradictory and leads people into what Casserley calls the "retreat into religion."[11] That is to say that the Christian experience becomes so exclusively subjective and individualistic that it stands in danger of losing a sufficient emphasis on the historical objectivity of the Christian religion.

Christianity is not "my experience" with Christ, as important as that may be, rightly understood. Rather, Christianity is the objective event of God incarnate in Jesus Christ who died and was raised again to establish a new humanity, the church. It is in and through the church as Christ's body that the experience of Christianity is realized.

This desire to recapture the corporate community life of the people of God in the church lies at the heart of current church renewal, especially among charismatic evangelicals and churches which have taken a more open attitude toward the reality of the Spirit in the life of the church. It has found specific expression in the many communities which have been formed recently in the United States such as Reba Place Fellowship in Evanston, Illinois, Koinonia Partners in Americus, Georgia, and Bethany Fellowship in Minneapolis, Minnesota.[12] Other forms of community are taking shape in local churches such as the Church of the Redeemer in Houston, Texas, and Circle Church[13] and LaSalle Church,[14] both in Chicago. The emphasis of each of these communities, and many more like them, is to break through the institutionalized individualism and the facade it wears to create new, open, and dynamic Christian relationships which demonstrate, by the presence and power of the Holy Spirit, a new fabric of relationships more akin to the early experience of the church described in the opening chapters of Acts.

Evangelicals must not stop, however, with the recovery of the local church as community alone. Granted, the focus of community for each Christian is the local body of believers, but beyond that we must face the implications of our relationship to the global community in faith, as well as our relationship to the church throughout history, and the departed saints who are now with Christ. In a mystical way we are members of the whole church, the living and the dead who constitute the fellowship in faith.

THE BODY OF CHRIST

The fourth image of the church, the body of Christ,[15] brings the other images together and puts the church into an incarnational focus:[16] The people of God who are a new creation, who share a common life together in Christ constitute His body. Christ is still present in the world, no longer physically and literally, but spiritually and mystically in His body, the church.

In Paul the "body of Christ" is understood in antithesis to the "body of death." This contrast is expressed in Romans 5:12-21. Here there are two humanities: those who stand in solidaric relationship with Adam and constitute the body of death; and those who stand in a solidaric relationship with Christ and constitute the body of life.

Throughout Romans Paul discusses the place of the believer in the body of Christ. In Christ's body the believer has "died to sin" (6:2); been baptized "into his death" (5:3); "buried with him in death" (6:4). Now that the believer participates in his body (7:4) the believer is to die to the body of death and live in the new life. The believer is no longer a slave to sin (6:20-23) because there has been a deliverance from "the body of death" (7:24), a freedom "from the law of sin and death" (8:2).

The body represents the whole self, including will and heart, soul and mind, as well as the physical parts. For this reason, *membership* in the body is not a casual joining of a group of people, but an incorporation into the body of Christ, the visible body of people here on earth who belong to Him. These members have various gifts as Paul details in 1 Corinthians 12:1-14. And these gifts are to be used for the edification of the body, the building up of each other to a mature and growing faith. There is such a solidaric relationship between these members, such as interdependence, that "if one member suffers, all suffer together; if one member is honored, all rejoice together" (1 Cor. 12:26).

Paul's reference to the church as the body of Christ is therefore not a mere metaphor containing social and psychological value, but a statement about the humanity of that relationship which exists between Christ and the redeemed. As Casserley states, "To say that the church is the body of Christ is to say that He is entirely one with it, that the existence of the church is an essential aspect or dimension of His existence."[17] From an incarnational perspective, the church is not a human organization, but a divine creation which, in a mystical, yet real way, coinheres with the Son who is made present in and through it.

This mystical concept of the church is rooted in the holistic conception of reality which the early Christians inherited from the Old Testament. Like the Jews, the early Christians did not function with the dualistic distinctions between spirit and matter, secular and sacred. They believed in the coinherence of the spiritual and the material, not in such a way that there is a side-by-side conjunction, but through a real union which did not destroy the identity of each property. This incarnational theology, the union of the divine and the human, regulated the early Christian perception of the church. If affirmed the church as the divine and visible body of Christ—in whom Christ is mystically present. Christ is seated at the right hand of the Father *and* really present in the world through the church. Ray Stedman captures this idea when he states "the holy mystery of the church . . . is the dwelling place of God. He lives in the people. That is the great calling of the church . . . to make visible the invisible Christ."[18]

The "body" image of the church is not a mere organization of human persons, but a new revolutionary society of people. Because the church has been reconciled to God, the people of God stand in a new relationship to each other and the world. As a new order, a new humanity, the church has always had within it the power to be an explosive force in society and in the history of the world. For it is called not to *contain* its message, but to live and to proclaim its message, calling all people into a repentance from the old body, the old humanity, the old creation, Satan's kingdom, the former age, into the new body, the new humanity, the new creation, the new kingdom, the new age.

How does this image of the body of Christ relate to evangelicals?

A major problem among many evangelicals is the failure to have an incarnational understanding of the church. This failure has caused many to view the church as a social institution, a psychiatrist's couch, an evangelistic tent, or a lecture hall. The current attempt to bring renewal by putting chairs in a circle, singing with a guitar, meeting in homes, and studying the Bible in small groups without the rediscovery of the incarnational nature of the church may be less the beginning of renewal than the last gasp before death.

The origin of this atheological approach to the church lies in the process of secularism. The world has in a real sense gotten into the church. During the last four centuries the church has been unknowingly shaped by social, political, and philosophical forces: democracy and capitalism have given rise to the rugged individualism expressed in the fierce concern for independence among many of our autonomous churches; denominationalism reflects the social divisions of society as suggested by H. Richard Niebuhr in *The Social Sources of Denominationalism;* [19] the industrial movement has produced wealth and with it the church has become a landed institution, a corporation wielding economic power through heavy investments; and enlightenment rationalism has robbed the church of her mystical self-conception so that by many she is regarded as little more than a human organization.

This identification with the structures of society and culture in the modern period differs only in kind from the accommodation of the Roman Catholic church to Roman law and social structure in the medieval period. *What is needed now as much as was needed in the sixteenth century is a theological reform of such a nature that the evangelical church will be shed of its social, political, and cultural identification. It must allow the true nature of the church as the mystical presence of Christ in the world through His people, the body, to transcend worldly identification, allowing the church to be the church.* Certainly this recovery must be central to the agenda for evangelical ecclesiology.

CONCLUSION

In this chapter we have explored the biblical images of the church and their implications for the practice of popular evangelicalism. The image of the church as the *people of God* calls us to abandon our ahistorical and exclusivistic notions of the church for a broader perspective—putting us in touch with the church throughout history and around the world. The church as the *new creation* bids us make visible Christ's victory over evil, to be the new humanity in the midst of the old. This newness is concretized in the *fellowship-in-faith*, the visible form of God's people who constitute the new creation. And this church is called *the Body of Christ* because in it and through it the presence of Christ in the world is mystically experienced and known.

It must be kept in mind that these images come from the world view of the New Testament which was Hebraic rather than Greek. For this reason the idea of the church is captured through images rather than logical propositions. These images point to the reality of the church as many sided, one which lies beyond logical definition.

They bear witness to truths that lie beyond a full human comprehension. Consequently, when we sense even an inkling of their depth, we can no longer treat the church light-heartedly or view it as a mere human organization. Instead, our involvement in the church and love for the church becomes a visible and tangible way of relating concretely to Jesus Christ.

In addition to these images the Christians of the early centuries regarded the church as *one, holy, catholic,* and *apostolic.* We turn now to an examination of these terms as they were understood in the historic church, looking again for principles for an evangelical agenda.

Notes

[1](Philadelphia: The Westminster Press, 1970)

[2]See Rudolf Schnackenburg, *The Church in the New Testament* (New York: The Seabury Press, 1965), pp. 149-157; Minear, *Images*, pp. 66ff.

[3]*God's Forgetful Pilgrims* (Grand Rapids: Eerdmans, 1975), p. 15

[4]In this respect see the "Dogmatic Constitution on the Church" in *The Documents of Vatican II* (New York: Association Press, 1974), pp. 350ff.

[5]Minear, *Images*, pp. 105ff.

[6]*A Theology of the New Testament* (Grand Rapids: Eerdmans, 1974), pp. 105ff.

[7]Sider, Ron (ed.), *The Chicago Declaration* (Carol Stream: Creation House, 1974), p. 1

[8]Douglas, J. D. (ed.), *Let the Earth Hear His Voice* (Minneapolis: World Wide Publications, 1975), p. 5, Article 6

[9]Minear, *Images*, pp. 136ff.

[10]*Living Together in a World Falling Apart* (Carol Stream: Creation House, 1974), pp. 46ff.

[11]Casserley, J. V. Langmead, *The Retreat from Christianity* (New York: Longmans, 1952)

[12]For a description of these communities, see Jackson, *Living Together*

[13]Mains, David, *Full Circle, The Creative Church for Today's Society* (Waco: Word, 1976)

[14]See Jim and Marti Hefley, *The Church That Takes on Trouble* (Elgin: David C. Cook, 1976)

[15]Minear, *Images*, pp. 173ff. See also Ray Stedman, *Body Life* (Glendale: Regal, 1972); John MacArthur, Jr., *The Church: The Body of Christ* (Grand Rapids: Zondervan, 1973); Gary Inrig, *Life in His Body* (Wheaton: Harold Shaw, 1975)

[16]A distinction should be made between the principle of the incarnation and the literal incarnation. There is only one incarnation of God, and that is in Jesus Christ. Seeing the church in terms of an incarnational focus stresses the presence of Christ in the church in a mystical way. This avoids the error of seeing the church as a literal extension of the incarnation. See Alan Cole, *The Body of Christ* (London: Hodder & Stoughton, 1964), pp. 67ff.

[17]Casserley, J. V. Langmead, *Christian Community* (New York: Longmans, 1960), pp. 16-17

[18]Stedman, *Body Life*, p. 15

[19](New York: Word Publishing, 1972)

Chapter 4

The Historic "Marks" of the Church

In the words of the Nicene Creed the Christian declares, "We believe in one Holy, Catholic and Apostolic Church." This confession is not a belief *about* the church, but a belief *in* the church and in Christ's presence in the world through the church. In this sense, then, faith in the church is not limited to a belief in the "invisible" and "spiritual" church. Rather it specifically confesses to faith in the visible church—the church in history. And, as such, it points to the mystery of Christ's presence in the world in the church. These ideas are all very evident in the four "marks" of the church: *One, Holy, Catholic,* and *Apostolic.* We will try to determine now what the early church understood by these marks, and how we, as evangelicals, may benefit through a restoration of the historic meaning and practice of the truth embodied in these terms.

THE CHURCH IS ONE

One of the problems of evangelical Christianity is that some of us have relegated the oneness of the church to an "invisible" or "spiritual" church which exists in the mind of God. The oneness of the church, however, which is first expressed in the words of Jesus "that they may all be one . . . that the world may believe that thou hast sent me" (John 17:21), appears to have a distinctly visible emphasis.[1]

The early church fathers certainly understood Jesus' statement in terms of a visible unity. For them, any break with the church was taken as a serious breach against Christ's body. For example, in a letter to the Corinthian church on the occasion of a revolt by some of the younger members of the church against the elders, Clement, the Bishop of Rome (A.D. 96), pointed to the seriousness with which he took the unity of the body: "Why do we divide and tear to pieces the members of Christ, and raise up such strife against our own body and have reached such a height of madness as to forget that we are members of one another?"[2] Likewise, in the *didache* (c. 100), a prayer over the bread at the *agape* feast points to the esteem in which unity was held: "Even as this broken bread was scattered over the hills and was gathered together and became one, so let thy church be gathered together from the ends of the earth into thy kingdom."[3]

It was this kind of spirit which stood behind the more elaborate portrayal of unity found in *The Unity of the Church* by Cyprian, Bishop of Carthage (A.D. 250).

> The Church also is one, which is spread abroad far and wide into a multitude by an increase of fruitfulness. As there are many rays of the sun, but one light; and many branches of a tree, but one strength based in its tenacious root; and since from one spring flow many streams, although the multiplicity seems diffused in the liberality of an overflowing abundance, yet the unity is still preserved in the source. Separate a ray of the sun from its body of light, its unity does not allow a division of light; break a branch from a tree,—when broken, it will not be able to bud; cut off the stream from its fountain, and that which is cut off dries up. Thus also the Church, shone over with the light of the Lord, sheds forth her rays over the whole world, yet it is one light which is everywhere diffused, nor is the unity of the body separated. Her fruitful abundance spreads her branches over the whole world. She broadly expands her rivers, liberally flowing, yet her head is one, her source one; and she is one mother, plentiful in the results of fruitfulness; from her womb we are born, by her milk we are nourished, by her spirit we are animated.[4]

In spite of this stress on unity in the early church, there were some minor divisions. Nevertheless, S. L. Greenslade argues that there is a "relative truth" in describing the early church as undivided, especially given "the seriousness with which the early church viewed any breach of unity."[5] Their concern for union, he states, was not because it was "uneconomical in manpower or money" but *"because disunion is in itself sin, and therefore to be fought against."*[6] (Italics mine.)

However, this concern for union did not extend to the heretical bodies. For example, no attempt was made to secure union with the gnostic groups. Instead, the concern for union was always directed toward the schismatics, those who held the same beliefs but were separated from the church as a result of differing social and economic influences, differences in worship practices, and problems of discipline or rivalry.

Having the early church's concern for unity in mind, we now ask how this concern may apply to evangelicals today.

It is a recognizable fact that evangelical Christianity is characterized by a number of divisions: Fundamentalists vs. neoevangelicals; conservatives vs. progressives; noncharismatics vs. charismatics; covenantalists vs. dispensationalists; Arminians vs. Calvinists; premillennialists vs. amillennialists, to name a few. For these reasons it appears obvious that evangelicals could learn much from the early church's concern for unity.

To begin with, we need to recapture the early church's theological understanding that the oneness of the church belongs to the *essence* of the church. For this reason, evangelicals should consider the recovery of an adequate theological understanding of the church to be the first step in our agenda for the church.[7] It is not the task of this book to state a theology of the church. However, it is my concern to point toward the theology of the early church with her emphasis on the mystical union between the church and Jesus Christ. This unity is expressed in a common creedal confession, a common ministry passed down by the laying on of hands, a common worship in the single loaf and cup, and a common mission in the world. On the other hand, an adequate theology of the church cannot ignore the pluriformity of the church. The church has unfolded in many forms, and no one single external form stands alone as the *correct* visible expression. As the church settled in various geographical areas and as it penetrated through a variety of cultures, it found expression in multifaceted forms. Thus, the insistence that the church must exist in a single form is a denial not only of the richness of creation, but also of the complexities of the human response.[8]

Nevertheless, the existence of pluriformity dare not be used as an excuse for division. Our first task, then, is to develop a theology of the church which affirms both the unity and the diversity of the church as seen in the unity of truth and the diversity of form. The next step is to practice this conviction by assuming an open position toward each other. That is, instead of being divided over secondary issues such as separatism, the gifts, cooperative evangelism, or distinctions between fundamentalist, neoevangelical, confessing, radical, or ecumenical evangelicals, or the differences between Calvinists, Arminians, dispensationalists, etc., we must learn to accept this diversity as part of the life of the whole church. To some extent this already has begun to happen through the World Evangelical Fellowship. (This fellowship, founded after World War II, was the successor to the original Evangelical Alliance of 1846, and exists to organize and stimulate the growth of national evangelical fellowships of which there are more than forty already in existence.)

Next, we should begin to develop a conscious unity of evangelical Christianity throughout the world. Perhaps our model could be the unity of second-century Christianity: local congregations clustered around centers such as Jerusalem, Alexandria, Antioch, Carthage, and Rome. These centers expressed their unity by a common allegiance to apostolic truth. When the time came for these churches to confront an issue as they did in Acts 15 (the Judaizers), or as they did later in the Arian Controversy (Council of Nicea, A.D. 325), the church spoke out of consent and called on the local churches to weigh carefully the authority of their gathering. In this way the local church and the universal church sought to speak with one voice. It was not so much an organizational or hierarchical unity as it was a unity based on a common faith, ministry, worship, and mission. However, it did not lack structure, for the outward structure was established on the authority of the apostles passed down in the church through the ordained ministry.

For evangelicals today, a similar approach may be to recognize the various national evangelical fellowships organized into the world evangelical fellowships as the structure through which evangelical unity is expressed. However, the problem is much deeper than a mere superficial recognition of these organizations. Any serious attempt to deal with the problem will eventually force us to take a close look at the threefold office of the ministry (deacon, elder, bishop) as well as the question of apostolic authority.[9] I believe these questions are in order and will, in the near future, become an issue in the evangelical agenda. Since the limitations of this writing will permit us to discuss this subject no further here, let it be sufficient to say that an active world organization of evangelicals is a desirable and perhaps necessary step in the recovery of unity.

A world expression of evangelical unity, however, must be seen as an initial goal of evangelical ecclesiology. Beyond this, evangelicals ought to pray and work toward an expression of world-wide unity with all Christian communions. I do not speak of a world church— every Christian becoming a catholic or an orthodox, or an ecumenical, or an evangelical. Instead, we need to envision a unity which accepts pluriformity as a historical reality, one which seeks for unity in the midst of diversity. In this sense the catholic, orthodox, ecumenical, and evangelical churches would be seen as various *forms* of the one true church—all based on apostolic teaching and authority, finding a common ground in the witness of the undivided church. Again, this is not to advocate a superficial relativism. There are numerous theological and historical differences that now stand in the way of such a realization, not the least of which is coming to grips with the meaning of the church as holy, to which we now turn.

THE CHURCH IS HOLY

One of the major problems we face is the need to come to grips with the holiness of the church. This is expressed in the admonition of Peter: "You shall be holy, for I am holy" (1 Peter 1:16). We may understand this statement not only in the individual sense, but also in the sense of the whole body of Christ, for Peter defined the church as a "chosen race, a royal priesthood, a holy nation, God's own people" (1 Peter 2:9). While all Christians agree that the church is holy, not all concur on the specific content and meaning of her holiness. The majority of Christians admit that it does not refer to a state of holiness achieved by individual members of the church. Also, it is generally agreed that holiness belongs to Jesus Christ; that the church which is baptised into him is holy because of His holiness, and that Christ through the Holy Spirit summons the Church to holiness (Rom. 1:7; 1 Cor. 1:2).[10]

Even in the ancient church there was no consensus on the meaning of "holiness" at first. Some leaders demanded personal holiness of church members and made little allowance for the process of sanctification, either in the individual or in the corporate sense. The issue for these "rigorists" centered around the inclusion of sinners in the church. The issue revolved in particular around professed Christians who, in times of persecution, swore allegiance to the emperor. When the persecution was over many of these "traitors" wanted to return to the church. Church leaders were divided over the course of action to be taken. One leader, Novation, argued against read-mittance on the basis that a church which contains apostates and allows their reconciliation ceases to be holy and so ceases to be the church. Because the established church advocated leniency, Nova-tion broke with the church and, regarding it as apostate, rebaptized the baptized Christians who desired to be part of his communion. Likewise, the Donatists,[11] who were horrified by the many lapsed Christians during Diocletian's persecution of the Christians, insisted on the purity of the church tested by the "saintliness of its members."

But the church in general agreed with Callistus of Rome that the church is like Noah's ark containing both the clean and the unclean. Pointing to the parable of the tares, Callistus insisted that the rigorists were usurping the prerogative of divine judgment.[12] The argument was that the wheat and the chaff grow side by side, thus the church contains both sinners and saints. The emphasis was placed on holiness as a quality of perfection that belongs to Jesus Christ by virtue of who He is, and to His church by virtue of what He has done for her. Thus the holiness of Christ's church is not a realized holiness but an anticipated holiness. The church that is "holy and blameless" without "spot or wrinkle" is the one the Son will present to His Father. Therefore, the church on earth may be regarded as both holy and unholy.[13] It is both divine and human.

We must now ask how the early Christians' belief in a "holy" church may be applied to evangelicals today. In the first place, we may point to two problems which prevent some of us from practicing the holiness of the church as it came to be understood in the second century. First, some of us are characterized by a moral rigorism which demands too much of the church, acting as though the church in its earthly pilgrimage can attain holiness. This attitude is evident in the inflexibility of the contemporary rigorists who, having set high personal standards for church members, act with intolerance and a lack of love toward those who fail to meet these standards. Often, this rigorism becomes a group attitude evidencing itself in the approach of a particular church or denomination over against another (i.e. General Association of Regular Baptists vs. American Baptists). This rigorism fails to recognize the *sinfulness* of the members of the church, expecting too much by way of personal holiness.

The second problem is that the same group which demands moral holiness often is characterized by a lax attitude toward the sinfulness of division in the Body of Christ. This contradiction in practice often is expressed in a self-righteous attitude toward other denominations (they are apostate). Furthermore, it often is characterized by little or no concern to heal divisions in the church. The end result is a denial that holiness is eschatological.

The way out of the above dilemma may result from a twofold understanding: first, there is the need to emphasize the biblical teaching that believers in Christ are "saved solely by God's grace in the blood of Jesus Christ (Rom. 3:24f.; 2 Cor. 5:18; Eph. 2:5; Titus 2:14; 3:7) and sanctified by the Holy Spirit in order then to lead a holy life, thankfully and obediently (cf. 1 Thess. 4:3-8; Rom. 6:12f., 19)"[14] In this conviction evangelicals are united. Second, there is a need to recover an understanding of the church as *simul justus et peccator* ("at the same time righteous and sinner"). This conviction has not received adequate attention among some evangelicals. Thus, we will look at it more closely.

Although the *simul justus et peccator* term was first coined by Luther, the idea reaches back into the understanding and practice of early Christianity. Like the doctrines of justification and sanctification, it affirms the church's standing before God in Christ simultaneously with the church's life in the world. The church is sinless before God but sinful in the world. Luther himself speaks of the church in this manner:

> God deals so wonderfully with his saints that he constantly brings it about in the church, that the church is holy and nevertheless not holy, that someone is righteous and at the same time not righteous, that another is blessed and at the same time not blessed.[15]

This recognition of the church's sinfulness in no way supports an attitude of laxness toward the church. The Reformers urged their fellow Christians to bring the earthly church into conformity to the church which exists in the mind of God. Calvin, for example, said, "as then it is necessary for us to believe in the invisible church which is seen by the eyes of God alone, we are enjoined to regard this church which is so-called with reference to man, and to cultivate its communion."[16] This attitude explains the tireless efforts on the part of many to bring about union between the catholic and protestant churches.[17]

There are a number of ways this *simul* approach to the church may be of help to evangelicals. In the first place, it will help us recognize that all branches of the church are a part of the whole. No particular visible church entity has the right to lay exclusive claim to the nomenclature "body of Christ" for herself. The whole church is much greater than the sum of her parts, and the multitudinous variety of the church shows her fullness more than any particular branch. The church includes all who confess Jesus as Lord.

Second, a recognition of the *simul* will help us become more aware of the humanness of the church. Because of her humanity she is subject to worldliness and even heresy. Throughout history the church has repeatedly accommodated herself to the outward forms of culture. There has always been a tendency to identify the visible church with a particular ecclesiastical structure, drawn more from culture than the Scriptures. This was certainly the case with the Roman Catholic Church, which reflected the juridical, sociological, and political categories of the Roman Empire as well as the eastern church in her adoption of Byzantine law and the procedure of the Byzantine court. The situation became aggravated in the West as the Roman Church became what T. F. Torrance calls an "overlay of monolithic ecclesiastical structure."[18]

When the Roman Church subjected the historic conception of the church to its own magisterium and began to exercise spiritual coercion, the church was less a visible, spiritual community of believers than it was an ecclesiastical ruling class defined by canons, regulations, and hierarchical authority. This is the reason why the Reformation *had* to take place. And because the Reformers recognized the tendency of the church to become influenced again and again by the standards of the world, they insisted that the earthly church must always be *ecclesia semper reformanda* (the church always reforming itself).

Third, the recognition of *simul* will help us become more tolerant of the weaknesses of the church. By recognizing that the church is caught in that tension between the "now" and the "not yet," we can learn to live with a true historic perspective in mind, anticipating the completeness and fullness of the church's holiness in the eschaton and working now on earth toward a tangible and visible demonstration of what the church is called to be. In particular we will have to take seriously the ontological oneness and holiness of the church and seek to manifest these by both our attitudes and our deeds.

In summary, we have seen that the holiness of the church is like that which belongs to the justified sinner—holy before God, yet sinful in the earthly working out of her holiness. We turn now to the third "mark" of the church—catholicity.

THE CHURCH IS CATHOLIC

A third problem of popular evangelical Christianity is her failure to understand what it means to participate in the full catholicity of the church.

The word "catholic" was first used by Ignatius when he wrote "wherever Jesus Christ is, there is the catholic church."[19] By this designation he pointed to the fullness of truth, i.e., the church that is catholic has all the truth. It has Jesus Christ.

A more definitive insight into the early church's use of the word catholic is provided by St. Cyril of Jerusalem in his *Catechetical Lectures:* It is called catholic then because it

> extends over all the world, from one end of the earth to the other; and because it teaches universally and completely one and all the doctrines which ought to come to men's knowledge, concerning things both visible and invisible, heavenly and earthly; and because it brings into subjection to godliness the whole race of mankind, governors and governed, learned and unlearned; and because it universally treats and heals the whole class of sins, which are committed by soul and body and possesses in itself every form of virtue which is named, both in deeds and works, and in every kind of spiritual gifts.[20]

In St. Cyril we see that the world catholic not only refers to that which the church possesses, but also to her task, i.e., to bring the whole world into an obedience to Jesus Christ.

Bela Vassady, a modern Protestant, in an attempt to come to grips with the full meaning of the word catholic, defines it by such words as "universal," "identical," "orthodox," "continuous," and "wholeness or fullness."[21] The church is *universal*, he argues, not only in the sense that it is world-wide, but also in the sense that it is grounded in the universality of the Atonement. The church is *identical* in that it always remains true to itself in history, that is to say that the church is always to remain *orthodox*. Consequently to identify with catholicity is to believe in the *continuity* of Christ's work in history and to affirm the *whole* faith.

The significant issue we must face is this: is there any one church which is catholic? Is there any one body which meets all the above requirements and has within it the *whole* catholic faith? There is a tendency among orthodox, Roman Catholic, and some evangelicals alike to regard their church and *only* their church as being the true catholic church of Jesus Christ. Such a claim is a denial of the present earthly, sinful condition of the ONE HOLY church. The full church is not seen in any one denomination or body. Rather, every branch of the church should be seen as part of the whole. The church catholic therefore needs every branch of the church to be complete.

For this reason there are two trends which we ought to overcome if we would affirm the catholicity of the church. The first is the spirit of sectarianism and the second is the pat answer of the "spiritual" unity of the church.[22]

Sectarianism is the spirit which regards its own position as the right one. This attitude has kept some evangelicals from associating with other Christians and, thus, from the contribution they could make toward the fullness of evangelical Christianity. We tend to affirm the unity that stands at the center of our mutual confessions and then act with an open attitude, an inquiring mind, and an accepting heart toward those churches with which we disagree. On the other hand, however, we must avoid an affirmation of spiritual unity on grounds that are theologically superficial and inadequate. To say, "We are one in the Spirit" or "We are one in Christ" really doesn't mean much apart from the content attached to the statement. The early church understood that her catholicity was built on apostolic doctrine and authority. Likewise, evangelicals must avoid the dangers of a cheap unity—one based on slogans and experiences rather than truth.

The fact is that the differences between churches *do* matter. The question is not, "How can we overlook these differences?" but, "How can we achieve a church which includes the many facets of truth?"[23] In other words, how can we have unity without conformity, recognizing the manifold and diverse nature of the church, affirming it whole, both in its many expressions throughout history and its many expressions in culture now? This is true catholicity; it is not obtained by overlooking differences but by accepting them and understanding them as a vital part of the nature of the church.

There are two steps then that evangelicals should take to recover catholicity. The first is to establish unity and catholicity among evangelicals. It is difficult to imagine evangelical Christianity having a world-wide impact as long as it continues to be divided against itself. Evangelical leaders, representing their various traditions, ought to meet together in a council to work through their theologies, attempting to distinguish between that which is primary and that which is secondary. Prime consideration ought to be given to apostolic Christianity, to that which has been affirmed in history and passed down through the centuries. Then, a concerted effort should be made to determine the historical causes which stand behind our theological differences. Such a course of action would unify evangelical Christianity in that which is essential as well as allow freedom in doctrinal matters where Protestants have generally agreed to disagree.

The second step is to enter into dialogue with Roman Catholics, orthodox, and ecumenical Christians. In this situation an even more challenging test of catholicity would occur. For, although evangelicals would find that the vast majority of other Christians would agree with them on such essentials as the Trinity, Christology, and the death and resurrection of Christ for salvation, they would also find strong differences of opinion in such subjects as the church, ministry, sacraments, and authority, to name a few. Catholics and orthodox do *not* regard these areas as secondary, but as a vital aspect of apostolic Christianity. In such a dialogue a healthy exchange could occur in which evangelicals could communicate their "evangelical spirit" while receiving from the other Christian bodies a deeper appreciation for the "historic substance" of Christianity.

I have no illusions about the difficulty of the task of catholicity. I am aware of how complex the issues are and have only succeeded in hinting at the reorientation that must take place within evangelical Christianity to recover a truly catholic understanding of the church. Some obviously will want to shrink from the challenge or deny the necessity of it. But most evangelicals, I believe, are becoming increasingly aware of the depth of the Christian faith and desire a more catholic expression of it in the ecclesiastical life of evangelical Christianity.

We now examine the fourth mark of the church, apostolicity.

THE CHURCH IS APOSTOLIC

A major concern of evangelical Christianity is to remain true to the apostles. Unfortunately, in popular evangelicalism, apostolicity often has been affirmed without a full knowledge of what the term implies.

To begin with, apostolicity means to be connected with the past. The emphasis here is both on the *past* and the *connection* with the past. It points to the church built "upon the foundation of the apostles and prophets" (Eph. 2:20) and in this way affirms a view of continuity from one generation to the next. This concept of continuousness reaches back into the way God made Himself known in Israel's history. For a Jew, Israel's past is always present. Abraham, Moses, David, and the prophets as well as the fortunes and misfortunes of Israel as a people, has always been looked on as a present reality— guiding, informing, and directing Hebrew life. In the same way apostolicity means that the witness and authority of the apostles, passed down in the church, is a present reality in the church today. In this way the church is not "a contingent phenomenon or a transcendent 'event' apart from any earthly connections and components, but she is shown and confessed in all her earthly, historical and human connections in time."[24]

To make the historical connection between the past and the present through the apostles more concrete, we may think of apostolicity as being "in the school of" or "under the authority of" the apostles. That is to say that the apostles constitute a *norm* for the church. Thus apostolic precedent must be taken seriously, for it is apostolic precedent by which the church is always to be tested.

For this reason the early church soon recognized two questions of supreme significance: (1) How is apostolicity passed on in the church? and (2) How does apostolicity function? We need to look at the answer provided by the early church to both of these questions in order to understand how the church is "under the authority of" the apostles.

First, how is apostolicity passed on in the church? The second-century church fathers stressed the office of the ministry as the locus through which apostolic authority was passed down in the church. For example, Clement of Rome summarizes the early church consensus: "The Apostles have preached the Gospel to us from the Lord Jesus Christ; Jesus Christ, (has done so) from God. Christ therefore was sent forth by God and the Apostles by Christ."[25] Although the prevailing conviction of the early church was that apostolic authority was passed down *via* the laying on of hands in historic succession from the apostles, this view was challenged by the Montanists who argued for a charismatic continuation of apostolicity.

Montanism appeared in A.D. 156 and spread quickly by the end of the second century. The emphasis was on the Holy Spirit, the charismatic gifts, rigorous bodily discipline, and the immanent second coming of Christ. The concern to capture the original enthusiasm of New Testament Christianity was certainly appropriate, but Montanists went to the excess of teaching Christians to expect new revelations just at the time the church was faced with the heresy of the Gnostics, who claimed a secret revelation superior to the Scripture. They questioned the authority of the church as an institution and broke with the order of the church to ordain those who were under immediate inspiration. For them the true church was not to be identified with the historic institution, but with the Spirit. Wherever the Spirit was, there was the true church. But in their repudiation of the order and authority of the church, there was no objective standard to keep them from going off into an excessive subjectivism, which they later did.

Little is known about the history of Montanism.[26] We do know that the church rejected its excessive emphasis on the charismatic gifts in favor of a ministry recognized and ordained within the church, and organized under the bishops. This did not mean that the church rejected charismatic gifts. It simply insisted that these gifts were to be recognized within the framework of the divinely ordained church. Nevertheless, their decision did have the long-range effect of replacing charisma with office. It should be noted, however, that both charismatics and traditionalists were showing a concern for continuity with the apostolic church.

The primitive church was charismatic in nature but gradually, as the church faced the disorder and chaos of individualism and subjectivism, the element of *order* had to be introduced. The Corinthian church is a case in point. In 1 Corinthians 12–14 Paul does not deny the charismatic nature of the church, but, instead, sets forth an orderly procedure through which the gift of tongues is to be expressed. Here already we see the tension between *charismata* and the *office,* a tension which has flourished again and again throughout history, and one which is evident today as a result of the modern charismatic movement, a movement rejected by some evangelical groups.

An answer to the dilemma of apostolic authority and succession is suggested by Hans Küng.[27] He argues first that "the whole church and every individual member share in this apostolic succession." The argument is that the "church as a whole is the successor to the apostles." The church is not an institution but a community of faithful Christians, all of whom stand in apostolic succession in the broadest sense of the term. Within this apostolic succession there is a special succession of the apostolic *pastoral* services. The implication is that a church to be apostolic ought to have within it all the charismatic gifts which were present in the primitive church, and they should be practiced within the body. There is, however, within the many pastoral functions, a specific succession of particular functions through the imposition of hands. These are the charismatic offices of *presbyter* (pastor), *episkopos* (bishop), and *diakonos* (deacon) which stood out with increasing prominence in the early church. The church recognizes in these offices a special authority to service the whole church.

The second question, "How does apostolicity function?" may be best approached with the second-century structure of the church in mind. A summary of the writings of Clement, Ignatius, and Cyprian on the function of apostolicity is as follows:

1. There is only one body of Jesus Christ, although scattered over the entire world.
2. Over this body God has appointed Jesus Christ, the ultimate authority, and under Him the apostles, then the bishops who continue the apostolic ministry. Under the bishops are the elders (ministers), the deacons, and the people. These are offices of service in and through the authority of Christ.
3. The truth of Jesus Christ is taught to the apostles, handed down to the bishops, and received by the church where it is preserved.
4. The bishops preside over the affairs of the church—its worship and the exercise of discipline. Because of the proliferation of the church, the ministers and deacons carry out the work of the ministry under the jurisdiction of the bishop and are answerable to him. The authority for ministry and sacraments is derived from Jesus but transmitted by the laying on of hands in the episcopate.
5. Congregations are to submit to the authority of the appointed ministers under the bishop. The bishop submits to the authority

of the collegiality of bishops. Together they submit to Jesus Christ who submitted to the will of God.

6. Through this line of authority the unity of the body of Christ will be maintained in the oneness of truth.

7. Anyone who breaks from the church is a schismatic and endangers his relationship with God.

Without entering into questions of whether church order is a doctrine or a matter of convenience, the second-century model will be used as an example for our question—how does apostolicity function? Although the early church model appears to be hierarchical (a later Roman model should not be read into it), the two main concepts that dominate the structure are *submission* and *service.*

In order to understand the meaning of submission and service in the early church, we should recall its incarnational model. In the Incarnation God did not "lord it over" mankind in Christ. Instead He "emptied himself, taking the form of a servant, being born in the likeness of men. And being found in human form he humbled himself" (Phil. 2:7-8). The key to the function of true apostolicity, then, is not *power* but mutual submission and service. The model is provided by Jesus Christ Himself who submitted to the Father and served mankind. The members of the church, which is His body, the mystical extension of Himself in the world, have been called to serve each other and the world.

This emphasis on submission and service highlights the need for evangelicals to address the problem of authority in the church for this reason: many evangelical pastors and leaders of organizations have fallen into the worldly model of authority—domination. Ray Stedman points to the problem in his article "Should a Pastor Play Pope?"[28] He writes, "Authority among Christians does not come from the same source as worldly authority, nor is it to be exercised in the same manner. The world's view of authority places men *over* one another, as in a military command structure or a business executive hierarchy." Stedman sees this "domination" approach among Christians who "operate churches, mission organizations, youth works, schools, colleges, and seminaries . . . in no way different from corresponding secular structures." The answer, he urges, is found in the model of Jesus—"Rather than being lords, disciples are to be servants of one another. The greatest would be servant of all (Mark 10:42-43)."[29]

The urgency to rediscover the incarnational model of submission and service is accentuated by the rapid growth of evangelical Christianity around the world as well as the current attempts to organize evangelicals on a world-wide scale. If the World Evangelical Fellowship and the National Evangelical Fellowships are modeled along the lines of corporations, and if the leaders of these organizations become obsessed with their power and "lord it over" the evangelical church, evangelical Christianity will become little more than a huge organization with programs and gimmicks.

The possibility of a technocratic-evangelical church makes the need to recover an incarnational theology of the church a matter of high priority. Popular evangelicalism seems to agree with the view of an evangelical leader who said "when Jesus Christ ascended into heaven, he cut the apron strings from the church and left us on our own." As long as this kind of view dominates our thinking, we will never be able to transcend the notion that the church is nothing more than a human institution. We will be left to the changing views of authority in secular society. We may at one time model our church on the basis of *dominion* or at another time model our church on *shared authority* similar to that advocated by some avante garde corporations. In the end, however, neither approach will be better than the other, for neither has a theological basis. We must go back to the incarnational principle, to mutual submission and service in the body of Christ as it was understood and practiced in the second-century church. The church can be apostolic only as long as it takes apostolic teaching and precedent seriously.

CONCLUSION

We have attempted to show that the church has a concrete existence in the world, and that this existence may be defined by four historic marks. The oneness of the church points not only to the unity we have with Jesus Christ, but also to the unity we have with all believers by whatever name they are called—Roman Catholic, orthodox, ecumenical, or evangelical. The holiness of the church points to the eschatalogical hope of the church when she will be complete in Christ, and reminds us of our present sinfulness and the need to be tolerant of each other's weaknesses. The catholicity of the church reminds us of the whole truth which the church possesses and points to the need to be inclusive of her many branches as opposed to an exclusivistic view that one branch contains the whole truth. The apostolicity of the church calls us to remain continuous with the past, to recognize the normative nature of apostolic doctrine and practice, and to function in the church through submission and service.

An agenda for the recovery of the church among evangelicals dare not disregard these marks of the church which go to the heart of the nature of the church.

Our current emphasis on the pragmatic side, "How can we get our churches to work?" needs the balance of the theological side which asks "What is the church?" There is a relationship between recovering the true nature of the church and seeing our church's "work." Any long-range renewal of the evangelical church must take evangelicals beyond the purely practical questions into the more difficult theological issues. For, as we recover what it means to *be* the church, that which we seek to recover through gimmicks will be achieved more naturally as we recover the real nature of the church.

Notes

[1]For a more detailed treatment of the biblical passages on the oneness of the church see G. C. Berkhouwer, *The Church* (Grand Rapids: Eerdmans, 1976), pp. 24-50

[2]*The First Epistle of Clement*, 56. All quotations from the early church fathers are taken from *The Ante-Nicene Fathers* and *The Nicene and Post-Nicene Fathers* (Grand Rapids: Eerdmans, 1960)

[3]*The Teaching of the Twelve Apostles*, 9

[4]*On the Unity of the Church*, 5. See also Benson, Edward White, *Cyprian, His Life, His Times, His Work* (London: Macmillan & Co., 1897)

[5]*Schism in the Early Church* (London: SCM, 1953)

[6]Ibid., 33

[7]For a theology of the church, see Paul Roberts, *The Church in Search of Itself* (Grand Rapids: Eerdmans, 1972), pp. 283ff.; also Hans Kung, *Structures of the Church* (New York: Thomas Nelson, 1964)

[8]For an expansion of this idea see Berkhouwer, *The Church,* pp. 51ff.

[9]See Eugene P. Heideman. *Reformed Bishops and Catholic Elders* (Grand Rapids: Eerdmans, 1970); John Kromminga, *All One Body We* (Grand Rapids: Eerdmans, 1970); J. S. Whale, *Christian Reunion* (Grand Rapids: Eerdmans, 1971); E. L. Mascall, *The Recovery of Unity* (New York: Longmans, Green & Co., 1958); Bonaventure Kloppenburg, *Ecclesiology of Vatican II* (Chicago: Franciscan Herald Press, 1974); Raymond Himelick (translator), *Erasmus and the Seamless Coat of Jesus* (Lafayette: Purdue University Studies, 1971)

[10]See Rudolf Schnackenburg, *The Church in the New Testament* (New York: Seabury, 1965), pp. 132ff.

[11]See W. H. C. Frend, *The Donastic Church; a movement of protest in Roman North Africa* (Oxford: Clarendon Press, 1952)

[12]For a modern interpretation of the parable, see Berkhouwer, *The Church*, pp. 367ff.

[13]For an expansion of this idea see Berkhouwer, *The Church*, pp. 334ff.

[14]Schackenburg, *Church in New Testament*, p. 135

[15]WA 39, 515

[16]*Institutes*, IV, 1, 7

[17]See John McNeill, *Unitive Protestantism* (Richmond: John Knox, 1964)

[18]*Theology in Reconciliation* (Grand Rapids: Eerdmans, 1976), p. 37

[19]*Epistle of Ignatius to the Smyrnaeans*, 8

[20]XVIII, 23

[21]*Christ's Church: Evangelical, Catholic and Reformed* (Grand Rapids: Eerdmans, 1965), pp. 19ff.

[22]For a more extended treatment of this entire subject see Louis Bouyer, *The Spirit and Forms of Protestantism* (Westminster: The Newman Press, 1956). For an entirely different point of view see Leonard Verduin, *The Reformers and Their Stepchildren* (Grand Rapids: Eerdmans, 1964)

[23]See R. Newton Flew (ed.), *The Nature of the Church* (London: SCM, 1952)

[24]Berkhouwer, *The Church*, p. 202, and following for an extended treatment of apostolicity

[25]*First Epistle*, 42

[26]See Ronald Knox, *Enthusiasm* (New York: Oxford, 1961)

[27]"What is the Essence of Apostolic Succession," *Apostolic Succession: Rethinking a Barrier to Unity*. Edited by Hans Kung (New York: Paulist Press, 1968)

[28]*Moody Monthly*, July-August, 1976, p. 40

[29]Ibid.

Section II
Bibliography for Further Reading

To understand the church as the body of Christ there is a need to grasp the Hebraic mind-set which perceived reality from an integral and holistic perspective. This Hebraic approach to thought is the key to understanding the incarnational approach not only to the church, but to early theology in general, since early Christianity was decidedly Hebraic rather than Hellenic. A rather comprehensive work on the subject is Thorleif Boman, *Hebrew Thought Compared with Greek* (Philadelphia: Westminster Press, 1961). Another helpful work is *The Clue to History* by John MacMurray (London: Student Christian Movement Press, 1938), especially chapter 2 on "The Hebrew Consciousness." Ludwig Kohler's work, *Hebrew Man* (London: SCM Press, 1956) is quite practical, and Rudolph Bultmann's work, *Primitive Christianity* (London: Thames and Hudson, 1956), contains some helpful insights on the Jewish mind, although his suggestion that Christianity is a syncretism between Judaism and Hellenism is certainly questionable.

For a view of the church in the New Testament read Paul S. Minear, *Images of the Church in the New Testament* (Philadelphia: Westminster Press, 1960). The chapter on the church as the body of Christ is eminently helpful. Two other New Testament studies which are useful for the student include R. Newton Flew, *Jesus and His Church: A Study in the Idea of Ecclesia in the New Testament* (London: The Epworth Press, 1951) and Edward Schweizer, *Church Order in the New Testament* (London: SCM Press, 1961).

For the ancient church, read H. B. Swete, *Essays on the Early History of the Church and Ministry* (London: Macmillan, 1921) and S. L. Greenslade, *Schism in the Early Church* (London: SCM Press, 1964). Greenslade is particularly helpful because he raises the questions we face today in relation to similar questions in the early church. For more on Montanism and the charismatic approach in history read Ronald A. Knox, *Enthusiasm* (New York: Oxford, 1961). On the marks of the church I suggest select chapters in Vladimir Lossky, *The Mystical Theology of the Eastern Church* (London: James Clarke, 1973) and *In the Image and Likeness of God* (Jordonville: St. Vladimir's Seminary Press, 1974). A recent and thorough work by G. C. Berkhouwer, *The Church* (Grand Rapids: Eerdmans, 1976) is organized around the four marks of the church. The concern for the Reformers to maintain a historic church is detailed by John T.

McNeill, *Unitive Protestantism* (Richmond: John Knox, 1964).

For a brief overview on the development of the church after the Reformation, see James Hastings Nichols, *History of Christianity 1650-1950: Secularization of the West* (New York: The Ronald Press, 1956). H. Richard Niebuhr's classic, *The Social Sources of Denominationalism* (New York: World Publishers, 1972) is most enlightening. James I. McCord's book, *Divisions in the Protestant House* (Philadelphia: Westminster Press, 1976) is also useful in getting at the origins of our difficulties.

Much material has been written by modern Catholics on the subject of the church. Of particular value is "Dogmatic Constitution on the Church," the "Decree on the Catholic Eastern Churches," the "Decree on Ecumenism," and the "Decree on the Pastoral Office of Bishops in the Church," from the *Documents of Vatican II* (Grand Rapids: Eerdmans, 1975). The various Catholic approaches to the church are summarized by Avery Dulles, *Models of the Church* (New York: Doubleday, 1974); read also Bonaventure Kloppenburg, *Ecclesiology of Vatican II* (Chicago: Franciscan Herald Press, 1974); Hans Küng, *Structures of the Church* (New York: Thomas Nelson, 1964). A helpful book on the various approaches to authority is *A Pope for all Christians? An Inquiry Into the Role of Peter in the Modern Church* (New York: Paulist Press, 1976), edited by Peter J. McCord. Other valuable works include Oscar Cullmann, *Message to Catholics and Protestants* (Grand Rapids: Eerdmans, 1959); Bela Vassady, *Christ's Church: Evangelical, Catholic, and Reformed* (Grand Rapids: Eerdmans, 1965); G. W. Bromily, *The Unity and Disunity of the Church* (Grand Rapids: Eerdmans, 1958); John Kromminga, *All One Body We* (Grand Rapids: Eerdmans, 1970); Robert S. Paul, *The Church in Search of Itself* (Grand Rapids: Eerdmans, 1972), and Eugene P. Heideman, *Reformed Bishops and Catholic Elders* (Grand Rapids: Eerdmans, 1970).

SECTION III
AN AGENDA
FOR WORSHIP

Chapter 5

The Meaning of Worship

THE PROBLEM

Among evangelicals there is a growing demand to change the form of worship, to incorporate more variety in the service, and to realize a more creative and meaningful expression of worship. Two reasons stand behind this concern to recover worship: man-centeredness, and the lack of biblical content in worship.

The man-centered nature of worship is expressed either in an overemphasis on reaching the intellectual aspect of the worshiper or an overemphasis on triggering an emotional response.

The overemphasis on the intellectual side of worship is committed when the thrust of worship is educational. Here the sermon is central. Everything else is geared around the sermon in a somewhat preliminary fashion. For example, once when I was acting as an interim pastor, a visiting dignitary asked me to "cut down the preliminaries" because, as he said, "I have a lot to say and need as much time as I can get." No evangelical would want to deny the importance of preaching for it is through preaching that God addresses His people. But worship which is oriented almost exclusively around preaching results in a loss of balance between God addressing His people and His people addressing Him. It turns worship into a one-way communication, which in the end is a denial of true worship.

On the other hand, the overemphasis on the emotional side of worship occurs when the goal of the service is to elicit an emotional response. In this situation the invitation usually is made central. The music, the testimonies, and the sermon are all designed to lead to the climax of the service in the invitation. People are asked to respond by accepting Christ, by coming forward for baptism, by accepting a call to Christian service, or by rededicating their lives. Of course, no evangelical would want to deny the activity of response as a vital aspect of worship, but when the entire service is geared toward the response of the congregation, the essence of true worship is missed.

The second problem, a lack of content, is closely related to the problem of man-centeredness. A man-centered approach to worship often occurs as a result of the failure to understand *why* content is necessary in worship, *what* that content should include, and *how* the content should be put together.

To begin with, there are some who fail to recognize why content is necessary. Most evangelicals agree that worship is not contentless. For that reason those who emphasize worship as a teaching ministry are strongly content-oriented. Sermons often are expositions of biblical texts—in many cases a series of sermons explicating a book of the Bible or a theme within the Bible. While the concern for content in Bible-oriented churches is certainly commendable, the focus is distorted when the content centers almost exclusively on the sermon, which, no matter how deep, can never present all the content which a full service of worship ought to contain.

In a full service of worship, the entire spectrum of Christian faith is included. Worship is a rehearsal of who God is and what He has done, and gives expression to the relationship which exists between God and His people. The focus of content in a sermon alone, or the emphasis found among the renewal churches where worship centers around a single aspect of God or a theme, misses the point of worship and fails to worship God in His entirety.[1]

In summary the historic Christian approach to worship which emphasizes the adoration of the Father through the Son has been replaced in some churches by a program with a stage and an audience. And the nature of worship as an offering up of the whole person, the entire community, the body, through the head, Jesus Christ, as a ministry of praise to the Father has been replaced by an emphasis which sees the minister as the agent of God to evangelize the lost and teach the saints. While evangelism and teaching are integral functions of the church, they should not, as they have in some churches, constitute the sum and substance of worship. For that reason we turn to the historic understanding of worship in search of some guidelines to lead us out of our overemphasis on man-centeredness and restore a more balanced biblical content to our worship.

WORSHIP IN THE EARLY CHURCH

The contemporary liturgical renewal has produced scores of books which have probed the origins and meaning of Christian worship. For this reason we cannot hope to do more than touch on the major themes developed at great length in liturgical studies. Although it would be beneficial to trace the development of worship through the Old Testament, the New Testament, and then into the early church, the limitations of this chapter force us to begin with the earliest full account of Christian worship in the early church and work backward in history from there to describe the origins of Christian worship. This account is found in Justin Martyr's *First Apology*, a work written to the emperor Antonius Pius, about A.D. 150. It contains two accounts of a Christian worship service. The first is a detailed description of the communion service (known as the Eucharist from the Greek word *euxarista*, to give thanks). The second is a description of the full service of worship containing both the liturgy of the Word and the liturgy of the Eucharist (the word liturgy comes from the Greek *leitourgia* and means service).

First Account

And when he has concluded the prayers and thanksgivings, all the people present express their assent by saying Amen. This word Amen answers in the Hebrew language to γένοιτο (so be it). And when the president has given thanks and all the people have expressed their assent, those who are called by us deacons give to each of those present to partake of the bread and wine mixed with water over which the thanksgiving was pronounced, and to those who are absent they carry away a portion.

And this food is called among us Εὐχαριστία (The Eucharist), of which no one is allowed to partake but the man who believes that the things which we teach are true, and who has been washed with the washing that is for the remission of sins, and unto regeneration, and who is so living as Christ has enjoined. For not as common bread and common drink do we receive these; but in like manner as Jesus Christ our Saviour, having been made flesh by the Word of God, had both flesh and blood for our salvation, so likewise have we been taught that the food which is blessed by the prayer of His word, and from which our blood and flesh by transmutation are nourished, is the flesh and blood of that Jesus who was made flesh. For the apostles, in the memoirs composed by them, which are called Gospels, have thus delivered unto us what was enjoined upon them; that Jesus took bread, and when He had given thanks, said, "This do ye in remembrance of Me, this is My body;" and that after the same manner having taken the cup and given thanks, He said, "This is My blood;" and gave it to them alone.[2]

Second Account

And we afterwards continually remind each other of these things. And the wealthy among us help the needy; and we always keep together; and for all things wherewith we are supplied, we bless the Maker of all through His Son Jesus Christ, and through the Holy Ghost. And on the day called Sunday, all who live in cities or in the country gather together to one place, and the memoirs of the apostles or the writings of the prophets are read, as long as time permits; then, when the reader has ceased, the president verbally instructs, and exhorts to the imitation of these good things. Then we all rise together and pray, and, as we before said, when our prayer is ended, bread and wine and water are brought, and the president in like manner offers prayers and thanksgivings, according to his ability, and the people assent, saying Amen; and there is a distribution to each, and a participation of that over which thanks have been given, and to those who are absent a portion is sent by the deacons. And they who are well to do, and willing, give what each thinks fit; and what is collected is deposited with the president, who succours the orphans and widows, and those who, through sickness or any other cause, are in want, and those who are in bonds, and the strangers sojourning among us, and in a word takes care of all who are in need.[3]

First, notice that Justin's summary of early worship consists of two parts: the liturgy of the Word and the liturgy of the Eucharist. A study of both of these above descriptions of worship suggests that the arrangement of these two parts of worship are as follows:

I. Liturgy of the Word

    Lessons from the Old and New Testaments
    Sermon
    Prayers
    Hymns (not mentioned by Justin)

II. Liturgy of the Eucharist

    Kiss of Peace
    Offering of bread, wine, and water

Prayers and thanksgiving over the bread and wine

Remembrance of Christ's death, including the narrative
of the institution of the Last Supper, and a command
to continue in it

Amen, said by all the people

Communion

Reserved portions taken by the deacons to those absent

One question which has exercised the minds of liturgical scholars is that of the origins of these two aspects of a single worship service in the early church. Without examining differences of opinion, let us say that the bulk of scholarship agrees that the liturgy of the Word is derived from the synagogue service and the liturgy of the Eucharist developed from the early celebrations of the Lord's Supper. A brief overview of both of these developments will help us focus on the meaning of these vital parts of Christian worship.

The origin of the liturgy of the Word

The relationship between the worship of the synagogue and Christian worship has received full treatment in C. W. Dugmore's *The Influence of the Synagogue on the Divine Office*[4] and *The Jewish Background of the Christian Liturgy* by W. O. E. Oesterley,[5] and more recently in Louis Bouyer, *Eucharist: Theology and Spirituality of the Eucharistic Prayer*.[6] All three authors show that the four essential elements of the liturgy of the Word—readings from the Holy Scripture, a sermon, prayers, and the singing of psalms—were all adapted from the Jewish synagogue worship.

References to the reading of Scripture in Christian worship is common in the literature of the third century. The Reader, as in the synagogue, usually went up to the reading desk (pulpitum), and read from the Old Testament, the gospels, and the epistles. Likewise the custom of expounding from the Scripture is derived directly from the synagogue. Even the custom of inviting a visitor or a member of the congregation (as in the case of Jesus at Nazareth) to read and speak was not uncommon among early Christian congregations.

The earliest recorded Christian prayers are also reminiscent of the synagogue, especially in the general content and sometimes in language. Prayers calling on God for help, for healing the sick, for forgiveness, and for peace show similarity in wording. But an even greater parallel is found in the subjects of prayer. Christians prayed for faith, peace, forbearance, self-control, purity, and temperance in words which Dugmore claims the rabbis would have "heartily endorsed." Christians were told by Polycarp to pray for "kings, potentates and princes, and for those that persecute and hate you, and for the enemies of the cross." All these, except for the last, were objects of prayer in the synagogue.[7]

The Jewish liturgical use of psalms was also continued in the church as evidenced by 1 Corinthians 14:26, "When you come together, each one has a hymn"; "addressing one another in psalms and hymns and spiritual songs" (Eph. 5:19). Pliny in his letter to the Emperor Trajan in A.D. 110 makes reference to the antiphonal singing of Christians.[8] And, according to Ruth Messenger in her pamphlet "Christian Hymns of the First Three Centuries," psalms "formed the bulk of Christian Hymnody" in the early centuries of the church.[9]

We may conclude with Oesterley that "the earliest Christian communities continued the traditional mode of worship to which they had become accustomed in the synagogue . . . so that when the time came for these communities to construct a liturgy of their own, it would be the most natural thing in the world for them to be influenced by the form and thought of their traditional liturgy with which they were so familiar."[10]

The origin of the liturgy of the Eucharist

The second half of early Christian worship, known as the liturgy of the Eucharist (thanksgiving), is also rooted in Judaism as demonstrated by Frank Gavin in his work, *The Jewish Antecedents of the Christian Sacraments.* Gavin traces the Jewish origin of the Christian thanksgiving to the "blessing of the table," the Jewish grace at meals which included the invocation of the divine name, the expression of thanks, and the act of blessing God for the food. These elements of thanksgiving were part of the Last Supper, which Jesus celebrated with His disciples on the eve of His death. He broke the bread and presumably spoke over it the typical prayer of blessing ("Praised be Yahweh, our God, the King of the world, who brings the bread forth from the earth"), then distributed it saying, "Take, eat; this is my body" (Matt. 26:26).

During this same ritual, the cups were filled four times and drunk. The third cup, the "cup of blessing," held particular significance for the Jews for the prayer said in connection with it not only thanked God for meat and drink but also for His benefits, particularly redemption from Egypt, for the land, the covenants, and the law. It was probably after this cup that Jesus said, "Drink of it, all of you; for this is my blood of the covenant, which is poured out for many for the forgiveness of sins" (Matt. 26:28). In this act, Jesus had taken a Jewish custom filled with religious meaning and had given it new meaning in relationship to Himself, His death, and the new covenant.

We know from Acts 2:46 that the earliest form of Christian worship was a meal—"breaking bread in their homes." This Christian meal is linked to the Last Supper through the postresurrection appearances of Jesus where, in what may be interpreted as a remembrance of the Last Supper and an anticipation of the coming kingdom and the messianic banquet, Jesus *ate* with His disciples (Luke 24:30-31, 41-43; John 21:9-12). Equally significant is the fact that Jesus was known to them in the breaking of the bread: "then they told what had happened on the road, and *how he was known to them in the breaking of the bread*" (Luke 24:35).

It is generally agreed by scholars that the earliest form of the liturgy of the Eucharist was patterned after the Jewish meal prayers: the breaking of the bread in the beginning of the meal followed by the thanksgiving prayer over the cup of wine mixed with water at the end.[11]

The picture that emerges through liturgical studies is that the early Christian meal was gradually replaced by a ritual symbolizing the meal. The continual growth of the church into large communities made it increasingly difficult to share an entire meal together. Consequently, the tables were replaced by a single table, the table of the Lord; and the complete meal gave way to the symbols used by our Lord at the Last Supper—bread and wine. The emphasis on the Lord's Supper as fellowship with Him and one another, the presence of Christ, the remembrance of Christ's death, and the anticipation of His return were all part of the church's thanksgiving.

This brief examination of the two parts of Christian worship suggests that the origins of Christian worship lie in the Hebrew forms. As Alexander Schmemann observes in *Introduction to Liturgical Theology*, "We have here a dependency of order, not simply a similarity of separate elements, but an identity of sequence and of the relative subordination of one part to another, which defines from within the liturgical significance of each part."[12] The significance of this similarity of form can be understood only when we grasp the meaning of worship for both the Hebrews and the Christians, a concern which we may discover through an understanding of (1) the meaning of worship and (2) the incarnational nature of early Christian worship.

THE MEANING OF WORSHIP

It must be remembered that the early Christians came into worship from a different perspective than modern Christians. We accept the Old because we have been informed by the New. But they accepted the New because they had been informed by the Old. As Schmemann remarks, "They believed in the New because they had seen, experienced and perceived the fulfillment of the Old. Jesus was the Christ; the Messiah; the One in whom all the promises and prophecies of the Old Testament were fulfilled."[13]

The earliest Christians, then, saw the coming of Jesus as the fulfillment of their worship. Their theology of creation, sin, the redemption of Israel out of Egypt, and the covenantal relationship they had with God found fulfillment and new meaning in Jesus Christ. Christ did not abolish the Old, but fulfilled it by actualizing it in Himself. Salvation was an actual and accomplished fact. History had come to a unique turning point. Consequently the worship of the church became the primary and fundamental expression of the content of both the Old and New covenants. The Old, which anticipates the New, was preserved in the liturgy of the Word, and the New, which fulfills the Old, was expressed in the liturgy of the Eucharist, the remembrance of Christ's death and resurrection which inaugurated the New.

The work of liturgical scholarship in this area suggests that the twofold form of worship described by Justin was no accident of history, but the result of a Christianity which accepted *both* the Old and the New revelations of God as authoritative. Consequently the form of worship itself is rooted in biblical convictions and betrays a particular theological stance. In particular, worship is based on the *character* of God and the *acts* of God.

In the first place worship is grounded in the character of God. We worship God for who He is. God, as the words of the *Gloria in Excelsis* describe Him, is the only God, the highest, the Lord God, the heavenly King, the almighty God and Father, the Holy One. These ascriptions are central to the vision of worship in Revelation 4 and 5. Here a whole host of creatures, angels and men in ever-expanding concentric circles, are constantly worshiping the Lord, ascribing to Him all honor and glory and praise. He is to be worshiped simply because of who He is—God.

Recently, when I was discussing this view, a young person objected to what she felt was the "egocentricity" of God. Why does God want everything created to praise Him? Or what value is it really? Another person more mature in the faith and wise in his understanding of worship responded to her question. "God," he said,

> only wants us to speak the truth about him. Even as in our own personal worth we appreciate people telling the truth about us and shy away from those who either overestimate or underestimate us, so God wants us to speak the truth about him. The truth is that he is the Creator, that he is ultimate, that he is the highest, the holiest, the one most perfect in his being. Now what would you think of God if he were to shuffle his feet in celestial dust and say, "Aw shucks," refusing to be honest about himself?

In worship we simply tell God the truth about Himself. In doing so we see ourselves in the proper relationship to God, which, in fact, is also an essential aspect of worship. Like Isaiah who, when he saw "the Lord sitting upon a throne, high and lifted up" and heard the cry "Holy, holy, holy is the LORD of hosts; the whole earth is full of his glory," responded by crying, "Woe is me! For I am lost; for I am a man of unclean lips, and I dwell in the midst of a people of unclean lips; for my eyes have seen the King, the LORD of hosts!" (Isa. 6:1-5). To see the Lord in all His glory is to see ourselves as sinful and in need of grace. And that realization is an indispensable aspect of worship.

Not only is worship grounded in the character of God, it also is based on three acts of God: creation, redemption, and covenantal relationship.

The first act of God is creation. In Revelation 4:11 the elders worship God because all things exist and were created by His will. The fourth commandment, which instructs Israel to set aside one day of worship to remember God's act of creation, implies that all of life is sacred, that Israel is to live worshipfully toward God in every aspect of life. The whole of life—eating, drinking, sleeping, working, studying, loving, and playing—is related to God. Creation affirms that life is more than what we see, feel, touch, taste, and smell. There is an interiority to the universe that provokes a worshipful position toward the Creator. For this reason, God set aside one day to be a sign of His lordship over all our time and activity. Through it we recognize God's rightful claim to every moment of our life.

The second act of God is redemption. In Revelation 5:12 the myriads of angels worship the Lamb that was slain. In the Old Testament Israel is commanded to worship God because He had redeemed them from Egypt with a mighty hand and an outstretched arm (Deut. 5:15). Israel's worship, particularly in the Psalms, abounds with this praise of God for His mighty acts of redemption. God was no remote deity or abstract idea. He had entered into their history, and through power and love redeemed them from their bondage. In the New Testament we worship God because He has personally entered into history through the Incarnation to redeem us and make us His people.

The central act of Christian worship in the history of the church has always been the Communion. The earliest church was found "breaking bread daily." Although this is not a reference to Communion as we know it today (most scholars feel it refers to the Agape feast), it nevertheless points to the fact that the early church celebrated the *presence* of Christ in their midst in every service of worship through the "breaking of the bread."

The "breaking of bread" looked back to the postresurrection appearances of Jesus on the road to Emmaus, in the upper room, and by the Sea of Galilee where He *ate* with them. It also looked forward to His return when they would all eat together in the great messianic banquet. By daily breaking of the bread, Christ's followers were celebrating the presence of the risen and soon-coming Lord in their midst, who was made uniquely present in the "breaking of the bread."

Later, in Corinth, Paul connected the "breaking of the bread" with the institution of the Lord's Supper at the last Passover. After that the "breaking of the bread" included the cup, and gradually evolved into Communion. Evidence from the literature of the early church as it developed through the centuries, shows that the church always celebrated Communion as the focal point of worship until after the Reformation when the focus of worship shifted to preaching.[14]

The third act of God to which we respond in worship is the covenantal relationship He has established between us. Revelation 5:9 ascribes worship to God because He has made His people to be a "kingdom and priests to our God." At Mount Sinai God entered into a covenantal relationship with Israel, sealed with blood. They became "a people holy to the LORD. . . chosen . . . to be a people for his own possession" (Deut. 7:6). The Lord became Israel's God, and Israel became God's peculiar people. And in this relationship there emerged tangible signs of the union between God and His people—the sanctuary, the priesthood, the offerings, and the appointed feasts and seasons.

In the New Testament there is another covenant, sealed with the blood of Christ, through which the church becomes Christ's peculiar possession, "a chosen race, a royal priesthood, a holy nation, God's own people" (1 Peter 2:9). This new relationship is the Body—the body of Christ, an extension of the Incarnation, the continued presence of Christ on earth, a divine organism inhabited by the presence and power of the Holy Spirit. In it there are tangible signs of the presence of Christ—the Word, the sacraments, the priesthood, discipleship, discipline, power, worship, prayer, and love.

It is in the twofold form of worship—word *and* sacrament—where the full impact of the Christian content is rehearsed by the Christian community. Unfortunately, this twofold form became much more elaborately developed in history, to the point where in the late medieval period the pomp and ceremony of the form crowded out the meaning of it. Nevertheless, the Reformers of the sixteenth century uniformly insisted on maintaining both the Word and the sacrament as necessary parts of a full service of worship.

William D. Maxwell in his work *An Outline of Christian Worship,* details how both Luther and Calvin insisted on keeping the historic twofold shape of worship. "To imagine," writes Maxwell, "that Calvin wished to replace sacramental worship by a preaching service is completely to misunderstand his mind and work and to ignore all that he taught and did. His aim was twofold: to restore the Eucharist in its primitive simplicity and true proportions—celebration *and* communion—as the central weekly service, and, within this service, to give the Holy Scriptures their authoritative place.

The Lord's Supper, in all its completeness, was the norm he wished to establish."[15] This conclusion concerning Calvin's desire to maintain both the liturgy of the Word and the sacrament is stated by Calvin in the preface of his *Service Book of 1545:*

> We begin . . . with confession of our sins, adding verses from the Law and the Gospel . . . and after we are assured that, as Jesus Christ has righteousness and life in Himself, and that, as He lives for the sake of the Father, we are justified in Him and live in the new life through the same Jesus Christ, . . . we continue with psalms, hymns of praise, the reading of the Gospel, the confession of our faith, and the holy oblations and offerings. . . . And . . . quickened and stirred by the reading and preaching of the Gospel and the confession of our faith . . . it follows that we must pray for the salvation of all men, for the life of Christ should be greatly enkindled within us. Now, the life of Christ consists in this, namely, to seek and to save that which is lost; fittingly, then, we pray for all men. And, because we receive Jesus Christ truly in this Sacrament . . . we worship Him in spirit and in truth; and receive the eucharist with great reverence, concluding the whole mystery with praise and thanksgiving. This, therefore, is the whole order and reason for its administration in this manner; and it agrees also with the administration in the ancient Church of the Apostles, martyrs, and holy Fathers.[16]

THE INCARNATIONAL NATURE OF EARLY CHRISTIAN WORSHIP

The incarnational nature of early Christian worship points to the mystery of God's plan of salvation known through signs and symbols in the Scripture and enfleshed in the incarnation of Jesus Christ, the chief mystery of the church. Because the worship of God's people, whether in the Old or New Testament points ultimately to the mystery of the Incarnation, the worship of God is always through Christ.

This early Christian understanding of the incarnational nature of worship is rooted in Jewish thought. As Gavin points out in *The Jewish Antecedents of the Christian Sacraments,* "A sound Christian definition of sacrament (incarnation) proceeds from the characteristically Jewish premise that the material world is not evil, but good—since God made it and saw it to be good."[17] Consequently this holistic approach to reality always relates the phenomena of nature to God as Gavin writes:

> From Psalm xix. to the countless benedictions of Jewish liturgical

devotion, all of the phenomena of nature were related to God. Nature as such expressed God. Man in using the good things of this world partakes of God's bounty and sanctifies the gift in acknowledging it. Social and family life were alike hallowed by the recognition of the love of God which made them possible. No feature of human life lay outside the eternal stream of God's interest. That in expressing his indebtedness and voicing his thanks man "sanctified" the world which he used, is a commonplace in the prayer forms of Judaism. Normally the "benediction" began with the words "Blessed art thou, O Lord God, King of the Universe," whereupon followed the ascription. Sanctification lay close to this eucharistic attitude: the expression of thanks sanctified the gift. The family meal, the annual Passover *seder*, the frequent meetings in fellowship of a group of friends, all adumbrate the Eucharist of Christianity. Nothing in the ordered scheme of Jewish life, lived as under the eye of God, was common or unclean. It was all knit up by dedication, consecration, thanksgiving to the Living One from whom the colourful multiplicity of good things had come.[18]

The specific rites and institutions of Judaism illustrate the basic principle of the coinherence of God in His creation. And Christian theology stands in direct line with the Hebrew conception of wholeness and coinherence in her theology of the Incarnation (that God became malllen); her Christology (that the human and divine exist together in a single person); her ecclesiology (that the church is both divine and human); her understanding of Scripture (the human is divinely inspired) as well as other doctrines which can be understood only through this incarnational model.

Because early Christianity affirmed a holistic concept of reality, it continued to stand in the Hebrew conviction that we can see God through the material world, that material things may be signs and symbols of sacred realities. For the early church the most significant material symbols which communicated eternal realities were the bread and wine of the Eucharist. The incarnational aspect of Christian worship was realized in the Eucharist, the bread and wine being symbols of the death of Christ, by which man is redeemed. The purpose of worship, to praise the Father for redemption through the work of His Son, is proclaimed both by the liturgy of the Word and the liturgy of the Eucharist.

But the climax of worship is the Eucharist, for the symbols of bread and wine are the material objects which in a mysterious manner are connected with the broken body and shed blood of Jesus Christ, through whom man worships the Father. For this reason the early church had a high view of the symbols of bread and wine and their place in Christian worship as indicated by the following statement from St. Cyril of Jerusalem written about A.D. 315.

> After this ye hear the chanter inviting you with a sacred melody to the communion of the Holy Mysteries, and saying, "O taste and see that the Lord is good." Trust not the judgment to thy bodily palate; no, but to faith unfaltering; for they who taste are bidden to taste, not bread and wine, but the anti-typical Body and Blood of Christ.
>
> In approaching therefore, come not with thy wrists extended, or thy fingers spread; but make thy left hand a throne for the right, as for that which is to receive a King. And having hollowed thy palm, receive the Body of Christ, saying over it, 'Amen'.
>
> Then after thou hast partaken of the Body of Christ, draw near also to the Cup of His Blood; not stretching forth thine hands, but bending and saying with an air of worship and reverence, 'Amen', hallow thyself by partaking also of the Blood of Christ. And while the moisture is still upon thy lips, touch it with thine hands, and hallow thine eyes and brow and the other organs of sense. Then wait for the prayer, and give thanks unto God, who hath accounted thee worthy of so great mysteries.[19]

The Roman Catholic medieval view of transubstantiation, which taught that the essence of bread and wine became the substance of body and blood, is a perversion of the early Christian affirmation of the real presence. The early Christians refused to define exactly what happened to the bread and wine. For them it was something more than a mere physical bread and wine, for Christ was actually present in a renewing and nourishing way. But it was something less than a crass physical presence like that taught later by some eleventh-century theologians who insisted that if "you bite the bread you have bitten the body of Christ." The early Christians wished to maintain the mystery of the Eucharist as the culminating point of worship which pointed to the redemption of Christ and served as a means of receiving the benefits of the death of Christ.

Calvin and Luther wished to retain the incarnational character of worship, recognizing that God is worshiped only through His Son by means of Word and sacrament, those tangible signs of eternal realities. But they rejected the medieval practices as having lost the true meaning of worship and called for a return to the simpler, more holistic, incarnational understanding of the early church.

CONCLUSION

in this chapter we have identified the two problems of evangelical worship as man-centeredness and a lack of content. We have argued that the origins of Christian worship lie in the synagogue worship and in the "breaking of the bread," which, although it had its origins in the Jewish meal prayers, found new meaning in an identification with the body and blood of Jesus. We have also argued that the meaning of worship is rooted in the character of God (who He is) and in His acts of creation, redemption, and covenantal relationship. Furthermore, we have suggested that material things may be signs and symbols of sacred realities, even as God Himself took a human body. If evangelicals are to overcome their man-centeredness and lack of content in worship, it would seem necessary to return to these principles and practices of Christian worship as the basis for a worship agenda. Before specific suggestions are made as to how this may be accomplished, we must turn first to an examination of the form of worship in the early church.

Notes

[1]See for example David Mains, *Full Circle* (Waco: Word, 1976), ch. 4

[2] *The First Apology of Justin,* LXV, LXVI

[3]Ibid., LXVII

[4](London: Oxford, 1944)

[5](Oxford: Clarendon Press, 1925)

[6](Notre Dame: University of Notre Dame Press, 1968)

[7]Dugmore, *Influence,* pp. 11-25

[8]See Henry Bettenson, *Documents of the Christian Church* (London: Oxford University Press, 1973), pp. 3-4

[9](New York: The Hymn Society of America, 1942)

[10]Oesterley, *Jewish Background,* p. 90

[11]See Bouyer, *Eucharist,* chapter 5

[12](London: The Faith Press, 1966), p. 44

[13]Ibid., p. 47

[14]See Gregory Dix, *The Shape of the Liturgy* (London: Dacre Press, 1945), pp. 613ff.

[15](London: Oxford University Press, 1936), p. 112

[16]Ibid., quoted by Maxwell, p. 116

[17](New York: Ktav Publishing House, 1929), p. 23

[18] Ibid., pp. 14-15

[19]*Catechetical Lectures* XXIII, 20-22

Chapter 6

The Form of
Worship

THE PROBLEM

A story in the Russian *Primary Chronicle* tells of Vladimir, Prince of Kiev, who sent several of his followers in search of the true religion. First, they went to the Moslem Bulgars of the Volga, but found "no joy," only a "mournfulness and a great smell." Then they went to Germany and Rome and found the worship more satisfactory, but still lacking in beauty. Finally they came to Constantinople, and attending the Church of the Holy Wisdom, they discovered what they were seeking. Consequently, they reported to Valdimir. "We knew not whether we were in heaven or on earth, for surely there is no such splendor or beauty anywhere upon earth. We cannot describe it to you: only this we know, that God dwells there among men, and that their service surpasses the worship of all other places. For we cannot forget that beauty."[1]

In this true story, the subjects of Vladimir put their finger on three important aspects of worship: the first is found in the statement *we knew not whether we were in heaven or on earth;* the second in the words, *God dwells there among men;* and the third in the phrase, *for we cannot forget that beauty.* All three of these statements points to the unity between form and spirit.

Among evangelicals there are some who take great pride in insisting that worship is "spiritual" and not "formal." There are several problems with this view: first, it evidences a docetic tendency, second, it fails to recognize that nothing exists without form, and third, it fails to concern itself with beauty in worship.

93

First, the insistence on "spiritual" worship over against "formal" worship is similar to the docetic tendency to reject the material in favor of the heavenly or invisible. Docetism denied the goodness of creation, the Incarnation as a taking on of real human flesh, and the presence of Christ in the Eucharist. The early church fathers recognized that this rejection of the visible and tangible undermined the very basis of faith, i.e., that God who created became in Jesus Christ a part of His creation.

Second, the tendency to pit form against spirit fails to recognize that nothing exists without form. Robert Bellah in his contribution to *The Roots of Ritual* points to the absolutely basic nature of form in worship. "For most of us," he writes, "the only place we can start is mutely, with gesture, motion, and dance, with liturgy and sacrament. In our moral confusion and our intellectual doubt perhaps the ordering of gesture—of the most elemental gestures, kneeling, eating, drinking, touching—is all that we are capable of. There is a natural movement from liturgy, which is communion, to brotherhood, to caring and curing, to social concern, though for the most of us social ideology has sagged and collapsed as utterly as theology. Being men, we must speak, and speech is first of all praise—praise for all that is given, and praise for all that we see through what is given. And, then, tentatively, speech about brothers, speech about community. Intellectual speech about ultimate things comes last— is now in abeyance and must wait until we have a fuller and less fragmentary imaginative vision."[2]

The fact is that form is so much a part of life that living is unthinkable apart from form. The real issue then is not "form" vs. "spiritual," but what kind of form is the best means through which worship may be expressed. This leads us to the third problem, that of beauty in worship. Beauty is expressed through form. Thus the lack of form results in a failure to reach the whole person on a meaningful aesthetic level. What is needed is a restoration of balance which will allow both the intellectual and aesthetic aspect of persons to respond to God in worship.

Stephen G. Meyer in his article, "Neuropsychology and Worship," argues (on the basis of research findings in neuropsychology) that the left hemisphere of the brain appears to be specialized in verbal functions while the right side of the brain centers on spatial functions and other non-verbal skills. He concludes that, "the mind consists of at least two minds, a verbal analytic left hemisphere and a subjective, spatial, gestalt oriented right hemisphere." From this he argues that the Scripture, which communicates both through rational discourse and highly symbolic apocalyptic literature, supports both a rational and symbolic approach to worship: "good sound theology is not independent of symbol, but based on symbol. In other words, theology which is learned from books and theology which is learned from experience should reflect the same reality on different levels."[3]

We must now ask why some churches fail to achieve a balanced worship which emphasizes both the rational and the aesthetic side of persons. There are three causes: first, an overemphasis on reason;[4] second, the influence of scholastic Protestantism; and third, the influence of a misguided kind of revivalism.

The overemphasis on reason

In the case of worship, the overemphasis on the rational side of man in worship was first advocated by Ulrich Zwingli, the Swiss reformer. Bard Thompson in *Liturgies of the Western Church* writes:

> Zwingli was convinced that faith is given and nourished solely by the Holy Spirit, apart from any physical channels, any external means, especially anything so crass as eating. Thus the Supper remained to him a vivid spiritual exercise in which the elements of bread and wine were but reminders, not vehicles, of grace. As symbols of Christ's body and blood, their value lay in engaging the senses and fixing the mind upon the great moment of our redemption on Calvary, so that the believer might be brought "to consciousness of the actual thing through faith and contemplation." The Eucharist was above all a contemplative experience of the goodness of God manifest on the Cross of Christ—so vivid to the man of faith that he could "grasp the thing itself." Even so, Zwingli apparently decided that such an occasion need only be offered to Christians four times a year: at Easter, Pentecost, autumn, and Christmas. With that decision, the Eucharist was disconnected from the normal service of the Lord's Day; and Zwingli was left to devise a new type of Sunday worship around the sermon.[5]

In the summer of 1524 Zwingli and his helpers began their "cleansing" of the church. They took out the relics, whitewashed the paintings and decorations, removed all the statues, ornaments, gold and silver equipment, and vestments. They even took away the song books and closed the organ permitting no more music so people could only hear the Word of God.

Zwingli's insistence that the Lord's Supper is not a means of grace and that the Word is the norm for Christian worship created a wedge between Word and sacrament, and broke with the ancient Hebraic and early Christian notion of the union between spirit and matter. Eric Heller in *The Hazard of Modern Poetry* points out that this shift is the "theological climax of a deep revolution in the thoughts and feelings which must find it more and more difficult even to grasp, let alone accept, what was in Luther's mind when he fought Zwingli's 'demythologizing' . . . lost will be that unity of word and deed, of picture and thing, of bread and the glorified body. Body will become merely body, and symbol merely symbol."[6] The practice and conviction of Zwingli laid the groundwork for what now appears to be the normal approach to worship in many churches—the emphasis on preaching and an approach to the sacrament which sees it as a "mere" memorial. But these convictions spread, not because of Zwingli, but because of the influence of Protestant scholasticism.

The influence of scholastic Protestantism

The result of the epistemological and cosmological revolutions of the age of enlightenment was to create a rationalistic, scientific way of looking at the universe, which opposed the mystical and supernatural. Although conservative Protestant Christianity resisted the full implications of the denial of supernaturalism, scholastic Protestantism was nevertheless influenced in its theology and worship by a more rationalistic approach to the faith which resulted in an emphasis on truth as propositional and thus knowable through analysis and intellectual inquiry.

The result of propositionalism in worship was to separate the spiritual from the natural, a shift already anticipated in Zwingli. Consequently worship became divorced from tangible and visible signs and separated from the whole man, and it became increasingly defined as the communion of spirit with Spirit, achieved through the medium of the intellect. This intellectual view became standard to Calvinistic worship. It overemphasized preaching, underemphasized the Lord's Supper, and denied the validity of tangible and visible signs as either channels for grace or means by which man is enabled to enter into worship through his senses.

Abraham Kuyper's *Lectures on Calvinism,* delivered in 1898 at Princeton Seminary, developed a rationale for this view of worship which has had an enormous influence on evangelical thought. In his chapter on "Calvinism and Art" he argues that Calvinism was not allowed to develop an art style of its own because the "alliance of religion and art represents a lower stage of religious, and in general human development."[7] For this reason, Calvinism "abandoned the symbolical form of worship."[8]

Kuyper goes on to recognize the relationship between worship and the symbolic in the Old Testament, but argues that "you find no trace or shadow of art for worship in all the apostolic literature. Aaron's visible priesthood on earth gives place to the invisible High-priesthood after the order of Melchizidek in heaven. The purely spiritual breaks through the nebula of the symbolical."[9] In support of his argument Kuyper paraphrases Von Hartmann:

> Originally Divine worship appeared inseparably united to art, because, at the lower state, Religion is still inclined to lose itself in the aesthetic form. At that period, all the arts, he says, engage in the service of the cult, not merely music, painting, sculpture and architecture, but also the dance, mimicry and the drama. The more, on the other hand, Religion develops into spiritual maturity, the more it will extricate itself from art's bondages, because art always remains incapable of expressing the very essence of Religion. And the final result of this historic process of separation, he concludes must be that Religion, when fully matured, will rather entirely abstain from the stimulant by which aesthetic pseudo-emotion intoxicated it, in order to concentrate itself wholly and exclusively upon the quickening of those emotions which are *purely religious.*[10]

Kuyper's view of worship is further supported by his argument that "our intellectual, ethical, religious and aesthetic life each commands a sphere of its own. These spheres run parallel and do not allow the derivation of one from the other . . . art is no side-shoot on a principal branch, but an independent branch that grows from the trunk of our life itself."[11] The sum of his argument is that worship, to be pure, must be separated from the tangible and concrete, freeing the spirit to commune immediately with the Spirit of God. With this insistence much of the mystery of worship has been taken away and replaced by an overemphasis on the mind.

The influence of revivalism

The third factor contributing to the breakdown of aesthetically pleasing worship is the adaptation of revivalistic worship to the morning service. Although modern revivalism is to some extent the product of the seventeenth-century pietistic movement and the evangelical revivals of Wesley, we must recognize that Wesley's revivalism and his understanding of worship are not to be confused.

Ole E. Borgen in *John Wesley on the Sacraments*, effectively argues that Wesley's view of worship and the sacraments was that of historic Christianity. Wesley believed the sacraments ought to occupy a "prominent place" in worship. He believed in the practice of fasting, hearing, and prayer as effective means of grace. But "none of them"could "surpass the sacrament of the Lord's Supper; it is the richest legacy which Christ has left for his followers."[12] Horton Davies in *Worship and Theology in England* reports that Wesley two years after his conversion "received the sacrament 98 times. Forty-five years later, in 1785, he communicated 91 times."[13] Further, Davies claims it was Wesley's high view of the sacraments which prepared the ground for the Oxford Movement by reviving the frequency of communion:

> In the light of the sacramental and ecclesiological emphasis of the Oxford Movement, it is customary but nonetheless erroneous to suppose that the evangelicals, in appreciating the pulpit, deprecated the sacraments. So far is this from the truth that the evangelicals can rightly be claimed as pioneers in restoring the Sacrament of Holy Communion to its central place in the Anglican cultus.[14]

This rich perception of worship and the sacraments was not maintained by the followers of Wesley. According to Borgen, the Methodists changed the emphasis "little by little" until "the Word, preached and heard" became the chief means of grace. For this reason "Wesley's rich and balanced views on the relative worth and position of the various means of grace are reduced, and the balance destroyed." The regrettable consequence of this shift was that "the heirs of Wesley, without realizing the consequences, open up the road to a future revivalism in danger of shallowness; to conceptions of holiness that have lost the Wesleyan anchorage in the eternal wonder of Christ's atonement."[15]

Revivalism has taken Wesley's experience of conversion without

Wesley's theology. This emphasis on experience apart from an incarnational understanding of theology has caused the emphasis in revivalism to center around the experience of God through personal conversion. As Daniel Stevick says in *Beyond Fundamentalism,*

> The shape of this cult has so altered the religion of the New Testament and Christian tradition that the chief communal action is no longer the Lord's Supper, but the invitation. The real presence of Christ in active, grace-giving, miraculous power which is quite generally ruled out of the sacraments by Fundamentalists is shifted instead to this evangelistic device. The great ritual of death, rebirth, and communion which the church, at her Lord's direction has found in baptism and the eucharist is now relocated by Fundamentalists in their (altarless) "altar call."[16]

From the outset it has been argued that we need to combine the "evangelical spirit" with "historic substance." Some evangelicals may fear that the incorporation of historic substance will result in the demise of a strong personal faith in Jesus Christ. On the contrary, the historic Christian understanding and practice of worship will provide forms through which a committed personal faith in Jesus Christ will find greater depth and meaning. These forms, which must constitute part of the agenda for the evangelical church if evangelical Christianity is going to stand in the historic faith, are three: 1) the restitution of the historic shape of worship; 2) the restitution of the Lord's Supper as a source of spiritual nourishment; and 3) the restoration of the Christian concept of time, especially as it relates to the restitution of the church year.

RESTORATION OF THE HISTORIC SHAPE OF WORSHIP

There is an immediate need to return to the biblical-historic shape of worship. One reason for returning to the classic shape of worship is that there is a close relationship between worship and living. Whenever some aspect of true worship has been lost, a change in the living of the people inevitably occurs. Gregory Dix in *The Shape of the Liturgy* cites an example from the fifth century when Christians began to make the sacrament of Christ's body and blood something to be pondered, rather than consumed. This unhealthy approach to worship, he believes, laid the groundwork for certain practices that developed in the medieval period and against which the Reformers reacted.[17]

A second example, and one closer to home for evangelicals, is the emergence of post-Renaissance individualism which has replaced the corporate experience of the church around the body and blood of Christ with the individual experience of salvation. This introduction of individualism with the simultaneous loss of the communal aspect of the Eucharist has had ramifications particularly in our loss of the church as the body of Christ. Interestingly, the current recovery of the body of Christ is attended by the recovery of worship, particularly the Eucharist where the single body of Christ gathers in union around the signs of redemption. These two examples, which could be multiplied extensively, are sufficient to point out the fact that a close relationship exists between the way we worship and the way we live out our Christianity.

Worship as a corporate action

In the first place then, we must return to worship as the corporate *action* of the body of Christ. Worship is not something done in front of the congregation or to the congregation as though there are actors and an audience. In the early church participation of the entire local body of Christians, as in 1 Corinthians 12–14, was accomplished, as Cullmann observes, through "free and unrestricted spiritual utterances" which found "their place alongside fixed liturgical forms."[18] Every one had a gift which was contributed to the whole body.

According to Justin's description of worship, worship as a corporate action is accomplished by the spontaneous prayer of the president (elder) who "sends up prayers and thanksgivings to the best of his ability, and the congregation which assents, by saying Amen." The Amen, Justin explains, means, "so be it" in the Hebrew language. It means more than a mere listening to the prayer, and points to an actual participation in the prayer. Because the body of Christ is *one,* the one who presides and the ones who respond are only engaging in differing functions in the single unified action of worshiping the Father through Christ. Current evangelical worship tends to be passive—the believer sits in the pew as something is done for him and to him. In evangelical free worship we sing, put money in the plate, and sometimes say Amen. If the relationship of these responses, minimal as they are, to the whole activity of worship was understood, it would make worship more meaningful.

Worship as rehearsal

We should also recapture the conviction of the early church that the corporate action of worship is a *rehearsal* of God's plan of redemption. Worship sets forth the gospel. It proclaims the entire faith of the church. This action is an offering to God through Jesus Christ who has accomplished the Father's will. It is an act of worship and praise to the Father for the redemption offered in His Son. Worship is also an action for the entire congregation of believers, that in it they may be nourished and strengthened by feeding on Christ in both Word and sacrament. Furthermore, although the action takes place in a local congregation, it is the worship of the whole people of God, the church, both the living and the dead—for together they constitute the body of Christ.

A detailed examination of the early Christian services of worship suggests that there was a real attempt to develop worship in such a way that it represented the living theology of the church. Fortunately, for our study, we have manuscripts of actual liturgies from the third and fourth centuries which show us the theological structure of worship, leading to the conclusion that worship was a rehearsal of the Christian faith. In summary, the basic structure of early worship revolved around Word and sacrament and may be diagrammed as follows:

Here, we have in Word and sacrament the two means of knowing God and entering into a relationship with Him. By Word and sacrament God has made known His plan of redemption. The Word proclaims it and the sacrament re-enacts it, and both Word and sacrament by the power of the Holy Spirit bring us the grace of God, the benefits of Christ when we hear and receive by faith.

Inside this general framework of worship, which centers on revelation and incarnation, all the other aspects of the church's confession of faith are to be found. The preparation for worship includes a recognition of sin, especially in light of the holiness and majesty of God. After a confession of sin is made, the worshiper is ready to hear the Word. In the Scripture readings, taken from the Old Testament, the Epistles, and the Gospels, the authority and primacy of Scripture in the church is expressed. Hearing and responding to the Word of God is followed by a sermon declaring God's grace and calling the church into an imitation of Christ. The prayers recognize God as creator, provider, sustainer, and ruler over all as well as remind the worshipers of their dependence upon God.

After these responses to the Word, the worshiper prepares to receive the mysteries which are signs and symbols of the redemption proclaimed in the Word. This preparation consists in the sharing of the kiss of peace, a sign of the reconciliation affected by the death of Christ which makes His church one body. The passing of the peace gives anyone who is out of fellowship with another member of the body an opportunity to make peace. The bread is a symbol of the "oneness" of the church, and anyone who is not at one with a brother or sister should not partake until reconciliation is achieved. Otherwise it makes a sham of the church's conviction that Christ's body is "one loaf." The sacrament is not only an ecclesiastical statement, it also, as the early liturgies suggest, points to the church's Trinitarian confession—that Jesus Christ is God; to the Christological confession—that He is both human and divine; and to the future return of Christ which is anticipated in the coming messianic banquet. It also contains significant social implications because of its stress on the "oneness" of the body gathered around the bread and wine. That is, it points to the responsibilities Christians have toward each other and the world.

The principle purpose of worship is not to teach but to worship God (although a person alert to the structure of worship will find it a constant means of learning the faith through rehearsal). God is praised as Creator, Redeemer, and Judge. The worshiper praises, magnifies, and glorifies Him not only for who He is, but also for what He has done in providing life, redemption, sustenance, hope, and many other blessings. In this way worship becomes an experience of God. The worshiper is carried through an experience in which the opportunity is given to make a fresh commitment to Jesus Christ as Lord and Savior.

This model of early Christian worship is an excellent example of the combination of evangelical spirit and historic substance and should be given serious consideration in evangelical circles as a model for worship renewal. The present structure of evangelical worship lacks the full content of the church's confession. Here is a "form" which incorporates the whole of evangelical and historic theology, yet provides for the freedom and spontaneity characteristic of evangelical Christianity. It avoids on the one hand the deadness of mere repetition, and on the other hand a zealous enthusiasm which neglects form and content.

An example of worship renewal which has succeeded in maintaining the historic shape of Christian worship with spontaneity may be found at Oral Roberts University. Kevin Ranaghan has written an article describing the worship practices of the Rev. Robert Stamps, a Methodist minister and chaplain of ORU. Although Stamps does not use a prayer book, his spontaneous prayers follow the ancient customs of the church and contain the content of historic Christianity. Ranaghan warmly approves of this renewal seeing it as "first of all a desire to worship God in fullness, a desire to celebrate the mystery of Christ's death and resurrection and thereby to be nourished. Secondly, it shows an openness to discovering the deep reality of Christ's saving action as he comes to us through Word and rite. . . . Thirdly, one must notice how well this liturgy is integrated with the life style of its worshiping community, how their faith life has both created this worship from experience and been simultaneously deepened by it. This is worship from life, oral, spontaneous, yet finding roots in the tradition of the church."[19]

If there is to be worship renewal in the evangelical churches we must at least be acquainted with the worship practices of the historic church. What Robert Stamps has done at Oral Roberts University has been accomplished through a thorough commitment to the study of worship and a recovery of the past shaped around the experience and need of His people. No one can dictate exactly how worship renewal is to take place. Each evangelical congregation or denomination will have to make a commitment to recover worship, then pay the price in study, time, and change that it will take. Certainly, the recovery of worship will help to break down the unhealthy individualism of evangelical Christianity and create the sense of community that belongs to the church, both in local worship, and in the larger global witness of the one body of Christ.

THE RESTORATION OF THE LORD'S SUPPER
AS THE CENTRAL AND CLIMACTIC POINT
OF WORSHIP

The second step we may take is to restore the Lord's Supper as the central and climactic point of worship. Evangelical worship represents, as we have seen, a departure from the *full* service of worship characteristic of the early church. Scholars are in general agreement that the norm of both biblical and early church worship was both Word and sacrament, although there were more than likely situations where only one or the other was celebrated. Nevertheless, any return to the historic shape of Christian worship, to be lasting and meaningful, should include an understanding of the biblical-historic shape of the Lord's Supper as the climax of worship in which we truly feed on Christ.

Gregory Dix in *The Shape of the Liturgy* informs us of the relationship between Matthew 26:26 and the classic shape of the service of the Sacrament.[20] In the Last Supper, Jesus *took, blessed, broke,* and *gave.* This is the fourfold form of the Lord's Supper. Although this was originally a sevenfold form because it involved the bread and wine separately, it developed into a fourfold form as the bread and wine were brought together in a single blessing. This fourfold emphasis is discernable in the literature of Hippolytus, a Bishop in Rome at the end of the second century, in his work, *The Apostolic Tradition.* Below are actual excerpts from his service to show the form and content of the Eucharist, the climactic point of worship as it was understood at the end of the second century. A close study of this form shows us the depth of content which the early church strove to incorporate in its worship.

The Form	The Content: From the prayers of Hippolytus

The Form

1. He *took*

   A. The kiss
      of peace

(The setting for this service is the ordination of a bishop, accounting for the reference to the bishop. Nevertheless it was ordinary practice to share the kiss of peace before every celebration of the Lord's Supper.)

   B. The offering

(The minister is standing behind the table with the elders of the church and the bread and wine are' carried to him by someone from the congregation representing the entire congregation.)

   C. The preface

2. He *blessed*

(The prayer of blessing contains the entire confession of the Christian church. Note that it begins with the essence of the Christian message and then emphasizes the unity of the Son with the Father, creation, incarnation, obedience, suffering (for the church), victory over

The Content: From the prayers of Hippolytus

"And when he is made bishop, all shall offer him the kiss of peace, for he has been made worthy."

"To him let the deacons bring the oblation and he with all the presbyters, laying his hand on the oblation, shall say giving thanks:"

M. The Lord be with you.
C. And with thy spirit.
M. Lift up your hearts.
C. We lift them up unto the Lord.
M. Let us give thanks unto the Lord.
C. It is meet and right so to do.

4 We render thanks unto thee, O God, through Thy Beloved Child Jesus Christ, Whom in the last times Thou didst send to us (*to* be) a Saviour and Redeemer and the Messenger of Thy counsel;
5 Who is Thy Word inseparable (*from Thee*), through whom Thou madest all things and in Whom Thou was well-pleased;
6 (*Whom*) Thou didst send from heaven into (the) Virgin's womb and who conceived within her was made flesh and demonstrated to be Thy Son being born of Holy Spirit and a Virgin;

evil through the Resurrection, recitation of the institution of the Supper as a remembrance (the word *anamnesis* means recall not mere memory), the power of the Holy Spirit to sanctify the elements and the congregation, and finally a recognition that the offering is one of praise to the Father *through* the Son.)

7 Who fulfilling Thy will and preparing for Thee a holy people stretched forth His hands for suffering that he might release from sufferings them who have believed in Thee;

8 Who when He was betrayed to voluntary suffering that He might abolish death and rend the bonds of the devil and tread down hell and enlighten the righteous and establish the ordinance and demonstrate the resurrection:

9 Taking bread *(and)* making eucharist [i.e, giving thanks] to Thee said: Take eat: this is My Body which is broken for you [*for the remission of sins*]. Likewise also the cup, saying: This is My Blood which is shed for you.

10 When ye do this [ye] do My "anamnesis."

11 Doing therefore the "anamnesis" of His death and resurrection we offer to Thee the bread and the cup making eucharist to Thee because Thou hast bidden us [or, *found us worthy*] to stand before Thee and minister as priest to Thee.

12 And we pray Thee that [Thou wouldest send Thy Holy Spirit upon the oblation of Thy Holy Church] Thou wouldst grant to all [*Thy Saints*] who partake to be united [*to Thee*] that they may be fulfilled with the Holy Spirit for the confirmation of [*their*] faith in truth,

13 that [we] may praise and glorify Thee through Thy [*Beloved*] Child Jesus Christ through whom glory and honour [be] unto Thee and *(the)* Holy Spirit in Thy holy Church now [*and for ever*] and world without end. Amen.

3. He *broke*

"And when he breaks the bread in distributing to each a fragment he shall say:
The Bread of Heaven in Christ Jesus."

4. He *gave*

"And he who receives shall answer:
Amen."[21]

The form and content of communion described by Hippolytus shows us how the ultimate focus of worship is on the cross and resurrection. Both Word and sacrament point to the cross and resurrection, but the sacrament is the climactic point of worship because of the intensity of its focus, because Jesus Christ is uniquely present, and because the church is nourished and strengthened by feeding on Him.

Unfortunately the development of the doctrine of Christ's presence is looked upon with disfavor by most evangelicals because of the Roman view of transubstantiation. However, the alternative of a mere memorialism is as much a departure from the early church as is transubstantiation. Leaving both transubstantiation and memorialism behind we should seek to understand what seems to be the historical view of the presence of Christ in the sacrament.

Oscar Cullmann and F. J. Leenhardt in *Essays on the Lord's Supper* have shown that the understanding of the early church was not a crass literalism but a mystical presence. The details of both New Testament exegesis and historical analysis are too complicated for discussion here.[22] Let it be sufficient, therefore, to point the way to a more symbolic and lively understanding of the Lord's Supper by the concluding words of Leenhardt which affirm the presence of Christ in the sacramental eating while avoiding the extremes of memorialism and transubstantiation:

> The presence of Christ to His Church is permanent because His promise is permanent. But, according to the promise itself, it takes place only when two or three are gathered together in His name. The likelihood of Christ being present to His own remains strictly personal. Christ's presence is not stabilized in a thing or in men. It is manifested in an action of Christ Himself. It is to be remembered that the declaration: "This is my body" is the comment on an action. The bread is the body of Christ only because it is Christ who gives this Bread. He can give it only if there is someone to take it, if the Church is there, if two or three are gathered together in His name, if faith welcomes this word.[23]

Those who have returned to this historical understanding of the climax of Christian worship, where the One who died and rose again to bring forgiveness and healing is believed to be present and received, have discovered the healing power of Christ through the Eucharist.[24] Worship, so conceived, breaks through the arid, dry, mechanical, and lifeless nature of what otherwise may be an empty form, and opens the worshiper to the joy and accompanying healing which comes from affirming the gracious and active presence of Christ in the sacrament as received again and again.

THE RESTORATION OF THE CHRISTIAN
CONCEPT OF TIME

The third step we may take toward the renewal of worship is to restore the Christian concept of time, especially as it relates to the restitution of the church year. The secularization of worship is perhaps most obvious in the typical evangelical church calendar. Generally the church year follows the secular year beginning with New Year's Day and ending with New Year's Eve. In between, our calendars are full of special events revolving around Mother's Day, Father's Day, Children's Day, Memorial Day, Independence Day, Labor Day, and in some churches special attention is even given to Boy Scout and Girl Scout Day as well as other national or even local days. This strange mixture of the patriotic, sentimental, and even promotional shows how far we are removed from a Christian conception of time. It may be objected that evangelicals do have a Christian year because Christmas and Easter are observed. While these surely are Christian events, they sometimes lack real meaning because they often are entered into with haste, and sometimes even take commercial or promotional shape.

The Christian concept of time

The Christian concept of time takes its starting point in the Eucharist. Here, we have, as Dix observed, "The enactment before God of the *historical process* of redemption, of the historical events of the crucifixion and resurrection of Jesus by which redemption has been achieved."[25] From a Christian point of view the life, death, and resurrection of Jesus Christ are at the *center of time*, for from Christ we look backward toward creation, the fall, the covenants, and God's working in history to bring redemption. But from the event of Christ we also look forward to the fulfillment of history in the second coming of Christ. For this reason time is understood from the Christian point of view in and through the redemptive presence of Jesus Christ in history.

Oscar Cullmann has dealt with the biblical concept of time in his well-known book *Christ and Time*.[26] Without entering into the details of his argument, it is sufficient to say that time is rendered meaningful by the Christian concept of eschatology, for the Christian believes that history is moving toward a fulfillment, not an ending. In this sense, the Christian view of time is similar to the Hebraic understanding. The Old Testament looks toward the fulfillment of time in the coming of the Messiah. His coming does not render the events of the Old Testament (and especially here we may think of the Hebrew sacred year) meaningless, but by fulfilling them it establishes their meaning. In the same way the Christian believes that the end of time will fulfill and complete the life, death, and resurrection of Jesus Christ which anticipate the future consummation of all things. For this reason the Christian year is based on the events of the life of Christ which shape the Christian understanding of time.

The application of the Christian concept of time to a recovery of the church year

The two earliest events which the church adopted from the Jewish sacred year were Passover and Pentecost. Christ had died as "our Passover," and on the day of Pentecost the Holy Spirit brought into being the church, which marked the beginning of time for the church. We need not go into the details of development here, except to say that the church year developed in relation to Easter and Pentecost. The first half of the church year moves back from Easter to the birth of Christ. The second half moves from Pentecost to the birth of Christ. Consequently the first half of the church year recounts the life and death of Christ, while the second half recalls the birth and spread of the early church. The following graph summarizes these main events which shape the Christians' understanding of time:

1. Advent. The word *advent* means "coming." It not only signals the beginning of the church year (four weeks before Christmas), but points to the three comings of Jesus: His birth, His second coming, His personal coming into our hearts. During this season the church anticipates Christmas in a manner different from the purely secular and materialistic connotations placed on it by society.

2. Christmas. Christmas season, which celebrates the Incarnation, consists of Christmas Day and the following two Sundays. The emphasis falls on the birth narratives, the Incarnation, and the adoration of the shepherds.

3. Epiphany. The word *epiphany* means "manifestation" and points to the manifestation of Christ to the world as the Messiah. It begins twelve days after Christmas (known as the twelfth night) and continues for nine Sundays. During these Sundays the church celebrates the manifestation of Christ in such events as His miracles and early teachings which reveal His messianic character.

4. Lent. Lent begins six weeks before Resurrection Sunday and signals a time of renewal and preparation for the major events of the Christian understanding of time. The emphasis of this period is on repentance and preparation including fasting, prayer, and Bible study. It is begun on Ash Wednesday with ashes symbolically placed on the forehead, an Old Testament custom which was a sign of grief and mourning. It concludes with Holy Week, including services of worship centering around the triumphant entry on Palm Sunday, the Last Supper and agony of Christ on Thursday, His death on Friday, and ends with the Resurrection which signals the beginning of Easter.

5. Easter (Resurrection Day). Easter is a seven-week celebration of the resurrection of Christ which ends with the Ascension and Pentecost. This is a period of much joy and celebration emphasizing the teachings of Jesus during His postresurrection appearances.

6. Pentecost. Pentecost season lasts until Advent. The emphasis during this season is on a variety of things, including the growth and development of the early church.

This brief introduction into the church year shows how, if adopted by evangelicals, worshipers may be sensitized to a more Christian perception of time. The constant reminder of time, revolving around the life of Christ and the early church, will serve to break down those unhealthy distinctions we make between the secular and the sacred, causing us to realize that all time belongs to the Lord who has created it, redeemed it, and will consummate it in His coming. In addition it is an excellent teaching tool, a means by which we can assure our congregations of keeping in touch with the events and teaching of the entire Scriptures.

CONCLUSION

We have attempted to show that worship is a *primary* function of the body of Christ. Because the tendency of the evangelical is toward a private and individual approach to worship through prayer and Bible study, we have stressed the act of public worship, the worship of the entire body of Christ. It is important for evangelicals to maintain private worship, for public worship was never meant to replace private worship. But the need right now in our churches is for a recovery of public worship.

For evangelicals, the restoration of public worship may involve the rethinking of the order of worship toward a more inclusive rehearsal of the entire faith, an increased use of the Lord's Supper as the focal point of worship, and a return to a creative use of the church year. Perhaps in this way we will be able to overcome the man-centeredness and the lack of content which has helped to create the yearning for a more fulfilling experience of worship.

Notes

[1]Cited in Timothy Ware, *The Orthodox Church* (Baltimore: Penguin Books, 1963), p. 269

[2](Grand Rapids: Eerdmans, 1973), p. 232

[3]*The Journal of Psychology and Worship*, Fall 1975, p. 288

[4]I do not deny that man is a rational being. What I am concerned with is the view that man is predominantly or exclusively rational.

[5](New York: Meridian, 1961), p. 143

[6](Folcroft: Folcroft Library Editions, 1953), p. 12

[7](Grand Rapids: Eerdmans, 1931), p. 146

[8]Ibid., p. 147

[9]Ibid.

[10]Ibid., p. 148

[11]Ibid., p. 150

[12](New York: Abingdon Press, 1973), p. 15

[13](Princeton: Princeton University Press, 1961), V. III, p. 187

[14]Ibid., p. 223

[15]*Wesley on Sacraments*, p. 16

[16](Richmond: John Knox, 1964), p. 57

[17](London: Dacre Press, 1945), p. XII

[18]*Early Christian Worship* (London: SCM Press, 1953), p. 21

[19]"The Liturgical Renewal at Oral Roberts University," *Studia Liturgica*, V. 9, 1973, p. 125

[20]Dix, *Shape of Liturgy*, pp. 48ff.

[21]See Burton Scott Easton, *The Apostolic Tradition of Hippolytus* (Hamden: Archon Books, 1962), pp. 33-36.

[22]See Joseph M. Powers, *Eucharistic Theology* (New York: Seabury Press, 1967)

[23](Richmond: John Knox Press, 1958), p. 76

[24]See Francis MacNutt, *Healing* (Notre Dame: Ave Maria Press, 1974), pp. 275ff.

[25]Dix, *Shape of Liturgy*, p. 305

[26](Philadelphia: Westminster Press, 1964)

Section III
Bibliography for Further Reading

Because of the twentieth-century renewal in worship, there are so many books of value that it is difficult to know what to exclude from the list. Let me suggest, first, that the need for worship renewal is awakened by reading *The Roots of Ritual* (Grand Rapids: Eerdmans, 1973) edited by James D. Shaughnessy. Also, no student of worship should be without *A Dictionary of Liturgy and Worship* (New York: Macmillan, 1972), a very useful resource edited by a well-known scholar in liturgical studies—J. G. Davies. Another useful resource book is *Liturgies of the Western Church* (New York: Meridian, 1961). This work, edited by Bard Thompson, contains the major liturgies from Justin Martyr to John Wesley.

For an introduction to the relationship between the Old Testament patterns of worship with the emergence of New Testament worship, be sure to read C. W. Dubmore, *The influence of the Synagogue upon the Divine Office* (London: Oxford, 1944); W. O. E. Oesterley, *The Jewish Background of the Christian Liturgy* (Oxford: Clarendon Press, 1925) and F. Gavin, *The Jewish Antecedents of the Christian Sacraments* (New York: Ktav Publishing House, 1929). A more recent publication is the outstanding scholarly work of Louis Bouyer, *Eucharist* (Notre Dame Press, 1968). Dugmore and Gavin are available through St. Vladimir's Bookstore. *Jewish Liturgy and its Development* (New York: Schocken Books, 1960) by A. Z. Idelsohn is another must on the list.

For the study of worship in the New Testament, read Ralph Martin, *Worship in the Early Church* (Grand Rapids: Eerdmans, 1975); Oscar Cullmann, *Early Christian Worship* (London: SCM Press, 1953); and C. F. D. Moule, *Worship in the New Testament* (Richmond: John Knox, 1961).

Once you have a fair grasp of worship in both the Old and New Testaments you will want to study the development of Chrishian worship in history. The classic in this area is Dom Gregory Dix, *The Shape of the Liturgy* (London: Dacre Press, 1945), also available through St. Vladimir's Bookstore. A work that is more compact than Dix, and highly regarded for its scholarship, is Josef A. Jungmann's *The Early Liturgy: to the Time of Gregory the Great* (Notre Dams Press, 1959). An easier work to read, which also gives a quick survey of the historical development, is William D. Maxwell's *An Outline of Christian Worship* (London: Oxford University Press, 1936). For an Orthodox point of view read Alexander Schmemann, *Introduction to Liturgical Theology* (London: the Faith Press Ltd., 1966), available through St. Vladimir's Bookstore. For a Presbyterian view read John M. Barkley, *Worship in the Reformed Tradition* (Richmond: John Knox, 1967); Hastings Nichols, *Corporate Worship in the Reformed Tradition* (Philadelphia: Westminster, 1968) and Julius Melton, *Presbyterian Worship in America* (Richmond: John Knox Press, 1967). An excellent little work by a Baptist is John E. Skoglund, *Worship in the Free Churches* (Valley Forge: The Judson Press, 1965). And of course, everyone should be familiar with "The Constitution on the Sacred Liturgy" found in *The Documents of Vatican II* (Grand Rapids: Eerdmans, 1976). An excellent Lutheran work has been written by Luther D. Reed, *The Lutheran Liturgy* (Philadelphia: Fortress Press, rev. ed., 1960).

For a deeper inquiry into the meaning of the Lord's Supper read Joseph M. Powers, *Eucharistic Theology* (New York: The Seabury Press, 1967) and *Essays on the Lord's Supper* (Richmond: John Knox Press, 1958) written by Oscar Cullmann and F. J. Leenhardt.

If you are interested in studying the church year or introducing it in your church, *The Christian Calendar* (Springfield: G. & C. Merriam Co., 1974) edited by L. W. Cowic and John Delwyn Gummer will be helpful. This is a complete guide to the seasons of the Christian year containing many full color prints of church art. Merrill R. Abbey has written *The Shape of the Gospel* (New York: Abingdon, 1970) to serve as a preaching guide for ministers. Adam Foxe, Gareth and Georgina Keene's work, *Sacred and Secular* (Grand Rapids: Eerdmans, 1975) is an excellent daily devotional guide through the church year.

Finally, the serious student should purchase and study the prayer books of various church bodies. The *Worship Book Services* (Philadelphia: Westminster Press, 1970) is helpful. But by far the most helpful and complete prayer book, containing a rich variety of liturgies both historic and modern, is *The Draft Proposed Book of Common Prayer and Other Rites and Ceremonies of the Church* (New York: The Church Hymnal Corporation, 1976).

SECTION IV

AN AGENDA
FOR THEOLOGY

Chapter 7

Scripture, Tradition, and Authority

THE PROBLEM

A difficult problem we face is that of putting ourselves back into the position of faith before formulation. Because we live on this side of theological formulation, we have the advantage of the cumulative thought of almost two thousand years. However, if we are to succeed in grasping truth as the early church did, we may have to regard our two thousand years of cumulative theology, and especially our current "position," as a disadvantage. In a manner of reflective analysis and self-criticism we may have to suspend our theological presuppositions, denominational teachings, and personal bias in order to stand with the earliest Christians who stood on the other side of theological debate and formulation.

For example, if we were to ask a Christian of the first century, "What is your theology?" the answer would probably be little more than a bewildered stare. It would be much more appropriate to ask, "What do you believe?" or "What is your doctrine?" Doctrine, which is the word for Christian teaching, was closely associated with several other terms familiar to the early Christian: *kerygma*, *catechesis*, and *didascalia*. *Kerygma* points to the essential message that Christ died and was raised from the dead (Rom. 8:34) and to the manner in which this message was announced (preaching); *catechesis* refers to the oral teaching about Jesus, especially to the basic and primitive facts of the faith which the New Testament writers called the "milk" of the Word (Heb. 5:12-14; 1 Cor. 3:1-3); and *didascalia* embodies the doctrinal content of the Christian faith as it came to be understood and affirmed in the church, the meatier and heavier matters of the faith which the writer of Hebrews called "solid food" (5:14).

The point is that the early Christian was more familiar with terms such as belief, doctrine, and confession than with the term theology. Theology comes from the Greek word *theologia* and means study of God. But it was not used by the church as a technical term until the eleventh century when Abelard used it to apply to the whole of Christian teaching. However, it was primarily Thomas Aquinas in the thirteenth century who worked out a theory of theology as a science of revealed truths. Ever since Aquinas, the term has been used to refer to the analysis, application, and presentation of Christian belief, doctrines, and confession.

Today we can use the word theology in an inclusive or exclusive way. If we talk about the theology of Christianity we refer to *all* the theologies or attempts to explain Christian truth in the history of Christian thought. On the other hand we can use the term in an exclusive manner and speak of the theology of Calvin or Luther, Arminius, or our local pastor. Therefore, as we approach the subject which has come to be known as theology, we must separate what the church believes, teaches, and confesses from the human systems of theology which persons have developed. The fact that these can be two very different things, and that contemporary evangelicals sometimes confuse their personal theology with what the church has always taught, underscores the necessity to recover the historic theology of the church. An example of this is found in the current debate over inerrancy.

The major problem in the current debate over inerrancy is to achieve balance and perspective. A balanced theology affirms the many parts of Christian teaching in such a way that each facet of truth is taught in a balanced relation to the whole; a theology with perspective sees Christian truth in relation to history. The failure to achieve balance and perspective results in an *overemphasis* on one or more points of theology, and thus, on the other hand a *reduction* of theology from the whole to a part.

An example may be drawn from the fundamentalist-modernist controversy in the early part of the twentieth century. Here, a conflict of real depth was gradually reduced to five issues which ultimately became little more than slogans among fundamentalists:

(1) verbal inspiration; (2) virgin birth; (3) substitutionary atonement; (4) bodily resurrection; (5) second coming. It now appears evident that the emphasis placed on the defense of these classic aspects of Christian truth detracted from the emphasis on other aspects of the Christian faith. American fundamentalism has neglected other truths which taken together with the five fundamentals provide a more complete and whole picture of Christianity. Consequently, fundamentalists have been characterized by a failure to develop an adequate view of the church, authority, worship, the sacraments, and life style. In other words, the overemphasis on these five points has produced an underemphasis on other aspects of Christian faith leaving fundamentalist Christianity less healthy and mature than it could otherwise be.

I mention this because a similar phenomenon faces the evangelical community today in the battle for the Bible. Unfortunately, in many cases, twentieth-century evangelical Christianity has not understood the *historic* relationship of Scripture, tradition, and authority. The result of doing theology without respect to historical perspective and balance can be disastrous. In the case of fundamentalism in the early part of this century and now again in the case of inerrancy, the chief result has been a schismatic approach to the church.

The urgent need in the "inerrancy crisis" is not to create new schisms but to recover the basis of authority as understood by the early church. Here authority is seen in its proper relationship to the rest of Christian teaching. We turn now to an explanation of Scripture, tradition, and authority in the early church and offer their perspective as an alternative to those who would base authority on inerrancy alone.

SCRIPTURE, TRADITION, AND AUTHORITY IN THE EARLY CHURCH

The second century was a decisive period for the early church, for it was during this time that vicious attacks were made against apostolic Christianity. These attacks, far from destroying or even modifying the faith, provided the church with a situation in which apostolic Christianity was able to emerge in a clear-cut fashion, both as to its substance and its authority.

The two most decisive conflicts were with Marcion and with the

Gnostics. The first of these debates resulted in the clarification of the *authoritative source* for Christian truth while the second resulted in the clarification of the *authoritative substance* of that truth. Because a knowledge of these conflicts and their results are indispensable for evangelical authority, we turn to an examination of each.

The authoritative source of Christian truth

The conflict of the church with Marcion resulted in a clear understanding of the authoritative source of truth. Although Marcion, who came to Rome about A.D. 140, was influenced by Gnosticism, it is not entirely correct to call him a Gnostic. He rejected the basic gnostic myths about the aeons which had supposedly come forth from an original divine being. But he accepted the gnostic premise that the Old Testament was the product of an inferior God. Irenaeus informs us that Marcion accepted the teaching of Cerdo, a Gnostic whose chief doctrine was that "the God proclaimed by the law and the prophets was not the Father of our Lord Jesus Christ."[1] For this reason Marcion wanted to rid the church of any connection with the Old Testament or Jewish practices. The issue Marcion raised was simply this: Did the Old Testament belong to the Christian tradition?

The answer to the place of the Old Testament in the church was determined by the tradition which had already been set by the apostles. They understood the Jewish past in terms of Christ's coming. This is evident in their attitude toward the Old Testament. They regarded the law and the prophets as well as the events and worship of Israel as part of the Christian tradition because they believed them to testify to Jesus Christ. Paul, for example, in 1 Corinthians 15:3-4, insisted that everything regarding Christ took place "in accordance with the scriptures." Soon, a typological interpretation of the Old Testament as reflected in Hebrews became a standard way of interpreting Jewish Scriptures in the church. This is evident in the so-called *Epistle of Barnabas*, a treatise written around 135 in Alexandria, in which the author wrote: "the prophets, having obtained grace from Him, prophesied concerning Him."[2] In the *Homily on the Passover* by Melito of Sardis written around A.D. 170, Melito's explanation of the paschal lamb in Exodus 12 is that it typologically points to Christ, the true Paschal Lamb.[3] And Justin Martyr in his *Dialogue with Trypho the Jew* argues that the entire Old

Testament points to Jesus Christ. Consequently, the Old Testament Scriptures were regarded as the Scriptures of the New Testament church because the apostles had received this precedent from Jesus.

Marcion's opposition to the Old Testament as well as his concern that the writings of the apostles (which were already read widely in the church and regarded as the authoritative voice of apostolic Christianity) were entirely too Jewish, led him to the formation of his own canon. He took the Gospel of Luke and the Epistles of Paul, with the exception of those written to Timothy and Titus, and edited out everything that came from the Old Testament. As Irenaeus wrote:

> He dismembered the Epistles of Paul, removing all that is said by the apostle respecting that God who made the world, to the effect that he is the Father of our Lord Jesus Christ, and also those passages from the prophetical writings which the apostle quotes, in order to teach us that they announced beforehand the coming of the Lord.[4]

The reason for this drastic action on the part of Marcion is found in his interpretation of Paul's doctrine of grace. He was convinced that Paul's doctrine of grace stood in absolute antithesis to the Old Testament. He saw the Old Testament God as just, vengeful, and demanding. Salvation in the Old Testament was by law, keeping the commands, and doing good. But the New Testament God was loving and kind, practicing mercy and forgiveness, giving salvation in Christ, and making no demands. Consequently Marcion would have nothing to do with the Old Testament. For him, it represented another God, another salvation, another way of life. His conviction was that if Christianity continued to mix with the doctrines of this inferior religion, it would lose its distinction.

Marcion's attitude toward the Old Testament and his abuse of the apostolic writings created a crucial situation for the young church. For one thing the apostles themselves had already set a precedent by interpreting the Old Testament through the death and resurrection of Christ. Were they right? On the other hand, the second-century church had already received the writings of the apostles as authoritative. Were they right in doing so? Consequently the young church was forced into the position of asserting the *authoritative source* of Christian teaching. Before the end of the second century the church affirmed the Old Testament, the four Gospels, and the letters of Paul as authoritative in their entirety (the canonicity of some of the

Catholic Epistles and the Book of Revelation remained controversial for some time).

Even though the canon was not officially ratified by a church council until the second half of the fourth century, the church had made a decisive step toward establishing a norm for doctrine and order by the end of the second century. The authoritative norm for Christian faith and practice was the apostolic testimony to the Old Testament and the apostolic writings. In this way the church continued to stand in the tradition of Paul who had entrusted the gospel to Timothy and commanded him to pass it on to other faithful men.

Marcion's rejection of the Old Testament as well as his selective use of apostolic writings put him and his group outside the church. Although Marcionism continued with some following for a time, it gradually disappeared. After the seventh century it is heard of no more. In the meantime, the church in the middle of the second century made it clear that she had an authoritative norm for Christian teaching—the apostles—which meant that both the Old Testament and the apostolic writings were the *authoritative source* for Christian truth.

The authoritative substance of Christian truth

The second test for the second-century church was its conflict with Gnosticism. Through this conflict the church clarified her understanding of the *substance* of the historic faith. Christianity had already begun to be tested in the New Testament period by Judaism and esoteric religious ideas from Egypt and Persia. The acid test of the substance of her faith came, however, in conflict with the Gnostics who claimed to have a superior knowledge handed down in a secret tradition. This knowledge, while it varied somewhat from sect to sect, basically taught the existence of two Gods—one the Spirit God who was responsible for the good, the other the Creator God (often identified with Yahweh in the Old Testament) responsible for evil. Because the evil God was the creator, matter was regarded as evil. Naturally then, man's body, which was a product of evil, was looked upon as the prison of his soul. Salvation, then, was the release of the soul from the body so it could ultimately unite with the good Spirit God. To accomplish this, the good God sent Christ, an emanation, to bring knowledge (gnosis) which would free the soul from the body.

This knowledge which Christ gave to the disciples, the Gnostics declared, was what one needed to know to be saved.

It is obvious that the teaching of the Gnostics is diametrically opposed to apostolic teaching. What was needed therefore by the Christian to combat this perversion of Christian truth was a summary of the Christian faith, an authoritative answer to the gnostic threat. Consequently, summaries of apostolic Christianity began to emerge independently of one another in various parts of the Roman Empire. The similarity of content among these statements which came to be known as "rules of faith" are remarkable. Here is the rule of faith written by Irenaeus about A.D. 190:

> The Church, though dispersed throughout the whole world, even to the ends of the earth, has received from the apostles and their disciples this faith: (She believes) in one God, the Father Almighty, Maker of heaven, and earth, and the sea, and all things that are in them; and in one Christ Jesus, the Son of God, who became incarnate for our salvation; and in the Holy Spirit, who proclaimed through the prophets the dispensations of God, and the advents, and the birth from a virgin, and the passion, and the resurrection from the dead, and the ascension into heaven in the flesh of the beloved Christ Jesus, our Lord, and His (future) manifestation from heaven in the glory of the Father "to gather all things in one," and to raise up anew all flesh of the whole human race, in order that to Christ Jesus, our Lord, and God, and Saviour, and King, according to the will of the invisible Father, "every knee should bow, of things in heaven, and things in earth, and things under the earth, and that every tongue should confess" to Him, and that He should execute just judgment towards all; that He may send "spiritual wickednesses," and the angels who transgressed and became apostates, together with the ungodly, and unrighteous, and wicked and profane among men, into everlasting fire; but may, in the exercise of His grace, confer immortality on the righteous, and holy, and those who have kept His commandments, and have persevered in His love, some from the beginning (of their Christian course), and others from the date of their repentance, and may surround them with everlasting glory.[5]

The issue which the Gnostics had raised by their teaching was simply this: what is the substance of Christian teaching? And the second-century church responded with a resounding affirmation of the faith which came from the apostles. The following brief comparison of gnostic teaching with apostolic teaching clearly shows that the second-century church rejected the false teaching of Gnosticism by asserting a summary of apostolic Christianity.

	Gnostic	Christian
God:	Dualism (two gods)	One: Father, Son, Holy Spirit
Authority:	Secret tradition	Tradition passed down from the apostles and their disciples; Holy Spirit through prophets.
Creation:	An evil god made matter. Thus matter is evil.	The Father, the Almighty, who made the heaven and the earth.
Jesus Christ:	An appearance, Jesus could not partake of flesh because flesh is matter and matter is evil. Known as Docetism (to seem); a great teacher.	Son of God Made flesh Born of a virgin Suffered Resurrected Ascended Will come again
Eschatology:	Absorption into divine. No resurrection of the flesh.	To restore all things Raise up all flesh Judgment
Salvation:	Knowledge	By His grace Give life incorruptible

It is important to recognize that the existence of these rules of faith represent a strong case to the effect that the *substance* of the church's belief and teaching was widely understood in the second century. Irenaeus did not pull his doctrine out of the air or create a counter-doctrine to the gnostic point of view. He himself states that his doctrine was no novelty, that it was, in fact, widely known, received, and confessed throughout the church universal:

> As I have already observed, the Church, having received this preaching and this faith, although scattered throughout the whole world, yet, as if occupying but one house, carefully preserves it. She also believes these points (of doctrine) just as if she had but one soul, and one and the same heart, and she proclaims them, and teaches them, and hands them down, with perfect harmony, as if she possessed only one mouth. For, although the languages of the world are dissimilar, yet the import of the tradition is one and the same.[6]

In summary then, by the end of the second century the church had an *authoritative source* and an *authoritative substance* of what she believed and taught. The authoritative source was the apostles. They had received their message from Christ and passed it on in the church. Consequently, both the *oral* and *written* tradition of the apostles which they had transmitted to the church, and which the church had received and guarded and passed on was authoritative. In this sense, the Scriptures, both the Old Testament and what had been by that time recognized by the church (the four Gospels and the Pauline

Epistles), was the authoritative source, which had been handed down by the apostles.

But the early church also recognized an authoritative substance within the authoritative source. This substance was a summary of the facts of faith, what came to be known as "the rule of faith." This rule, which appeared in various geographical areas of the Roman Empire independently of one another, was regarded as a key to the interpretation of Scripture. Tertullian and Irenaeus both contended that the Scriptures, the authoritative source, could not be interpreted apart from the rule, the authoritative substance. It was the key to understanding the message of the apostles, handed down in their writings to the church, the keeper and guardian of the truth.

Authority, then, was not based on inerrancy in the early church, but on the apostolic witness handed down in their writings, summarized in the rule of faith, and preserved in the church. We must now ask how this view may be applied to the current dilemma over inerrancy among evangelicals.

AN AGENDA FOR AN EVANGELICAL APPROACH TO SCRIPTURE, TRADITION, AND AUTHORITY

In the first place evangelicals should recognize that a doctrine of inerrancy is not a sufficient basis for authority. The Jehovah's Witnesses believe in an inerrant Bible as do the Christian Scientists. Mary Baker Eddy in *Science and Health* claims "as adherents of truth, we take the inspired Word of the Bible as our sufficient guide to eternal life."[7] It is a well-known and documented fact that every heresy in the church, including Arianism and Pelagianism, has been based on the Scriptures. For this reason it is simply inadequate to assert certain positions because they can be "proved" by the Bible. Bruce Shelley, a leading evangelical historian, recognizes the fallacy of the simplistic approach in his work *By What Authority?* He asks:

> Is the evangelical committed to an unqualified Biblicism? Is there no place for "tradition" in any sense? . . . Must the evangelical be a rebel against the communion of saints and 2000 years of spiritual history?[8]

In the second place evangelicals should recognize that the church's authority is the tradition of the apostles.

It is impossible to deny the presence of tradition in faith. The question is really not "Do I believe in tradition?" but, "Which tradition will I follow?" Every evangelical subculture is laden with traditions peculiar to its own history. As Shelley says, "Any Biblicist who will carefully examine his own denomination will find characteristics that fail to rally explicit New Testament support."[9]

F. F. Bruce in *Tradition Old and New* describes a situation in a biblicist church where 1 Corinthians 13:10 ("when the perfect comes, the imperfect will pass away") was applied to the emergence of glossolalia and similar manifestations of the Spirit. A circular letter was sent with an appeal to the effect that this was the "standard" interpretation of 1 Corinthians 13:10 in their churches. Bruce points out that this interpretation was made "quite apart from the validity of the exegesis" and that the basis of it was really "an appeal to tradition, even if those who made it believed they were appealing to scripture."[10]

The disturbing truth is that because of our human frailty we all are subject to the misuse of Scripture, to the creation of a tradition which is really false, and to a legalistic insistence that all who would be in our camp must hold our view (even if incorrect). For that reason alone it is imperative to recover the original apostolic tradition.

In the third place evangelicals should recognize that the content of apostolic tradition was first and foremost the writings of the apostles.

R. Laird Harris, in his work *The Inspiration and Canonicity of the New Testament*[11] has effectively shown that the reason why some books were accepted as inspired and therefore canonical and others were not was the test of apostolicity. If a book was written by an apostle it was regarded as authoritative. As Clement wrote, "The Apostles have preached the gospel to us from the Lord Jesus Christ; Jesus Christ (has done so) from God. Christ therefore was sent forth by God and the Apostles by Christ."[12] Irenaeus tells us that Polycarp "always taught the things which he had learned from the Apostles, which the church has handed down, and which alone are true."[13] H. E. W. Turner in *The Pattern of Christian Truth*[14] has successfully demonstrated the reverence of the Fathers toward Holy Scripture. They were not, as Harnack once suggested, metaphysical theologians, but biblical theologians. Any reading of Justin Martyr, Irenaeus, Tertullian, Clement, Origen, Athanasius, Basil, Jerome, or Augustine shows that they are steeped in the Scriptures. And that they would agree with the judgment of St. John Chrysostom:

Tarry not, I entreat, for another to teach thee; thou hast the oracles of God. No man teacheth thee as they; for he indeed oft grudgeth much for vainglory's sake and envy. Hearken, I entreat you, all ye that are careful for this life, and procure books that will be medicines for the soul. If ye will not any other, yet get you at least the New Testament, the *Apostolic Epistles,* (italics mine) the Acts, the Gospels, for your constant teachers. If grief befall thee, dive into them as into a chest of medicines; take thence comfort of thy trouble, be it loss, or death, or bereavement of relations; or rather dive not into them merely, but take them wholly to thee; keep them in they mind."[15]

In the fourth place evangelicals should recognize that the key to interpreting Scripture is the "rule of faith." Because of the faithful witness of the second-century church, we are able to see that there is a "tradition within the tradition," a "canon within the canon." This is the tradition of the gospel summarized in the rule of faith (standardized in the Apostles Creed) which clarifies the essential biblical framework which the church proclaims, believes, guards, and passes on. This is the tradition of the church which is common to the whole church—Catholic, Orthodox, Protestant, Evangelical. Shelley comments that this rule of truth is "that teaching which distinguished Christianity from heresy. It was drawn from scripture but was found also in the living message of the church."[16] Cyril of Jerusalem in his *Catechetical Lectures* argues that each part of the creed can be confirmed out of Holy Scripture and that "just as the mustard seed in one small grain contains many branches, so also this faith has embraced in few words all the knowledge of godliness in the Old and New Testaments."[17] The church throughout history is called to be a witness to this truth. It is not to change it, to alter it, to add to it, or take away from it. It is to guard, preserve, transmit, expound, and teach it. That is, in all of its interpretation it is to remain faithful to it by doing its thinking in such a way that it always points to it as the truth revealed, received, and kept. The church's understanding of this truth may grow and deepen as it is called within a particular geographical place, cultural situation, or historical time to proclaim, explain, and defend it intelligently and perceptively, but the church is to proclaim no new doctrine or deny that which has been given.

In the fifth place evangelicals should recognize that apostolic tradition has always been guarded in the church. The Scriptures and the rule of faith were not set in a false and artificial isolation from the judgment of the church. The church had from the beginning given witness to her faith in preaching and in worship. The church as the body of Christ with her worship and her faith was in existence before the writings of the New Testament. The Old Testament Scripture gave rise to the church and the church gave rise to the New Testament. Thus, the writings were not written to create faith but were written in the context of faith to confirm and guide the faith which was already implanted in the heart.

Consequently, the truth which second-century Christians received and acclaimed was the tradition of the church. Evangelicals should come to grips with the fact that the Bible belongs to the church. It is the living church that receives, guards, passes on, and interprets Scripture. Consequently, the modern individualistic approach to interpretation of Scripture should give way to the authority of what the church has always believed, taught, and passed down in history. The second-century church in its battle with the false teaching of Marcion and the Gnostics crystalized both the *source* of the church's authority and the *substance* of the church's teaching, providing a clear-cut example of what Paul had admonished Timothy to do: (1) "guard the truth" (2 Tim. 1:14); (2) "entrust to faithful men"; (3) "who will be able to teach others also" (2 Tim. 2:2).

CONCLUSION

Theology, we have argued, is a reflective exercise and, as such, is human thinking about the truth. The facts of faith, however, are not the result of human thinking, but of divine revelation. These facts of faith were received by the apostles and transmitted to the church for safekeeping. They came originally through the oral witness of the apostles and were eventually committed to writing which became the authoritative source for Christian truth. Within this source there is an authoritative substance of truth—namely the message of the Christian faith as outlined in apostolic preaching and summarized in the earliest confessions such as the "rule of faith," the baptismal creeds, and later the Apostles Creed.

It is important for us as evangelicals to recognize the implications of apostolic authority. First, it implies that we ought not make the basis on which we determine a person's allegiance to apostolic Christianity any more narrow or broad than the basis determined in the early church. This means that a person who would advocate "you cannot have any right to the term evangelical unless you believe in my view of inerrancy, millennialism, spirituality, or whatever" is *adding* to the criterion set by the early church. On the other hand, anyone who would accept as apostolic or evangelical someone who would deny the authority of Scripture, the divinity of Christ, or the Second Coming is *reducing* the criterion of apostolic Christianity. In both instances the criterion by which the judgment is made is no longer *the tradition* but the personal preference of an individual or a group.

To create a new standard, whether it be authority based on inerrancy, the correctness of pretribulation rapture, tongues as a sign of the Holy Spirit, congregationalism as the only form of church government, Calvinism as the only true theology, dispensationalism as the key to interpretation, or any other teaching that represents a *distinction* and insists that adherence to this distinction is the criterion of being an evangelical, is a dangerous usurpation of the historic substance of the gospel, an addition to it, which will result in an imbalanced and unhistorical Christianity. Evangelicals must "stand fast" in the essence of the faith once for all delivered, neither adding to it nor taking away from it. Evangelicals should return then to the authority of apostolic tradition, the source of which is the Scriptures, the essential substance of which is the rule of faith. This view provides a broad but secure basis, and allows for the distinction between faith and formulation, the subject of the next chapter.

Notes

[1] *Against Heresies* I, XXVII, 1.
[2] 5:1
[3] See "A New English Translation of Melito's Paschal Homily" in *Current Issues in Biblical and Patristic Interpretation* (Grand Rapids: Eerdmans, 1975), p. 147, edited by Gerald F. Hawthorne
[4] *Against Heresies* I, XXVII, 2
[5] Ibid., I, X, 1
[6] Ibid., I, X, 2
[7] (Boston: A. V. Stewart, 1917), p. 497
[8] (Grand Rapids: Eerdmans, 1965), p. 148
[9] Ibid., p. 149
[10] (Grand Rapids: Zondervan, 1970), pp. 14-15
[11] (Grand Rapids: Zondervan, 1957)
[12] *The First Letter of Clement*, XLII, 1-2
[13] *Against Heresies* III, 4
[14] (London: Mowbray, 1954)
[15] Colossians, homily IX
[16] Shelley, *By What Authority?*, p. 83
[17] V, 12

Chapter 8

The Problem of
Faith and Formulation

THE PROBLEM OF FAITH AND FORMULATION

In order to arrive at a clear sense of the problem of "faith" and "formulation," we will begin with a definition of the terms.

The word "faith" is not being used here in the sense of subjective response such as trust *(fiducia)* or relationship *(fides)*. Instead it is being used in the sense of the propositions of faith, the corpus of Christian doctrine, the convictions which are a necessary part of the Christian view of things *(credentia)*. Paul refers to this body of doctrine as the "gospel," the "pattern of the sound words," the "truth" (2 Tim. 1:11-18). This is the truth taught by Jesus, transmitted by the apostles, and received in the church. It is the truth that is basic, fundamental, and apostolic. While there are summaries of the truth in the New Testament such as the sermons in Acts, Paul's creedal statement in 1 Corinthians 15:3-5, and the confessional hymn of Philippians 2:1-11, the full-orbed truth became more specifically organized in the church in the second century in "the rule of faith," which was the forerunner of the creeds. The word "faith" then is being used here in the specific sense of the *content* of Christianity as contained in the rule of faith, the Nicene Creed, and the Apostles Creed.

The word "formulation" is being used in the sense of theological thinking that goes beyond a mere affirmation of the faith, i.e., human thinking about the truth. The fact of historical theology is that Christians throughout history have, in their thinking about the faith, attempted to organize their thinking in various categories of thought

131

and to explain theological relationship between the parts of the whole to show their systematic unity. A glance at the history of theological formulations suggests that the articulation of theological systems is unavoidable. One only has to think of the outstanding systems of thought produced by the Cappadocian Fathers (Eastern Orthodox), Augustine, Aquinas, Luther, Calvin, and Arminius, to say nothing of the systems of thought propounded by theologians of lesser rank or movements such as Puritanism, Pietism, or Revivalism.

THE PROBLEM

The problem among many Christians is that because the distinction between faith and formulation is seldom made, there is a tendency to identify the peculiarities of a particular formulation as *the* truth. For example, as we have seen in chapter 2, each evangelical subculture stresses one or more issues which to some extent separates them from other subcultures. Consequently one group may stress separation, another tongues, another a particular hermeneutic. More obvious is the comparison that often is made between systems of theology. The Calvinists stress one system, the Arminians another, some try to bring the two together, and others stress no system at all. The fact is that beneath all these divisions there is a fundamental agreement. All evangelicals agree on the content of the gospel as defined by the early creeds. But not all evangelicals agree on the interpretation (formulation) of the facts of the faith.

The tragic result of our inability to separate formulation from faith and accept these differences is something like a theological legalism. Theological legalism is the insistence on a particular way of interpreting and organizing biblical data as the correct way of describing faith. It is what Bloesch calls orthodoxism, a tendency to view faith as assent to a particularization of dogma.

Among evangelicals, theological legalism often is built around the differences of strong personalities or clear thinkers who by the magnitude of their ministry have created a following. This appears to be a basic reason for the existence of so many evangelical subculture groups. Groups of people have fixed their leaders' theological insight into patterns of truth. Agreement with the leaders or founder, or in some cases with the interpretation given to the founder's insights, becomes a criterion for fellowship and ministry. Agreement with the teachings of Luther, Calvin, Menno Simons, Arminius, or Wesley marks a person as belonging to one group and not the other. Because correct belief often is associated with a person or that person's system, adherence to the system is sometimes maintained by means of a party spirit. Unfortunately, when a subculture clings to the letter of its own formulation, it stands in danger of minimizing the primary essence of the Christian faith through its preoccupation with the preservation of its own secondary concerns.

Although theological legalism grows out of a sincere desire to do right, to think correctly, to apply Scripture to life, and to please God, it can become a fixed and inflexible tradition characterized by a spirit of exclusivism, divisive and schismatic tendencies, a rigid and inflexible self-righteousness, a judgmental spirit, arrogance, and lovelessness. In short, it tends to make obedience and conformity to man-made insights the substance of Christian doctrine.

The origins of the legalistic theology lie in a legalistic methodology. Although all evangelicals accent the Bible as the final authority for faith and practice, there is much diversity among the subcultural groups on exactly how the authoritative word is to be interpreted. It is not the diversity of interpretation that produces a methodological legalism, but the attitude that a particular subcultural interpretation is the only one that is right.

John Newport in *Why Christians Fight over the Bible* describes the problem succinctly: "many denominational and confessional groups appear to feel that the view of the Bible and the interpretations expressed by their founders or early leaders are to be exalted (and in some cases deified)."[1] This attitude becomes particularly suspect when one considers the various approaches to biblical interpretation among evangelicals: the Lutheran emphasis on justification as the key to interpretation; the Reformed Covenantal approach; dispensationalism; literal *versus* spiritual interpretation of certain Old Testament prophecies; strict literalism *versus* openness to interpretation according to literary genre; and grammatical, historical, theological method *versus* certain types of devotional and subjective interpretation.

Methodological legalism occurs when a subculture treats its hermeneutical system as the one correct approach, excluding (at least in part) the other schools, without taking into consideration the fact that their school of interpretation is one among many. This closed-mindedness is what E. J. Carnell referred to as the "cultic mind." The variety that is found in the Bible itself is bound to produce a broad spectrum of emphasis. Unfortunately these variables allow for conditions where, "differences in interpretation interrupt the unity of the Spirit." Consequently Ramm argues, "It is well for conservative Protestantism to discover bases of fellowship rather than of divergence for a hermeneutical victory at the expense of Christian graciousness is hardly worth winning."[2]

While there are signs that this legalistic authoritarianism is cracking, the permeating and threatening presence of it restrains the winds of change and threatens to strangle the new spirit of a truly biblical and historic Christianity struggling to emerge in various stages in most evangelical subcultures.

We turn now to see whether the terms "faith" and "formulation" and the idea of the difference between the two is found in the early church.

FAITH AND FORMULATION IN THE EARLY CHURCH

Michael Green in *Evangelism in the Early Church*[3] discusses the content of Christian belief in relation to three terms: good news *(evangelizomai)*; to tell good news *(kerusso)*; and to bear witness *(martureo)*. He points out that the "good news" which Jesus proclaimed and embodied was nothing less than *the dawning of a new age*. It was introduced by the forerunner, John the Baptist, announced by Jesus at Nazareth in his reading of Isaiah 61, and preached by the disciples who declared "one subject and one only, Jesus." The central focus of this message was the redemptive death of Jesus, a death which the apostles said was for the whole world, although effective only for those who repented, believed, and followed Jesus.

The second word, to tell good news, means "to proclaim like a herald," and has reference to the same content as the "good news." In writers as varied as Matthew, Mark, Luke, and Paul, the good news preached is "the announcement of the climax of history, the divine intervention into the affirmations of men brought about by the incarnation, life, death, resurrection and heavenly session of Jesus of Nazareth."[4] Green also shows that the third word, "witness," which ordinarily means to attest facts or assert truths, also has reference to the same content. In Luke 24:48 Jesus commissions his disciples to be witnesses "of these things." As Green points out, these things include "the identification of Jesus as the Messiah, the fulfillment of all the scriptures in him, his suffering and death, his resurrection, and the proclamation of repentance and faith in his name to all nations, beginning from Jerusalem."[5]

The content of this apostolic preaching was soon challenged by those who would add to it as the Judaizers did, and those who would modify it as the syncretists did. For these reasons, Paul charged Timothy to "follow the pattern of sound words which you have heard from me" and to "guard the truth that has been entrusted to you" (2 Tim. 1:13-14). Here, as John Stott comments in *Guard the Gospel,* "Paul is commanding Timothy to keep before him as his standard of sound words, or as a 'model of sound teaching' what he had heard from the Apostles."[6] Timothy is not only to *guard* the gospel but also to *pass it on:* "What you have heard from me before many witnesses entrust to faithful men who will be able to teach others also" (2 Tim. 2:2). In these passages Stott sees a fourfold progression in guarding and passing on the faith:

> First, the faith has been entrusted to Paul by Christ. . . . Secondly, what has been entrusted to Paul by Christ Paul in turn has entrusted to Timothy. . . . Thirdly, what Timothy has heard from Paul he is now to "entrust to faithful men." . . . Fourthly, such men must be the sort of men who "will be able to teach others also."[7]

What we may see from this brief inquiry into the New Testament content of Christian truth is that the faith of the church, from the earliest times, has been characterized by a *specific content.* It is a recognizable body of truth. What was true in the New Testament period is equally true in the second century.

The picture of the church at the end of the second century is that of a number of churches (clustered around the major cities of Rome, Carthage, Alexandria, Jerusalem, and Antioch) united under their bishops, similar in worship, and grounded in the teaching of the apostles as summarized in the "rule of faith." Hegesippius, a church historian of the second century, wrote in his "Memoirs," a portion of which is still preserved in Eusebius' *Ecclesiastical History,* that he made a trip from Jerusalem to Rome and found, "In every succession . . . and in every city, the doctrine prevails according to what is declared by the law and the prophets and the Lord."[8]

The doctrine which Hegesippius referred to was not a theology, not theoretical thought, and not something which was the private possession of a few scholars. Instead his reference is to the contents of apostolic preaching, to the rule of faith, to the summary of Christian teaching which has been passed down from the apostles. This summary of the Christian faith which emerged with clarity in the second century is not theology but what we can aptly term "a biblical framework of thought." That is to say, the contents of biblical or historic Christianity which remained faithful to the biblical witness set forth the necessary presuppositions from which Christian thinking proceeds. Consequently, the contents of the rule of faith is not the result of Christian thinking, rather it is a summary of revelation: the apostles had summarized the data of revelation and passed it on. This "biblical framework" then became the framework which defined the perimeters within which the Christian church did her thinking.

When we move into the third century and beyond, the distinction between the faith of the church and the theological formulation of the church becomes more clear. In the third century the task of *theoretical thinking* became increasingly important to the church. Between A.D 300 and 600 the church was engaged in the task of formulating an explanation of what she already believed. This is evident in the Trinitarian, christological, and soteriological debates which dominated the third, fourth, and fifth centuries. (I do not deny formulation before the third century. Speaking in broad terms, the church at large began her formulation in the creedal controversies.)

An examination of these doctrinal controversies leads us to three observations: first, that the church always formulated her theology in conformity to the apostolic tradition. For example, Irenaeus' rule expresses faith in "one God . . . the Father Almigthy; one Christ Jesus, the Son of God; and in the Holy Spirit." In similar fashion the rule speaks of the full humanity and divinity of the Son—"The Son of God who was made flesh." And it refers to the sinful state of man: "and in the godless and wicked and lawless and blasphemers among men," as well as to the fact that the incarnation, death, and resurrection of Jesus was "for our salvation." The issue of the Trinitarian, christological, and soteriological controversies revolved around the *explanation* of these statements of faith. In other words, the church was engaged in a reflective exercise. She was thinking about the truths which the church had always accepted as *given* by God, *transmitted* by the apostles, and *received* by the church.

The second observation is that the church always thought about her faith within the context of her culture. For example, these controversies must be understood within the background of cultural, geographic, or philosophic differences. Both the Trinitarian and the christological controversies were at their center, exercises in communicating biblical truth into a Hellenistic frame of reference. The genius of both the Nicene Creed and the Chalcedonian definition is that the Fathers recognized the inadequacy of human language to capture the mystery of God as one yet three and the mystery of Jesus as fully human and fully divine. They rejected the dualistic notions that tended to separate the Son from the Father and the human from the divine, and affirmed within a culture that was dualistically inclined, the holistic faith of the church. In this way the church succeeded in remaining faithful to apostolic Christianity while communicating the faith in a cultural form different than that in which the truth had been originally received and understood.

The soteriological controversy, which has to do with the nature of man, of sin and grace, of election and free will, and of the means of receiving the benefits of the death of Christ, has never been as successful in uniting the church as the Nicene Creed and the Chalcedonian definition. While the Nicene Creed has gained universal acceptance and the Chalcedonian definition has been accepted by all except the Monophysites, the same cannot be said for the problem of man and salvation.

Although the entire church is united in its belief that man is a sinner and that Jesus Christ's death and resurrection procures salvation, there exist a number of explanations about man's sinful nature, and the means of receiving the benefits of Christ's death. The diversity on the soteriological question accounts for much of the diversity in the church. An examination of these differences can be accounted for, through the variety of influences which have given them shape—both cultural and philosophical. In other words, the church is divided not over her agreement to soteriological truth, i.e., that man is a sinner whose only hope is in the death and resurrection of Christ, but in her disagreement on *how* this is to be explained.

A third observation is that the existence of disagreement forced the church to face the issue of private judgment. How can we determine which of the many interpretations we should follow? If there are many explanations, many theologies, many formulations, is the church left in a sea of relativity or is there a criterion by which these various interpretations may be judged? The answer to this question was provided by Vincent of Lerins (d. 450) in his *Commonitory:*

> I have often then inquired earnestly and attentively of very many men eminent for sanctity and learning, how and by what sure and so to speak Universal rule I may be able to distinguish the truth of Catholic faith from the falsehood of heretical pravity; and I have always, and in almost every instance, received an answer to this effect: That whether I or any one else should wish to detect the frauds and avoid the snares of heretics as they rise, and to continue sound and complete in the Catholic faith, we must, the Lord helping, fortify our own belief in two ways: first, by the authority of the Divine Law, and then, by the Tradition of the Catholic Church.
>
> But here some one perhaps will ask, Since the canon of Scripture is complete, and sufficient of itself, what need is there to join with it the authority of the Church's interpretation? For this reason,—because, owing to the depth of Holy Scripture, all do not accept it in one and the same sense, but one understands its words in one way, another in another; so that it seems to be capable of as many interpretations as there are interpreters. For Novatian expounds it one way, Sabellius another, Donatus another, Arius, Eunomius, Macedonius, another, Plotinus, Apollinaris, Priscillian, another, Iovinian, Pelagius, Celestius, another, lastly, Nestorius another. Therefore, it is very necessary, on account of so great intricacies of such various error, that the rule for the right understanding of the prophets and apostles should be framed in accordance with the standard of Ecclesiastical and Catholic interpretation.
>
> Moreover, in the Catholic Church itself, all possible care must be taken, that we hold that faith which has been believed everywhere, always, by all. For that is truly and in the strictest sense "Catholic," which, as the name itself and the reason of the thing declare, comprehends all universally. This rule we shall observe if we follow universality, antiquity, consent. We shall follow universality if we confess that one faith to be true which the whole Church throughout the world confesses; antiquity, if we in no wise depart from those interpretations which it is manifest were notoriously held by our holy ancestors and fathers; consent, in like manner, if in antiquity itself we adhere to the consentient definitions and determinations of all, or at least of almost all priests and doctors.[9]

Vincent of Lerins wrote from a high view of the church. For him, the church was not a mere human organization of people who believe, but the body of Christ inseparably united with the Holy

Spirit. Consequently the Holy Spirit who is truly within the church brings consensus. Although the suggestion of Vincent does not represent a doctrine as such, it does offer a helpful way to look at much of the theological diversity within the church. In essence it suggests that the church in the fifth century was united in its affirmation of the biblical framework of thought, but sought to sort out the thinking about this framework to determine which theology stood in the tradition of the apostles by using the threefold rule of universality, antiquity, and consent as its criterion.

This brief summary suggests that the content of Christian faith is basic to and even prior to theological formulation. The content of the church, which is based on the apostolic preaching and writings, is common to the whole church, belonging to the simple believer, to the theologian, the philosopher, or any other Christian thinker. It is the basic framework of truth from which all Christians live and think. Theology, on the other hand, is the attempt to speak the faith through various cultural or philosophic forms in such a way that the biblical framework of truth is not violated. And the guide to Christian thinking, the means by which Christians hold their subjective interpretations in check, is the rule of universality, antiquity, and consensus. How these conclusions relate to the problems within evangelical Christianity and how they may set our agenda is the problem we must now address.

AN AGENDA FOR EVANGELICAL THEOLOGY

Coming to grips with faith and formulation

The first responsibility for evangelicals is to come to grips with the difference between "faith" and "formulation" and those implications which grow out of such an understanding. We may begin by looking at the major way of handling faith and formulation in the past—the old Roman Catholic view which argues for two sources of truth: Scripture and tradition. The argument is that God has given the church additional truths which complete the Bible. The Council of Trent (1545–1563) refers to these "truths" as the "unwritten traditions from the Apostles." A more recent Catholic view, though, is to regard these truths of the church as "living in 'the mind of the church' or preferably, in 'the present thought of the church in continuity with her traditional thought.'"[10] If this view is granted, then the church has within itself a kind of continuous inspiration, a view which obviously results in the correct formulation.

Although few evangelicals will allow the Roman Christian such an assertion, the strange fact is that many American evangelicals function with a similar attitude toward their tradition. One only has to look at the heated discussions between Calvinists and Arminians; premillennarians and amillennarians; dispensationalists and covenantalists; charismatics and noncharismatics. The exclusiveness and party spirit which denominational distinctives create is rooted in the conviction "I have the truth and you don't." This attitude forces us to conclude that some evangelicals act as though there are two sources of truth: the Scriptures *and* the particular tradition of the subculture, i.e., "I believe in the Scriptures *and* the Calvinistic interpretation of it."

Accepting the differences between summaries of faith
and explanation of the faith.

If we reject the two-source theory of truth, the alternative is to come to grips with the difference between the "summary of the faith" and a "formulation" of some aspect of the faith.

If we regard the summary of faith as the truth *inherited* from the apostles then we need to recognize that beyond these statements there exist many theological explanations, most of which have not had the universal consent of the church. For example, in the sixteenth century there were a baffling array of confessional statements: Lutheran, Reformed, Anabaptist, and Catholic. These "confessions" are distinct from the Creeds in that they are *more than* summaries of belief; they are *interpretations* of belief. Each confession constitutes a carefully designed interpretation of how the faith of the church is to be understood. Nevertheless, each interpretation is based on the universally accepted creeds of the early church.

This variety of interpretations raises the question of how we are to deal with the differences between us. Some will argue that one confession is true and the others are false. This is certainly a possible answer, but as we have noted above, such an assertion runs the risk of posing two sources of truth—the Bible and a particular interpretation of it. Others will insist that no confession is to be regarded as true, and will reject all statements of faith including the creeds in favor of a biblicism. This view, as already noted, runs the risk of failing to deal with the cults which also insist their views are derived solely and directly from an inspired and inerrant Bible. A third approach is to conclude that all theologies result from thinking about truth. This view recognizes the difference between faith and formulation, yet regards formulation as the necessary task of the church.

There are two arguments that support this latter position: in the first place interpretation of truth is based on human thinking. Confessions and books on systematic theology are the results of human thinking, not divine revelation. The limitations of the human mind are part of redeemed humanity so that, like Paul, all Christian thinkers, no matter how perceptive or scholarly, see "through a glass darkly." Consequently the tendency of human thinkers is to over-emphasize some aspect of truth and interpret everything else in relation to it. Luther, for example, developed his entire theology around justification by faith; Calvin around the sovereignty of God; and Menno Simons around the theme of discipleship. No one human or even a group of humans are able to overcome their limitations fully enough to write a comprehensive and all-embracing theology.

Second, all interpretations of the truth are conditioned by time, location, and culture. For example, the confessions of Luther and Calvin are understood best against the background of the late medieval interpretations of Christianity which they regarded as perverse. In that context, as they broke from the Roman church, they accented the Word so strongly that a weakened view of the church, ministry, and sacraments resulted. But what they did, although a "tragic necessity," as Jaroslov Pelikan describes it, was indeed a necessary corrective for that time and place. Nevertheless, it set into motion divisions and differences in the church which to this day have not been healed. The interpretation of truth therefore is the ongoing activity of the church. The church is always at work formulating her faith in such a way that it remains faithful to the original deposit, yet communicates within its own generation, geographical place, and cultural condition.

There are several important implications that proceed from recognizing the difference between faith and formulation. The first is that formulation does no violence to the essential truth of Christianity so long as the church accepts the historic substance of Christianity as the truth. In the case of a modern theological formulation, where the historic faith is regarded as untenable but the language of faith is retained, the formulation cannot be said to stand in continuity with the truth, for it denies the historic deposit, the apostolic testimony to the content of truth. However, where there is an honest acceptance of the historic contents of the faith, the thinking church is responsible to investigate the sources or attempt to articulate the faith within the context of a modern system of thought. But this thinking must always be brought under the judgment of the Scriptures and the testimony of history.

Second, however, the freedom to formulate human thinking about truth raises a certain cautionary note about the so-called doctrine of the private judgment of Scripture. Peter Toon in *The Right of Private Judgment* points out the fact that the careless subjective approach to Scripture, which is a denial of the doctrine in its Reformational sense, "has been abused in much contemporary Evangelicalism" in that "little concern seems to be shown for setting the right context in which the Bible is to be understood and interpreted."[11] He rightly argues that in the New Testament those who became converted were "expected to submit to the teaching of Christ and his Apostles" that in fact private judgment really meant "making sure that one held firmly to the genuine Apostolic tradition."[12] For this reason it is important that Christians make sure their ideas are tested by Scripture and the history of interpretation in the church. With so many subjective and ill-informed opinions filling the air, especially those coming from our current obsession with group discussions and sharing sessions, it is a good idea to test our insights by asking "What has the church said?" This is a surer and safer test for truth than the subjectivistic and individualistic insights that are being passed around in gatherings of well-intentioned believers.

A third implication is that it would be well for all of us to hold our theological formulations with a degree of tentativeness. This in no way means we are to be tentative about the gospel or the deposit of faith. The truth which has been revealed and passed down in history is unchangeable. Our conviction about it, our adherence to it, our propagation of it, is to be executed with firm assurance that it is true. But our formulation of that truth into a system, whether it be Calvinism, Arminianism, Dispensationalism, or whatever, must be expressed with tentativeness, even hesitancy. We must learn to say, "it seems to me" or "my interpretation of Scripture seems to suggest" or "our church follows the interpretation of so and so who saw it this way." Here in the area of formulation we must learn to be *inclusive,* not exclusive. Obviously, such an approach serves the gospel, for it accents what we are sure about and makes what has been passed down in history unmistakably clear. It avoids making nonessentials essential and sets forth an attitude of Christian humility and graciousness which makes us accepting of and open to other Christians who also stand in the historic faith, but articulate it through a different frame of reference.

A fourth implication is that thinking about the truth is the ongoing task of the church. To think about the truth and to articulate it in human form is consistent with the Incarnation. A mere biblicism is a denial of the human container through which truth is always known. The task of the church is to articulate truth within the context of history and culture. Such a task demands the critical use of human methods of thought—be they philosophical, psychological, anthropological, economic, or whatever. It is this task that leads us into the next step of an agenda for evangelical theology—namely learning to communicate truth in human garb in such a way that truth is not lost.

Communicating truth in human garb

As the church faces the task of doing theology, the inevitable problem is that of communicating truth in human garb without accommodating truth to the garb through which it is being explained.

The process is simply this: we interpret our faith through the glasses of the culture in which we find ourselves. We tend then to impose these cultural categories of thought on the faith, articulate our faith through these categories, and create an expression of Christianity peculiar to those cultural forms. Consequently the faith becomes inextricably interwoven with a particular view of life or method. Our orthodoxy, then, becomes not only believing the faith, but also believing it within the life-view or by the method through which it has been expressed. Consequently, the "grid" which is the garb of the faith becomes a matter of belief just as much as the faith itself.

Helmut Thielicke addresses this problem in his work *The Evangelical Faith* by making a distinction between a theology of *actualization* and a theology of *accommodation*. A theology of actualization "always consists in a new interpretation of truth . . . the truth remains intact.

It means that the hearer is summoned and called 'under the truth' in his own name and situation." On the other hand a theology of accommodation takes a different approach. It calls truth "under me" and lets me be its noun. It is pragmatic to the extent that it "assigns truth the function of being the means whereby *I master life.*"[13] (Italics mine.)

Thielicke names accommodation theology the "cartesian" approach after René Descartes, the seventeenth-century philosopher who insisted that the starting point for truth was man—"I think, therefore I am." According to Thielicke there are, broadly speaking, two approaches in which cartesian theology may be expressed—rationalism and experientialism. The reason these two approaches can be regarded as accommodation theologies is because "the receiving I is primary."[14] We might paraphrase it like this: "The Christian faith is a perfectly rational system about life. When *you* accept it and live by it *you* will really have life by the tail. *You* will be able to stand up strong and really face life"; or "What *you* need is an experience of Jesus Christ. When *you* let Him come into *your* life and take over, *you* will feel much better. Everything will fall in place for *you* and life will be beautiful." The emphasis is on the person, what the person does, how much better it is for the person, how much more in control of life the person will be.

On the other hand, actualization theology comes at a person's lost situation in an entirely different way. Because the person is "under the truth" an appeal is not made to the effect that the message of Christianity is "good for you." Instead, the truth is spoken in such a way that the person stands under the judgment of God, condemned because of sin, and under the sure wrath of God. Truth is proclaimed, not merely explained. Through this proclamation the person is confronted then by truth—the truth about the human situation, the truth about personal involvement and participation in that situation, and the truth about the way Jesus Christ has met that situation and overcome it by His death and resurrection. Such an approach is a return to the kerygmatic preaching of the apostles.

The theology of actualization is the historic approach to communicating the gospel. The emphasis is on the biblical proclamation as truth and not the explanation which often is reliant on current philosophical categories of thought as well as subject to creaturely limitations. Final truth, it says, is always deeper and much more complex, more mysterious than the best explanations we can offer.

This was the task of the church in the creedal era. How could it take the biblical concepts and articulate them within the framework of a Hellenistic mind-set, a Platonic or Neoplatonic philosophy? For example, the Trinitarian controversy employed Greek words like *homoousion* and *hypostasis* to communicate the unity and diversity of the Godhead. The christological controversy as well was settled through the use of Greek language and Hellenistic thought forms. However, the genius of the creedal formulations is that *they did not elevate the methodology or the final theological form as truth in and of itself. Instead, the Nicene and Chalcedonian creeds pointed to the truth contained in Scriptures and summarized in the rule of faith as ultimately beyond the possibility of being captured in a comprehensive form.* In other words, the creeds wrote a negative theology: Jesus is not a creature as Arius taught; Jesus' humanity is not lost into divinity as Apollinarius taught, nor is His divinity a mere appendage to His humanity as some alleged Nestorius taught. No, instead of allowing Jesus Christ to be defined as some wanted, the creeds affirmed the mystery of the unity of the Son with the Father and the completeness of full humanity and full divinity in the person of Jesus Christ. The point is that the creeds did not propagate a system, but affirmed the ultimate mystery of Christ through the thought patterns of the day. They spoke the biblical framework through a language and thought form different than the biblical language and thought forms without accommodating the truth to those forms.

The use of cultural forms as channels for truth has always been an issue in Christianity. Aquinas expressed the Christian faith through the Aristotelian system of philosophy; Hodge through a Scottish Realism and Strong through a Personal Idealism. These are simply a few samples of philosophical systems through which thinkers attempt to communicate the Christian message. The problem we face is that when the method and the results of the method are made authoritative, Christ and the Christian message then become blurred in the system.

The point is that the theology of the early church was able to deal with the ambiguities of the Christian revelation. It didn't try to explain everything through a system. Instead, it developed creeds and theologies as means to communicate truth, not as ends in themselves. Hopefully, as we learn to articulate an actualization theology we will become not only more tolerant of people we disagree with, but also able to see the complexity of doing theology more clearly, resulting in a reduction of our arrogance and pride as well as a growth in genuine humility. Furthermore such an attitude will free us to do theology within the framework of our own culture. We will begin to understand that the task of theology is not that of arriving at a fixed explanation which we forever freeze, but rather the calling to bring biblical thought to bear on ultimate questions in culture and in every generation in such a way that it communicates the truth of apostolic Christianity to that situation. Consequently, our systematic theology will forever become historical theology as the church will always be alive to the truth of Jesus Christ and the Word, not dead through a slavish allegiance to a system about the truth. This more biblical approach to theology will free us to make mistakes and to take the risk of thinking out loud—a risk which no one who is a slave to the system can take. Above all, this open-ended theology will free us to be related to Jesus Christ in a real and personal way by allowing Him and the truth about Him in the Scripture to be our final and ultimate point of reference.

CONCLUSION

We have attempted to argue throughout this section against an atomistic and unhistorical approach to theology. The fact is that all evangelical subcultures share the gospel as expressed in the apostolic tradition. The point is, however, that many of us lack the historical perspective to know how to deal with the differences that exist between us. It is not enough to ignore these differences, to dismiss them as though they were unimportant. Nor is it a wise course to stress our differences so strongly that they become divisive issues, breaking that spirit of harmony and love that ought to bind us together.

We may argue therefore, that the wisest and most biblical self-understanding is to recognize that differences are all rooted in an aspect of the truth. The fundamentalist concern for separation from those who do not believe; the charismatics' concern to return to the Spirit; the concern of Lindsell and others for inerrancy; the concern of the Restoration churches for unity as well as all the other *distinc-*

tives are all grounded in an aspect of the truth.

What is needed is a firm grasp on the apostolic deposit as the essential deposit of faith—the framework on which we all build. Then, recognizing that we belong to each other as a body, we need through love, understanding, patience, and acceptance to learn from each other to affirm and support each other in our differences as well as in our similarities. Only by recognizing theology as human thinking about truth will we be able to establish the basis from which the unity and reconciliation of evangelicals can be realized.

Notes

[1](Nashville: Thomas Nelson, 1974), p. 14
[2]Ramm, Bernard, *Protestant Biblical Interpretation* (Grand Rapids: Baker, 1956), p. 267
(Grand Rapids: Eerdmans, 1970), pp. 48ff.
[4]Ibid., p. 60
[5]Ibid., p. 71
[6](Downers Grove: InterVarsity Press, 1973), pp. 43-44
[7]Ibid., pp. 50-51
[8]*Ecclesiastical History* Book III, XXII
[9]*A Commonitory*, II
[10]See Bruce Shelley, *By What Authority?* (Grand Rapids: Eerdmans, 1965)
[11](Portland: Western Conservative Baptist Seminary, 1975), p. 6
[12]Ibid., p. 12
[13](Grand Rapids: Eerdmans, 1974), p. 27
[14]Ibid., p. 38

Section IV
Bibliography for Further Reading

It is difficult to find critical works dealing with the way evangelicals do theology. For one thing evangelicals are not generally self-critical, and for another evangelicals have only recently come to the attention of nonevangelical writers. One article I've found helpful is "Contemporary Evangelical Faith and an Assessment and Critique" by Paul L. Homer in *The Evangelicals,* edited by Wells and Woodbridge (New York: Abingdon, 1975). My own thinking about this has been stimulated by the study of historical theology since the time of the Reformation. I have summarized this material in the first five chapters of *Reshaping Evangelical Higher Education* by Mayers, Richards, and Webber (Grand Rapids: Zondervan, 1972). Also read Arthur Holmes, *Faith Seeks Understanding* (Grand Rapids: Eerdmans, 1971) and *All Truth Is God's Truth* (Grand Rapids: Eerdmans, 1977).

The situation is different with the early church. There is so much material on this subject that it is difficult to decide what to leave out. For general primary material I suggest Cyril C. Richardson (ed.), *Early Christian Fathers* (Philadelphia: Westminster Press, 1953); William A. Jurgens, *The Faith of the Early Fathers* (Collegeville: The Liturgical Press, 1970); and *Readings in the Early Fathers* (St. Charles, Ill.: St. Charles House, 1977). The best secondary work on the theology of the early church is J. N. D. Kelly, *Early Christian Doctrines* (New York: Harper & Row, 1959).

For the problem of authority, Scripture, and tradition in the early church the classic is H. E. W. Turner, *The Pattern of Christian Truth* (London: A. R. Mowbray & Co., 1954).

John R. Stott in *Guard the Gospel* (Downers Grove: InterVarsity Press, 1973) offers a helpful exposition of Paul's second letter to Timothy. His remarks regarding Scripture, tradition, and the gospel are pertinent. Also, I've benefited greatly by three other works by evangelicals: F. F. Bruce, *Tradition Old and New* (Grand Rapids: Zondervan, 1970); Bruce Shelley, *By What Authority?* (Grand Rapids: Eerdmans, 1965); and Bernard Ramm, *The Pattern of Religious Authority* (Grand Rapids: Eerdmans, 1959). Shelley's is the most helpful because he concentrates on the developments in the second century. A good selection of creeds are found in John H. Leith, *Creeds of the Churches* (New York: Doubleday, 1963) and B. A. Gerrish, *The Faith of Christendom* (New York: Meridian Books, 1963) although Philip

Schaff, *The Creeds of Christendom*, 3 vol. (New York: Harper, 1919) is the standard work in this area.

For the future of evangelical theology I suggest the writings of T. F. Torrance, especially *Theology in Reconstruction* (Grand Rapids: Eerdmans, 1965) and *Theology in Reconciliation* (Grand Rapids: Eerdmans, 1976). Torrance develops theology from an incarnational view and refers back to the early fathers frequently and in depth. Helmut Thielicke's work, *The Evangelical Faith* (Grand Rapids: Eerdmans, 1974) offers an excellent and thorough critique of the cartesian approach to theology. Ian C. Barbour in *Myths, Models, and Paradigms* (New York: Harper, 1974) suggests that we think of theological models in a fashion similar to our use of scientific models.

SECTION V

AN AGENDA
FOR MISSION

Chapter 9

The Mission of the Church in Evangelism

WHAT IS THE MISSION OF THE CHURCH?

The mission of the church is summarized by Matthew: "Go therefore and make disciples of all nations, baptizing them in the name of the Father and of the Son and of the Holy Spirit, teaching them to observe all that I have commanded you; and lo, I am with you always, to the close of the age" (28:19-20). The sequence is make disciples . . . baptize . . . teach.

Most mission models of the recent past are based on the concept that evangelism and education are two different functions of the church. This questionable view finds support in C. H. Dodd, *The Apostolic Preaching and Its Development.* Dodd's thesis is that "It was by kerygma . . . not by didache that it pleased God to save men."[1] On the strength of Dodd's arguments educators like Iris Cully in *Dynamics of Christian Education* have argued that "the method of the early church . . . was to proclaim the gospel as the way to faith; teaching as instruction came later to strengthen faith and to deepen the knowledge of faith."[2] James Smart, an educator who has consistently rejected this separation of evangelism and catechesis wrote in *The Teaching Ministry of the Church:*

> In alleging that in the Biblical period teaching was confined largely to ethical instruction, he (Dodd) has validated what is actually one of the chief sicknesses of education in the church, that it has been consistently *moralistic* (italics mine) in its character and has lacked the depth and power of the kerygma. He has done nothing less than detach the work of teaching from all essential relation to the kerygma.[3]

153

Not only has the loss of evangelism in education had an adverse effect on education, but the loss of education in evangelism is one of the root causes of superficiality in evangelism. The message of Christianity is a *historical* message with *content*. Whenever Christianity is preached without its history or content it is reduced to a social or psychological panacea, or worse yet, a mere manipulation of the feelings, moving the individual into a contentless response. On the other hand, whenever the content of Christianity is presented as factual or intellectual data without the accompanying call to commitment and change of life, Christian education loses its power to form character in the convert. Clearly, evangelism and education must stand together. There must be content in preaching and proclamation in teaching.

Although a number of scholars have questioned Dodd's conclusion, it wasn't until the publication of *Preaching and Teaching in the Earliest Church* by R. C. Worley that Dodd's conclusions were exposed by a full-scale treatment.[4] Worley shows as Michael Green suggests that in "both rabbinic Judaism and in early Christianity there was no such clear-cut distinction between the work of the evangelist and the teacher."[5] Paul's example at Ephesus where "he entered the synagogue and for three months spoke boldly, *arguing* and *pleading* about the kingdom of God" (Acts 19:8) suggests that the mission of the church to the unconverted was accompanied by a rigorous and stimulating intellectual activity.

Not only is the mission of the church to evangelize and educate, but also it is a mission to serve the world. The God of the Bible is a sending God. He sent the prophets; He sent His Son; He sent the apostles; He sends us. The mission of the church must therefore be understood in an incarnational sense. That is, as He sent His Son, so He sends us. "As the Father has sent me," Jesus said "even so I send you" (John 20:21). As Jesus was sent, His church is sent *into the world to serve.*[6]

Peter Beyerhaus, in his work *Missions: Which Way?*[7] believes the evangelical understanding of service is limited by the failure of evangelicals to have a truly biblical understanding of history. In other words the mission of the church must be based, not only on a few verses of Scripture, but on a firm grasp of the theology of history.

The failure to understand the biblical view of history is grounded in a simplistic theology that does not grasp the implications of the

Christian doctrines of creation, incarnation, and redemption. The Christian doctrine of creation affirms that God not only called the world into being, but that He also is active in it, purposefully moving it toward a final destination. The doctrine of the Incarnation affirms that God entered into human history, became a part of the struggles of life, shared in what it means to be fully human, and fully participated in life. The doctrine of redemption affirms that not only did Christ die for man, but also for his world. Consequently Christ's death affects history, for it inaugurates a new humanity (the church), which, as a historical people, has a responsibility to the ongoing process of God in history through which, by God's providence, the world is being directed toward its final consummation in the second coming of Christ.

According to Beyerhaus our failure to understand this historical dimension of the gospel has evidenced itself in a simplistic other-worldly gospel as well as an exclusion of salvation from history and society.

The present direction of evangelical mission, however, is a rejection of the antihistorical approach which has characterized its past. Evangelists are becoming increasingly aware of the need for content, and educators are becoming more aware of the need to teach the Bible in such a way that it makes a difference in *living*. Furthermore, evangelicals *are* beginning to take history seriously. For this reason there is much concern for crosscultural communication and a new interest in the relationship of the church to social issues. Consequently we will treat missions in this larger fourfold sense, under the following headings:

1. The mission of the church in *evangelism* (chapter 9)
2. The mission of the church in *crosscultural communication* (chapter 10)
3. The mission of the church in *education* (chapter 11)
4. The mission of the church to *society* (chapter 12)

THE MISSION OF THE CHURCH IN EVANGELISM: THE PROBLEM

That evangelism is the hallmark of evangelical Christianity, no one can question. In this century alone evangelicals have circled the globe and penetrated into the obscure parts of the world to present Christ's saving message to millions of people. Recently the Roman

Catholic church and the World Council of Churches have recognized the urgency of evangelization and are now giving greater attention to what has always consumed the energies of evangelical Christianity.

Although it is not popular to critique the evangelical efforts at evangelism, constructive self-criticism always has the value of strengthening the church rather than weakening it. It is in this spirit then that many evangelical leaders have come to recognize that the major fault of evangelism among evangelicals has been the tendency to oversimplify the Christian message.

The oversimplification of evangelism is rooted in what R. B. Kuiper in *God-centered Evangelism* calls man-centered evangelism:

> For too often the limelight is turned full upon the evangelist—his personality, his eloquence, his ability as an organizer, the story of his conversion, the hardships which he has endured, the number of his converts, in some instances the miracles of healing allegedly performed by him. At other times attention is focused on those who are being evangelized—their large numbers, their sorry plight as exemplified by poverty, disease and immorality, their supposed yearning for the gospel of salvation, and, worst of all, the good that is said to dwell in them and to enable men to exercise saving faith of their own free, although unregenerate, volition. And how often the welfare of man, whether temporal or eternal, is made the sole end of evangelism.[8]

Unfortunately this man-centered evangelism tends to create and support what J. V. Langmead Casserley in *The Retreat from Christianity*[9] calls the cult of the "simple Christian." This view supports the notion that the simple Christians who read the Bible, pray daily, attend church, and witness faithfully are the ones who really have a corner on God's presence and power in their lives. In turn, suspicion is sometimes cast toward those who think or question or attempt to probe more deeply into the meaning or the implication of the Christian faith in life. Consequently, it is not uncommon for evangelical intellectuals to be made to feel inferior because they do not feel at home with Christians who find virtue in simplicity alone. Nor is it uncommon for intellectuals to feel judged or pressured by those who elevate simplicity to a near creedal status. The warning Casserley makes in the case of this kind of self-satisfaction and pride which results from simplicity is to "avoid despising each other's gifts, lest we fall into the habit of congratulating ourselves overmuch on our own."[10] In any religious circles which indulge in the cult of the "simple Christian," this is precisely the sin to which the "simple Christian" himself becomes most prone.

There are at least two ways in which an oversimplification of the gospel is expressed: the first occurs when evangelism is divorced from theology; the second when Christian obedience as the result of faith is neglected.

It is a man-centered evangelism that tends to separate the message from the theology of the church. Whatever one thinks of Wesley, Whitefield, Edwards, or Finney, it will have to be admitted that they attempted to evangelize with a framework of theology. John R. Stott, in one of his earliest works, *Fundamentalism and Evangelism,* recognizes the need for an evangelism with content and urges "we shall be faithful in outlining the implications of the Christian life. We shall urge our hearers to count the cost of Christian discipleship . . . we shall preach the repentance which is a turning from all known sin and a readiness to make restitution where possible. We shall proclaim the lordship of Christ and the necessity of the unconditional surrender of every department of life to Him. We shall plead also for an open and unashamed allegiance to Christ in the fellowship of the church."[11]

Secondly, Jim Wallis in *Agenda for Biblical People* argues that evangelism has separated its message from obedience. "The great tragedy of modern evangelism," he writes, "is in calling many to belief but few to obedience."[12]

The separation of evangelism from obedience produces the cult of easy and attractive Christianity. All too often the faith is packaged through beautiful people who testify that Christianity has really been good for them: it has given meaning to life, saved a marriage and a home, or made life fun, exciting, adventuresome. Others testify that they are now happy, acceptable, in control of things, popular, and even rich. I do not mean to demean the positive effects of Christianity. Certainly many lives are given meaning and direction. Our major emphasis, however, must not be to make Christianity attractive, as attractive as it is; nor to make it a panacea for all ills, as much as it does give life meaning and purpose. Instead, we must emphasize the cost of discipleship, the absolute claim of God over our entire life, and the necessity of a faith that issues forth in obedience. It's a problem of balance and emphasis. The need is to return to the biblical message and its demands.

One reason why modern evangelism may be divorced from obedience is due to the purpose of evangelists. Evangelists seek to elicit a response, to get someone to make a decision, to make a commitment to Christ. For this reason evangelistic services sometimes play on the emotions. The music, the testimonies, the sermon, the invitation are all geared in such a way that the emotional level of the people can be skillfully and psychologically guided toward a decision. Often such a heavy emphasis is put on the decision that the inquirer may leave with the false impression that the sum and substance of Christianity is in making a decision. The result is an individualization of the Christian message. The need for pre-evangelism, for a return to the unity between *kerygma* and *didache,* for a follow-up program in the local church is being increasingly recognized as a healthy corrective to emotional evangelism.

Another reason for the divorce between evangelism and obedience may be found in "cultural conversions." That is, a person may make a radical break from a former way of living into a particular form of Christianity. For example, a person may be persuaded to give up bad habits and join a group whose identity is strongly defined by the absence of smoking, drinking, dancing, gambling, and the like. The problem is that the new convert may confuse an obedience to the forms of this "new culture" with an obedience to Christ. The person may be told that obedience means giving up bad habits, and taking on new habits such as Bible reading, prayer, witnessing, attendance at church, and tithing. As good as these new habits are, they do not get at the heart of Christian obedience, and the reduction of the Christian life to these few principles tends to obscure larger and deeper issues as well as to lead the convert who obeys them to substitute a cultural change of habits for a more far-reaching biblical change of life style.

Having summarized these problems, we turn now to look at the pattern of evangelism in the early church.

THE PATTERN OF EVANGELISM
IN THE EARLY CHURCH

When Jesus began to preach, His message was the kingdom of God. Although John the Baptist had already preceded Jesus and preached the coming of the kingdom, Jesus' proclamation was something new. The Baptist was speaking as a prophet of the One who was to come. But Jesus was the event John proclaimed, the kingdom had arrived in Him. To understand New Testament evangelism, then, we must understand the meaning of the kingdom.

The basic meaning of the Greek word *basileia* (kingdom) is twofold. First it refers to the *realm* of a king, and secondly it refers to the *rule* of the king. These two meanings may be applied in three ways as George Eldon Ladd, in his book *The Gospel of the Kingdom* has shown. Some passages refer to the kingdom as "God's *reign*"; others refer to God's kingdom as the "*realm* into which we may now enter to experience the blessings of His reign"; and still others refer to a "future realm which will come only with the return of our Lord Jesus Christ into which we shall then enter and experience the fulness of His reign."[13] These distinctions demand an exegetical integrity, forcing the serious Bible student to examine every reference of the kingdom in its context in order to know which of the aspects of the kingdom is being mentioned.

There is, however, despite different usages of the word kingdom, three underlying themes which permeate the "kingdom" uses.

First, the underlying theme is the *rule of God in Christ over all the areas of life*. It is this rule that Jesus proclaimed. In effect He was saying, "The ruler of the universe has come to rule in your life. . . . Turn away from all other demands for ownership of your life . . . enter into My reign. Let Me rule in the life of the world through My rule in you." Jesus called men away from following their false gods to follow the one true God manifested in Himself.

To grasp the meaning of the rule of Christ we must take into account the New Testament contrast between the kingdom of Christ and the kingdom of Satan. We see Christ's kingdom as a "rule" more clearly when we view His kingdom within the context of the antikingdom of Satan. It is of primary importance to recognize that the contrast is between two "rules" in the world order. Satan's rule in this world is not some kind of ownership of creation. (This is a gnostic doctrine which has crept into the thinking of many people, i.e., the world belongs to Satan and therefore it is bad and everything in it is evil.) On the contrary, the ownership of the world belongs to God by virtue of the creation. It is His world and it is good! However, due to the Fall, a new force or power had been unleashed—namely, the power of the evil one *who rules in the hearts of men and in the life of the world through men.* So the conflict between Jesus and Satan has nothing to do with the physical world. It has to do with persons. By whom will the life of persons be ruled? By the king of evil or by God's King?

The second underlying theme of the kingdom is that *it is a gift.* Jesus pointedly emphasizes that people must be born into the kingdom. The kingdom comes to a person without that person's help or actions (John 3:5-6,8; Mark 9:1; Luke 17:20-21). Although entrance into the kingdom is viewed as a gift, there are also correlatives which look at entrance into the kingdom from a person's point of view. The way a person is to receive the rule of God is as a child (Mark 10:15). The self-righteous Pharisees and other Jewish leaders won't get into the kingdom because of their refusal to repent (Matt. 21:31-32).

Also, to follow the king is no easy decision—no "cheap grace." Those who come under the King's rule must be willing to "give him first place" and "live as he wants you to" (Matt. 6:33). One must face God's kingly power with absolute honesty and openness. It is the deepest decision of a person's life—a sharp "either-or" decision which is irrevocable. One who enters under the rule of the King on a wave of enthusiasm, without thought and intent, is like the person who "built his house upon the sand" (Matt. 7:26-27). Even those who make it a habit to say "Lord, Lord" are not His—only those who truly do the will of the King (Matt. 7:21-23). The demand of the kingdom is so great that it can be set forth in such shocking appeals as insistence on the hatred of one's own family (Matt. 10:37), plucking out the eye of temptation, cutting off the hand that offends (Matt. 5:29-30), or making oneself a eunuch for the sake of the kingdom (Matt. 19:11-12). But who can do all that? Who can really enter as a child? Who can truly do all that the King demands?

The third underlying motif is that Jesus *Himself is the embodiment* of the kingdom (Matt. 19:29; 21:9; Mark 10:29; 11:9-10; Luke 18:29-30). It was the King-god who "became a human being and lived here on earth among us" (John 1:14). It is this King who was made flesh, who died and was buried, who was raised from the dead, who is present in the church, who is returning for those He rules. He is the One who is announced and is present in the proclamation. To preach Jesus Christ then is to preach the kingdom. The content of the Good News is the coming of Christ—who is Himself the Good News—the embodiment of the kingdom. In Jesus both the publication of the Good News and the actualization of the Good News are brought together. He not only proclaims the Good News but He *is* the Good News and He *does* the Good News. He is the content of His message.

We should note then that it is this theme (Jesus—the kingdom) that the apostles preached. Jesus sent the disciples "to tell everyone about the coming of the kingdom of God" (Luke 9:2, LB). The ministry of the apostles began after Pentecost and as a result of the persecution the believers who had fled Jerusalem went everywhere preaching the Good News about Jesus!" (Acts 8:4, LB).

For this reason, there are three aspects about apostolic preaching and teaching which are important to keep in mind in evangelism. The first is that the apostles were not preaching mere facts, but an interpretation of an event. The message was that Jesus lived, died, and rose again *for their sin!* Salvation is no mere assent to the facts about the King—but the actualization of repentance, faith, and obedience. This is the Good News "that saves" (1 Cor. 15:2).

The second aspect of apostolic preaching is that Christ is the inaugurator of a new age in the church.

The special feature of this new age is that God Himself has entered into human history (John 1:14). It is the age in which the King of glory has *appeared* in human flesh and lived out before the eyes of people the rule of the King. Because He is that King, He calls people to follow Him, to live under His rule, and establish Him as the Lord of their lives. The presence of His kingdom is within them (Luke 17:20-21) and some day will extend over the whole world (Rev. 11:15). The full-blown development of this kingdom concept as it relates both to the presence of the kingdom in the here and now and the ultimate fulfillment and establishment of the eternal kingdom, means that there can be no area of life or living that escapes the rule of the King. His rulership extends over all of life. His rule has to do with our material, physical, social, psychological, political, and cultural being. What we do, say, and think must be executed under His rule. Our eating, sleeping, drinking, judging, and loving must all take place under the rule of the King. He is the Lord of *life*—all of life. Thus the inauguration of the new age is not some mere intrusion into the secular world, nor a spiritual component that runs alongside of life. Rather it is the central dynamic to the whole of life and it involves the whole man in all his thinking, feeling, and living aspects.

A third aspect of apostolic evangelism in the New Testament is that it always led to baptism and entrance into the church, the realm where Christ rules. Baptism was a physical sign and seal of conversion, of a turning away from a former way of life, of a trusting in Jesus.

Baptism was no empty symbol, no mere external act, but an act which was a *necessary* aspect of conversion. The message was repent *and* be baptized. The doctrine of justification and the doctrine of baptism were all of one piece, in a holistic sense. It is no accident, as Green remarks in *Evangelism in the Early Church*, that Romans 6, the great chapter on baptism as an identification with Christ, comes after Romans 5, the great chapter on justification. They belong together and the pattern of the early church was always conversion and baptism.[14]

A brief consideration of the meaning of baptism in the New Testament period shows us how important baptism was regarded.[15] Baptism implies repentance and renunciation, its form symbolizes the main facts of the gospel, its content signifies an entrance into the New Age, an admission to the new community, and a mark of the reception of the Spirit. The cumulative evidence of all these notions which are filled with content suggests that conversion and baptism were not mere emotional experiences, but were entered into on the basis of understanding. Evangelism in the New Testament was not based on emotion, but on *content*. It was an appeal made on the basis of the truth of Jesus' person and what that meant for mankind.

AN AGENDA FOR EVANGELISM

The goal of evangelism should be to overcome the weaknesses of oversimplification on the one hand, and on the other to return to the biblical practice which emphasizes kingdom preaching.

Billy Graham set the agenda for this kind of evangelism at the Lausanne Conference in his address "Why Lausanne?" He said "as this congress convenes, four basic presuppositions should undergird our labors. These four foundation stones have guided our planning and should underlie everything we do at this congress."[16] A summary and paraphrase of Graham's four points is as follows:

1. Evangelicals must stand in the tradition of historic evangelism.
2. Evangelicals must act as one body, obeying one Lord, facing one world, with one task.
3. Evangelicals must re-emphasize those biblical concepts which

are essential to evangelism.

4. Evangelicals must be concerned about the unevangelized world and the church's resources to evangelize the world.

Graham's insistence on a return to a biblical and historical approach to evangelism is the key to an agenda for evangelism. This can be accomplished by, 1) a restoration of evangelism that centers on the kingdom of God; 2) a restoration of evangelism that stresses the rule of God; and 3) a restoration of evangelism that demands radical obedience.

First, an evangelism that centers on the kingdom of God will naturally speak to the entirety of human existence.

Dr. Visser 't Hooft in his retiring speech as general secretary of the World Council of Churches at the Uppsala Assembly said: "A Christianity which has lost its vertical dimension has lost its salt, and is not only insipid in itself, but useless to the world. But a Christianity which would use the vertical dimension as a means of escape from responsibility for and in the common life of men is a denial of the incarnation of God's life for the world manifested in Christ."[17] This statement contains in a nutshell the essence of kingdom evangelism. It is to bring the whole person in all vertical and horizontal relationships under the jurisdiction of Jesus Christ.

There is a cautionary note, however, that is in order here. It is to the effect that we must hold the vertical and the horizontal aspects of our relationship to the kingdom in balance. While evangelicals tend to overemphasize the vertical, the ecumenicals tend to overemphasize the horizontal. We need to bring them together.

Klaus Bockmuhl discusses the extremes of ecumenical horizontalism and evangelical verticalism in his paper "Presuppositions on the contemporary theological debate."[18] Ecumenical horizontalism sees salvation as liberation from economic injustice, the recovery of human dignity against political oppression, or the personal discovery of hope against despair and thus represents a *reduction* of biblical Christianity to a social humanism. It results in a man-centered evangelism where "the world sets the agenda." The hope of the world is not Jesus Christ, but liberation from oppression. Salvation becomes a participation in world liberation; conversion is involvement in social action; the church loses its identity and becomes one with the program of world development; eschatology becomes the utopian kingdom achieved by man's efforts; redemption is an ontological universalism; prophetic preaching is an identification of secular forces as God's tools; there is a relativity of truth in all religions; and today's mission is to discover truth together through a dialogue stripped of all presuppositions.

But the evangelical approach to evangelism is not altogether immune from criticism either. Evangelicals are all too often smugly satisfied in thinking that they represent New Testament Christianity in its original and complete form. Not so says Bockmuhl: "It would be an oversimplification," he writes, "to say that today's evangelicalism is a straight successor to that Biblicism which opposed and proved an alternative to theological liberalism at the beginning of this century. It is too little conscious of the task of theology for that." "Its theological thinking," he continues, "if there is any at all—often is more a kind of sentiment and conviction, less a developed, thought-through and ready representation of the teachings of the Bible."[19] Specifically, evangelicals overemphasize soteriology and a futuristic eschatology and lack a theology of creation and providence, a theology of ethics, a theology of the Holy Spirit, and a theology of the church and the sacraments. Clearly then evangelical Christianity is also a *reduction* of biblical Christianity.

What is needed is a return to a kingdom evangelism which not only *announces* the kingdom but also seeks to *inaugurate* the kingdom in the biblical sense. That is, our evangelism must also stress that obedience in the world which results in the application of kingdom teaching and living in every area of life. This emphasis may be realized more fully by restoring an evangelism that stresses the rule of God.

Second, by recovering the proper emphasis on the rule of God, new Christians will be brought face to face with what it means to live *under* His rule.

In the first place this means that we are called to forsake false gods. All too often we have identified false gods as personal sins only. There is no question that the Christian is called to flee the personal sins of immorality, impurity, passion, evil desires, greed, anger, wrath, malice, slander, abusive speech, lying, and the like. To live by these values is to live under the rule of Satan. But when we fail to recognize the controlling presence of these sins not only in our hearts, but in the very warp and woof of society, in the social institutions of people and in the cultural products of our minds, we miss both the depth of the biblical understanding of sin and the depth of the kingdom of God as the rule of Christ in every area of life. In other words, to reduce the rule of the kingdom to our personal experience apart from our activity in society and culture is to deny the Lordship of Christ over all of life.

To avoid this reduction of the Christian message, evangelism should regain the biblical understanding of the cosmic battle between the two kingdoms. A renewed emphasis must be placed on the battle between the rule of Satan and the rule of Christ and that, in this world, in the very structures of society and culture this battle now rages. Preaching of the kingdom must be set in the context of creation and sin. The whole of creation belongs to God and is good by virtue of His creative act. All the structures of creation are areas in which we are able to give praise to God by living according to His will. But because of sin, mankind has produced moral, social, political, and personal chaos. Because of sin God's world is full of hate, greed, selfishness, pride, violence, and oppression. The power of sin is, therefore, not only something that we must fight on the personal level, but also as it manifests itself in the structures of society—in the breakdown of the family, in oppressive laws, in war, in dishonest business dealings, in the dehumanization of impersonal work, in oppressive economic systems, in drunkenness, in the misuse of power, in the pollution of air and water, in the waste of natural resources, and in many other ways.

But also, evangelism should be characterized by a renewed sense of the victory of Christ over evil. Christ has put down and destroyed evil by His death and resurrection. He has dethroned principalities and spiritual powers (1 Cor. 15:24,26); He has "disarmed the principalities and powers and made a public example of them, triumphing over them" (Col. 2:15). This was a cosmic battle, a cosmic victory.

And now, in the interim between the resurrection of Christ and His coming in judgment, the church, His kingdom on earth where He now rules, is the scene of this cosmic struggle. Christ has extended to His body—His power, His authority, His victory over evil through the Holy Spirit in the church. Evangelism calls people into His kingdom, into His church, under His rule. It enlists the saved to participate in Christ's victory over evil, to *extend* Christ's victory in every area of life in which they live and serve, to bring all of life under the reign of Christ. Thus the Christian under God's rule is called to radical obedience.

Third, evangelism should return to a preaching that demands radical obedience. This obedience begins by demanding the full identification of the believer with Christ by baptism. Baptism in many evangelical churches has lost its meaning. This is so because in many cases the gospel has been reduced to "something good for you." To be baptized into Christ means to identify with His suffering, to enter into His death, and to be raised to new life in Him. In this way the Christian participates in the victory of Christ over evil and is called in His body, the church, to continue to wage war against evil, wherever it is found, in the name of Christ—in His power and authority.

Salvation means to participate in the new age. It means to be delivered from our sin, to be called into a new way of life. This is not only in an individual and personal sense, but also in the corporate sense of the church which is the New Creation. J. Nicholls in "The Kingdom of God, the church and the future of mankind," insists that evangelicals must begin where Jesus began—with the preaching of the kingdom. This kingdom is "the reign of God. Whenever Christ reigns there the Kingdom is manifest." But the kingdom of God is more than an eschatological hope, it is a present reality as well as a future hope. It is found now in the church, among the people God has called out and together: "both the Kingdom and the church," writes Nicholls, "are dynamic organisms which are manifest in redeemed people. The church is both the contextualizing of the Kingdom on earth and the divinely appointed agent for spreading the Kingdom throughout the world."[20]

CONCLUSION

We have attempted to show that evangelism cannot be divorced from the content of the Christian faith. We cannot entertain, manipulate, or even persuade people to accept Christ. Instead, evangelism must proclaim the inauguration of the kingdom, set forth the demands of the kingdom, and invite people to participate in the presence of the kingdom. This includes repentance, acceptance of Christ as Lord and Savior, baptism, and participation in the life of the church, which, as an extension of Christ in the world, is an active witness in history to the power of Christ over evil.

Notes

[1](New York: Harper, 1939), p. 8

[2](Philadelphia: Westminster, 1958), p. 117

[3](Philadelphia: Westminster Press, 1954), p. 19

[4](Philadelphia: Westminster Press, 1967)

[5]*Evangelism in the Early Church* (Grand Rapids: Eerdmans, 1970), p. 204

[6]See John Stott, "The Biblical Basis of Evangelism" in *Let the Earth Hear His Voice* (Minneapolis: World Wide Publications, 1975), pp. 66ff.

[7](Grand Rapids: Zondervan, 1971), pp. 53ff.

[8](Grand Rapids: Baker, 1961), p. 8

[9](London: Longman & Greens, 1952)

[10]Ibid., p. 71

[11](Grand Rapids: Eerdmans, 1959), p. 72

[12](New York: Harper, 1976), p. 23. See also David Moberg, *The Great Reversal: Evangelism Versus Social Concern* ((Philadelphia: Lippincott, 1972)

[13](Grand Rapids: Eerdmans, 1959), p. 22

[14](Grand Rapids: Eerdmans, 1970)

[15]Ibid., p. 153

[16]See J. D. Douglas (ed.), *Let the Earth Hear His Voice* (Minneapolis: World Wide Publications, 1975), pp. 22-36

[17]Quoted by George Hoffman in "The Social Responsibilities of Evangelization," *Let the Earth Hear His Voice,* p. 698

[18]See Bruce J. Nicholls, *Defending and Confirming the Gospel:* The Report of the 1975 Consultation of the Theological Commission of the World Evangelical Fellowship (New Delhi, India: WEF Commission, 1975), pp. 36ff.

[19]Ibid.

[20]Ibid., p. 45

Chapter 10

The Mission
of the Church in
Crosscultural Evangelism

THE PROBLEM

In the last decade or so evangelicals have discovered that it is one
thing to proclaim the gospel in a familiar culture and quite another
to communicate it in an entirely different culture. This issue has been
made increasingly clear by the voice of third-world Christian leaders
who resent the imposition of a Western theology on an African,
Asian, or South American culture. José Miguez-Bonino in an
eloquent and passionate plea in "The Present Crisis in Mission"[1]
captures the frustration of many third-world church leaders: "we
have discovered that the missionary enterprise of the last one hundred and fifty years," he said, "is closely related to and interwoven
with the expansion of economic, political and cultural influence of
the anglo-saxon world."[2] All of this, he continues, calls into question
not only mission "but the theology which has undergirded it, the
church which has supported it, and the message that it has proclaimed."[3]

The problem, as Eugene Nida points out in his work *Message and
Mission*,[4] originates in the way the message of Christianity is communicated. The people of the "third world" view life through a
different model than the West. They talk a different language. They
have a different "grid" through which ideas are communicated and
understood. For example, anthropologists point to the different
customs and rituals; psychologists have shown that people select,
organize, and interpret all they perceive; and information theory
which has to do with "encoding, decoding, feedback, redundancy,

169

noise, and transitional probabilities" shows how complicated communication really is. For these reasons communication of the gospel in a foreign culture can no longer be a superficial presentation of biblical Christianity. Instead, it must be a careful, thoughtful, and precise crosscultural communication which speaks in such a way that the biblical gospel is understood within the culture and native framework of thought. In the past missions have not taken into proper consideration these needs in crosscultural communication.

This lack of awareness in evangelical mission has produced a second problem—namely, the implanting of a Western Christianity in a non-Western culture. In many cases converts have had to completely give up their cultural background to become Christians. For example, symbols, rituals, patterns of dress, associations, and social customs often were regarded as evil by uninformed missionaries. Instead of expressing faith in and through accustomed social patterns, many converts were forced to adopt a Western life style and cultural habits. This practice wrenched new Christians from their past, set them against their own history and people, and put them in the uncomfortable position of being "outsiders" to their own native land and customs. Conversion was not only to Christ, but also to the Western way of thinking about Christ.

This led to a third problem—the domination of the new churches by Western leaders. The missionary became the Pope. He or she had all the answers, all the money, and therefore, all the power. Natives could not be trusted—they weren't intelligent enough, lacked the ability to be responsible, or tended to interpret the faith through their own cultural background. Consequently Western denominations or mission boards dominated the leadership structure of mission churches—and even today many continue to exercise paternal authority over mission churches.

These problems have become so acute that some emerging leaders in third-world countries are calling for a moratorium on missions. José Miguez-Bonino concludes: "this is my message for missions: go and die and come back afterward. I think there is no other message for missions today than the message that Christ gave to one man a long time ago, 'you must be born again.'"[5]

These concerns force us to ask the question: What possible direction does the early church offer us in the problem of crosscultural communication?

CROSSCULTURAL COMMUNICATION
IN THE EARLY CHURCH

The problem of crosscultural communication of the gospel is in no way unique to our century. As soon as the gospel was first proclaimed its messengers became involved in the task of making the message understood to a completely different culture than the one in which it originated.

Michael Green quotes Kirsopp Lake's insight into this issue:

> The good news was the Lordship of Jesus. This distinguishes very clearly the evolution of preaching. In the first stage, the "good news" was the coming of the kingdom of God; this was the message of Jesus himself. In the second stage it was now Jesus as "the man" ordained to be judge of the living and the dead: this was the preaching of the disciples to the Jews. The third stage was the announcement that Jesus was the Kyrios, which doubtless included the Jewish message which Peter delivered to Cornelius, but must also have meant much more to heathen minds, and had connotations quite different from anything contemplated by Jewish-Christian preachers.[6]

The original proclamation of Christianity was to the Jews. The disciples proclaimed their message in terms of the Old Testament messianic expectation, a method which obviously made sense to the Jews. They argued that the ancient Scriptures had been fulfilled, that Jesus was the goal of both the law and the prophets. The thrust of the early sermons of Luke and John center on the fulfillment of the past. According to B. P. W. Stather Hunt in *Primitive Gospel Sources,*[7] it seems almost certain that a collection of "messianic testimonia," a compilation of Old Testament messianic sources, were in existence and were studied and preached about in Jewish circles. The early Jewish preachers, then, spoke about Christ in the context of Jewish history, Jewish expectation, Jewish culture, and Jewish Scriptures.

But how could this Jewish message be spoken in a Gentile culture? How could Gentiles who had no knowledge of Jewish history, Jewish expectation, Jewish culture, and Jewish Scripture understand the Christian message? Must a Gentile become a Jew before the message can be understood? These were *real* questions in the minds of the early Christian missionaries. This question was at the heart of the Jerusalem Council (Acts 15) as well as the Jewish suspicion about Paul (see Gal. 1:2; Acts 21).

The answer did not come easy. But when it did, it was an affirmation of crosscultural communication. It affirmed that a Gentile could understand the Christian message through the context of his own cultural and historical background. Daniel Van Allmen describes the transition of preaching from the Jew to the Gentile and concludes "what the early Christians were aiming at was not a 'Hellenized theology' but the most faithful transcription possible of the primitive faith into terms intelligible to the Greek mind."[8]

This method of crosscultural communication which was established in the New Testament period continued to be the basic practice of Christian communicators in the second century. It is seen, for example, in the writings of the apologists, particularly in Justin Martyr's *Apology*. The task of the apologists was to attack paganism, to refute the accusations against the Christians, and to present the Christian message.

Justin claimed that in Christianity he had found the true philosophy. This accounts for one of his major interests in writing — to determine the relationship between Christian faith and classical culture. Justin "contextualizes" the gospel by emphasizing the unity between the Christian understanding of logos with the Greek idea of logos. The Greeks believed that all knowledge is a product of the logos. Justin capitalized on this conviction and argued that the logos is not only the rational principle of the universe, but is indeed the pre-existent Christ written about in John's prologue, the one who became incarnate and died for the sins of man.

Justin had succeeded in maintaining the content of Christian truth, but formulated it in such a way that it was understandable to the Hellenistic mind. (Justin's view was not the exclusive approach of the second-century church. Tertullian, for example, argued against rapprochement with philosophy. His attitude is captured in his famous statement "what has Jerusalem to do with Athens?")

Jean Danielou has shown in his work, *Gospel Message and Hellenistic Culture*,[9] that the communications of the gospel in the second century was neither an accommodation to an alien world view nor a syncretism with it. The object of the apologists in the missionary efforts with the pagans was to "wean men from their heathen errors" and thus "to win souls to the unique truth of the gospel." To do this, the apologists sustained a three-pronged attack on the pagan world view. They attacked 1) pagan myths because they gave expression to a false theology; 2) pagan morals because they were corrupt; and 3) pagan religion in its cultic aspects because it was fraudulent.

Over against this attack on heathen error the apologists presented the truth of Christianity. First, they counteracted the false theology of pagan myths with true doctrine. Their concern was especially with the oneness of God over against the polytheism of paganism and the judgment of God against unbelief. What they emphasized, however, related at least in part to the situation being addressed. Not all apologists were equally evangelical. Justin placed the Incarnation and the passion at the center of his presentation, but Tatian treated Christianity more as the true philosophy or knowledge. For the most part, however, the apologists presented the contents of the rule of faith, if not in its whole, at least in those parts which they felt needed to be emphasized. Proofs and arguments for the resurrection, for example, constitute a major portion of apologetical argumentations.

Second, just as the apologists contrasted Christian truth with pagan error, so they compared the Christian life against pagan immorality. Here, they drew particularly on the features of Christian living expounded in the Jewish-Christian catecheses such as the *didache* or the *Epistle of Barnabas*. Athenagoras wrote, "You will find uneducated persons and artisans, and old women, who, if they are unable in words to prove the benefit of one doctrine, yet by their deeds exhibit the benefit arising from their persuasion of its truth; they do not rehearse speeches, but exhibit good works; when struck, they do not strike again; when robbed, they do not go to law; they give to those who ask of them, and love their neighbors as themselves."[10]

Third, they counteract pagan cultic practices by the presentation of their own Christian worship. Here Justin in particular provides a detailed description of Christian initiation (baptism) and worship, with a particular emphasis on the Eucharist.

While these apologists communicated the Christian faith without accommodation and syncretism, they nevertheless sought for common elements in Greek culture with Christianity, so that the acceptance of Christ and Christian truth, although requiring a radical choice against pagan myths, conduct, and cult, nevertheless *fulfilled* truth in their culture which stood behind their religious perversions.

Justin, for example, argues in *The Apology* that reason itself requires the lovers of truth to seek for truth. The truth of the logos, he argued, was already found in their culture and it was for this truth (and the refusal to worship idols) that many pagans in the past had been put to death. Here Justin demonstrates that two traditions exist within Greek culture: the truth and the perversion of it. Consequently, the renunciation of pagan idolatry and practices is not "a betrayal of tradition" but an "act of loyalty to the best elements in it."

The apologists consistently appealed in this way to general reason and conscience, but they always insisted "above all on the divine authority of Christ" over against "the nature of human opinion." Furthermore, they confronted man with their "responsibility in light of the coming judgment" and called them to repentance and faith.

The work of the apologists, of course, was incomplete. Theirs was a special mission in a unique situation. It took the work of catechesis, the development of a full and well-rounded explanation of the entire gospel to correct the imbalance of the apologists. We will look at this in the next section on the education of the church. First, we must ask what bearing the apologists may have on our concern in crosscultural communication.

AN AGENDA FOR EVANGELICAL CROSSCULTURAL COMMUNICATION

The question of crosscultural communications has received much attention by evangelicals since the Wheaton Declaration on Missions in 1966. Spurred by the Fuller Theological Seminary School of Missions and the writings of Donald McGavern, Charles Kraft, Ralph Winter, Peter Wagner, Peter Savage, Peter Beyerhaus, and Marvin Mayers, as well as numerous writers from the third world, evangelicals have forged ahead to fulfill the mandate of the Wheaton Declaration "to seek under the leadership of our head with full assurance of His power and presence, the mobilization of the church, its people, its prayers and resources, for the evangelization of the world in this generation."

This revitalized sense of mission has forced evangelicals to face the relationship of Western theology to other cultures. The form in which this question has taken shape is known as the problem of contextualization.

The most simple and straightforward definition of contextualization is "doing theology in context." That is to say, contextualization takes seriously the difference between faith and formulation. It is a process of communication that recognizes the task of relating an eternal and changeless message within the particulars of a given culture or framework of thought in such a way that the truth of the gospel is clothed in a language and forms that communicate the truth without changing it. Ted Ward put it succinctly in an address at Wheaton College, May 6, 1975:

> The mission of the church, what is it? Is it the culture-bound gospel that simply exports what we have somewhere else as they did in the colonial period? Emphatically No. Is it the culture-free gospel that will ultimately make us look alike? Indeed emphatically No. Such a view is sterile, arbitrary, purely theoretical. It is the culture-relevant gospel that sees the gospel to say different things to different people in different situations, and expects the redeemed of the world always to look alike only in those realms of spiritual development, and not likely to look alike in terms of social, cultural, and even psychological development.

Peter Savage in an unpublished paper "Discipleship in Context: the Challenge of 'Contextualization,'" feels that the refusal by some evangelicals to recognize the earthen nature of theology as it relates to various cultures is an indication of a "docetic tendency," the refusal on our part to recognize the human garb in which truth is clothed.

The method of contextualization

It should be recognized, however, that there is no uniform consensus on the method of contextualization. In the same unpublished article Peter Savage outlines four approaches: accommodation; adaptation; "possessio"; transformation. He points out that all schools hold the necessity of conversion in common but disagree on the "relationship the Gospel will have to the cultural world view, or that the church will have to existing social institutions."

Accommodation, the Roman Catholic approach to culture, is premised on a strong sense of natural law which affirms the basic goodness of every culture as a result of God's creation and providence. For this reason accommodation will always retain what is good or neutral and purge the impure. Examples of the areas in which this process occurs are: *externals* such as clothing or greetings;

language such as various patterns of thought or symbols of communication; *aesthetics,* such as expressions of beauty in art and architecture, liturgy and music; *social practices* such as marriage, polygamy, dowry, or initiation rites; *intellectual* such as the view of culture, cultic writings, myths and legends; and the *religious and ethical* customs and practices. Accommodation seeks in all of these areas to adjust to the total culture in an organismic way as far as possible without a syncretism occurring which would rob Christianity of its unique truths.

Adaptation differs from accommodation in that it strives for an expression of the gospel through the cultural forms and ideas, rather than assimilate with them. The task of adaptation is to provide a translation of Christianity into the culture in such a way that a thorough grasp of the truth is communicated. Justin's use of the Greel *logos* idea is an example of adaptation. Instead of confronting the Greek idea of *logos* with an alternative, he capitalized on their use of the *logos* in such a way that he forced a translation to occur. The Greek idea of *logos* was adapted or modified through the input of a new perspective or data in such a way that its fundamental characteristic was modified. No longer was it a mere abstract philosophical idea. It was now a personal and concrete reality in the person of Jesus Christ, the incarnation of the *logos.*

"Possessio" is the classical reformation position argued for by Peter Beyerhaus. Instead of an accommodation or an adaptation to culture, possessio is the affirmation that a culture can be possessed for Christ. This notion can be understood only within the framework of the cosmic battle between Jesus as Lord or Satan as lord. Possessio pits the reign of Christ over all cultures against every particularization of culture which inherently reflects sin in all its institutional forms. The possession of culture, then, is realized in the conversion of individuals who, because Christ is Lord, function in the culture in such a way that the lordship of Christ over culture is reflected in the unfolding of its institutions. The possession of a culture occurs in three stages: the first is the establishment of Christian beachheads; the second is the continual conflict between the reign of Christ and the rule of Satan in culture; the third is the realization of cultural conversion in the drama of Christ's return.

The fourth approach, transformation, has emerged more recently in response to the new understandings resulting from the social sciences. Culture is seen as an extension of the person, constantly undergoing change as it keeps pace with the growth and development of persons. Instead of communicating from the "outside," transformation attempts to communicate from "within." Charles Kraft, a leader in the transformational approach, argues that this method is based on a theology of the incarnation:

> God had a choice of roles in his approach to men. He could have remained as God in heaven, or even come to earth as God, and retained the respect and prestige that is his right as God. He would have continued to have admirers but not friends. The risks would have been far fewer, but the real impact very low because the predictability would have been so high. But God chose not to go that route, choosing rather to become a human being within the frame of reference of human beings, so that, in spite of the tremendous risk involved, he might earn the respect of and, therefore, the right to be listened to by human beings. Likewise we as missionaries may choose to remain as gods above or as gods in the midst of the people we work among. Or we may seek to follow God's example and establish a beachhead within the frame of reference of the people to whom God has called us—a beachhead of "human beingness" according to their definition.[11]

CONCLUSION

We have argued that missions should be engaged in the *translation* of Christian principles from one culture to another, rather than the *imposition* of a Western culturized Christianity upon a non-Western culture. The Christian principle which stands behind this effort is that of the Incarnation. As God in Christ entered into humanity and history and became one of us, so we are to enter into another culture and to participate in it fully in order to communicate the gospel.

As we continue to probe, to experiment, and to discover new ways to communicate the gospel, the guidelines set forth in the Lausanne Covenant offer the perimeters within which our discussion and work should continue to take place. We conclude then, with these words:

> The development of strategies for world evangelization calls for imaginative pioneering methods. Under God, *the result will be the rise of churches deeply rooted in Christ and closely related to their culture.* Culture must always be tested and judged by Scripture. Because man is God's creature, some of his culture is rich in beauty and goodness. Because he has fallen, all of it is tainted with sin and some of it is demonic. *The Gospel does not presuppose the superiority of any culture to another, but evaluates all cultures according to its own criteria of truth and righteousness, and insists on*

moral absolutes in every culture. Missions have all too frequently exported with the Gospel an alien culture, and churches have sometimes been in bondage to culture rather than to the Scripture. Christ's evangelists must humbly seek to empty themselves of all but their personal authenticity in order to become the servants of others, and churches must seek to transform and enrich culture, all for the glory of God. (Italics mine.)[12]

Notes

[1]See Anderson, Gerald and T. F. Stransky (editors). *Mission Trends No. 1,* (Grand Rapids: Eerdmans, 1974)

[2]Ibid., p. 38

[3]Ibid., p. 39

[4](New York: Harper & Row, 1960)

[5]Anderson and Stransky, *Mission Trends,* p. 48

[6]See *Evangelism in the Early Church* (Grand Rapids: Eerdmans, 1970), p. 115

[7](London: James Clarke & Co., 1951)

[8]See "The Birth of Theology," *International Review of Mission,* Vol. LXIV, No. 253, January, 1975, p. 41; see also Michael Green, *Evangelism in the Early Church* (Grand Rapids: Eerdmans, 1970), chs. 4 and 5

[9](Philadelphia: Westminster, 1973)

[10]*A Plea for Christians,* XI

[11]"God's Model for Cross-Cultural Communication—Reincarnation," *Evangelical Missions Quarterly,* Vol. 9, No. 4, Summer, 1973, p. 212

[12]See *Let the Earth Hear His Voice,* edited by J. D. Douglas (Minneapolis: World Wide Publications, 1975), p. 6 (Section 10, Evangelism and Culture)

Chapter 11

The Mission of the Church in Education

THE PROBLEM

Michael Green argues that primitive evangelism "was by no means mere proclamation and exhortation; it included able intellectual argument, skillful study of the scriptures, careful, closely reasoned teaching and patient argument."[1] For this reason education and evangelism go hand in hand. We educate in evangelism and evangelize in education.

It is in this context then that three failures of Christian education may be cited: 1) the overemphasis on moralism; 2) the reduction of learning to factualism; and 3) the failure to see things holistically.

Most educators are aware of these three problems and much is already being done to overcome them, especially in the new curriculum models of our Sunday school literature.[2] Nevertheless, because altogether too many Sunday school programs are still subject to these errors, a brief explanation of them is in order.

Moralism resembles a do-goodism that neglects a more biblical understanding of Christian ethics as it grows out of the redemptive work of Christ. The moralistic teacher tends to find "the moral" in Bible stories and in the lives of biblical heroes. There is a tendency to emphasize how "doing good" and "being responsible" always pays off in the end. On this basis the teacher urges the students to be helpful, to be kind, and to share. In other words "moralism" is sometimes substituted for moral teaching.

The problem with this kind of teaching is not with the behavior suggested by moralism, but with the context in which it is found.

181

Sometimes moralism is a misinterpretation of what the Scripture *actually* says. Also, it fails to emphasize the redemptive nature of Scripture. The stories of Scripture often are explained as isolated incidents of interest. They are not set forth as examples of the way God is working to accomplish redemption. Thus the picture of Christianity as a superficial do-goodism is being unconsciously presented.

Factualism is similar to moralism in that it calls for the mere memorization of factual material apart from an understanding of the meaning of that material. It is good for a student to know the periods of biblical history and to know what happened in each period. But unless the student knows *why* what is happening is happening, the whole point is missed. A mere memorization of the names of the kings, or the important dates, events, places, and people of the Bible are only forgotten tomorrow unless the role they play in the unfolding of the redemptive process is made clear. What is the redemptive meaning of Seth, Abraham, Moses, David, and Jeremiah? How is God working in history to bring His Christ into the world? What does this mean in relation to the human predicament? What am I to do about it? Unless these questions are probed along with the teaching of facts the education given can make no claim to be really Christian at its root, because it does not shape perception and behavior.

The failure to see the complete picture is similar to moralism and factualism. A Christian education without a biblical framework on which to hang what is being taught provides only scattered information, bits and pieces of truth that never come together in a coherent whole. For this reason it is imperative to have a good grasp of the entire Christian faith. In this context education improves, deepens, and strengthens the learners' grasp of the claim Christ makes over the whole of life.

The basic problem with moralism, factualism, and the failure to see the complete picture is that they do not lend themselves to faith, to the increase of real growth, not only in the understanding of the Christian faith, but also in the living out of that faith. In short they do not educate and evangelize. These errors tend to support an individualistic and privatistic approach to the Christian faith. Consequently they provide an inadequate understanding of the faith, fail to further a deepening sense of commitment to Christ, and do not succeed in showing how the Christian faith relates to all of life. We turn, therefore, to the early church in search of some guidelines for an agenda for evangelical education.

CHRISTIAN EDUCATION IN THE EARLY CHURCH

There are three ways we can gain information about education in the early church. First, by looking at the initial response to the message; second, by examing the earliest Christian catechism; and third, by reviewing the content of catechetical instruction.

The initial response to the Christian message

The preaching of the apostles always called for a response to the gospel facts. Since the initial response of preaching was for the hearer to be baptized, it is through the earliest baptismal creeds that we gain insight into the *content* of early Christian teaching. These creeds appear basic, such as, "I believe Jesus is Lord" (Rom. 10:9) or "I believe Jesus is the Christ, the Son of the living God" (Matt. 16:16; John 20:31) or the more expanded creed of Paul in 1 Corinthians 15:3-5, "that Christ died for our sins in accordance with the scriptures, that he was buried, that he was raised on the third day in accordance with the scriptures, and that he appeared to Cephas." These early hearers of the gospel were hearing "the faith" and were not formulating the faith.

That a deeper education in the faith began immediately after conversion and an incorporation into the new community through baptism, is suggested by Acts 2:42. Here the new Christians "devoted themselves to the apostles' teaching and fellowship, to the breaking of the bread and the prayers." It is most natural that this pattern should develop since the Jewish synagogue was a place of instruction and worship. According to Acts 2:46, it appears that this postbaptismal instruction was on a "daily" basis. But what was the content of this instruction? To answer this question we turn to an examination of the earliest Christian catechism.

The earliest Christian catechism

Philip Carrington has attempted to reconstruct the early teaching of the church in his work *The Primitive Christian Catechism*.[3] His argument is that the earliest Christian catechisms were modeled after the Jewish form of instruction. The method of teaching was through both oral and written means. The emphasis was not so much on speculative matters as it was on behavior or on "walking." He argues interestingly and effectively that the New Testament documents yield traces of this teaching which drew on the Old Testament pattern.

Jewish teaching for example began with Leviticus, a catechetical summary of religious duties. The central chapters of this catechism are 19–20, the so-called holiness code. And within this code two verses are of supreme importance: The first is Leviticus 19:2, "You shall be holy; for I the LORD your God am holy" and second, Leviticus 19:18 "you shall love your neighbor as yourself." These two verses constitute the key to Jewish catechetical instruction. The theme of their instruction—the holiness of God and love—appear frequently and with some apparent organization in the New Testament literature, suggesting that parts of the New Testament are the actual material of the earliest catechetical instruction of the church. (Be holy: see Matt. 5:48; 1 Thess. 4:7; 1 Peter 1:16; 1 John 3:3. For love, see Matt. 5:43; 1 Thess. 4:9; 1 Peter 1:22; 1 John 3:10.)

While the actual catechetical nature of the New Testament documents remains a probability and not an uncontestable fact, the form of education along catechetical lines is without question the practice of the second-century church and even before that.

Second-century catechetical instruction

At some point between the age of the apostles and the second-century church, education prior to baptism became increasingly important. In the *didache* the author indicates that public instruction in the faith preceded baptism. By the time of Hippolytus (A.D. 215), according to *The Apostolic Tradition*, there is a considerable period of instruction before baptism: "let catechumens spend three years as hearers of the word. But if a man is zealous and perseveres well in the work, it is not time but his character that is decisive."[4]

We are at once confronted with a change in practice from New Testament times. In the New Testament converts were baptized immediately. By the end of the second century they were enrolled in a three-year program of study before baptism. Why such a change? No details are given us by any writer; so we are left to the mercy of historical reconstruction. There are probably two prominent movements which contributed to the change: heresy and persecution.[5] We know that the church was combating heresy within her own ranks by the end of Paul's lifetime (Pastoral Epistles). It may well be that the early church was too hasty in baptizing converts who had really not worked through the implications of the message they had heard, causing a syncretism between Jewish ideas, or the views of mystery religions, or one of the many Roman religions with the Christian faith. To prevent this from happening the church may have simply prolonged the period between initial conversion and initiation into the church through baptism to make certain that the convert knew what he or she was doing and that the church knew full well what kind of person she was receiving.

Persecution as a factor cannot be ruled out either. The church, because it was not regarded as a legitimate religion in Rome, had to practice the faith in a guarded manner. Although persecution was local and sporadic, the meetings had to be guarded against the intrusion of false converts who may have been there for the purposes of spying.

A second development different than the New Testament practice was the emergence of a pre-evangelism education screening. At least according to Hippolytus' *The Apostolic Tradition,* pre-evangelism education was the practice in Rome by the end of the second century. By this time prospective converts were organized into three groups: seekers; hearers; kneelers. The seeker was an inquirer, the hearer one who was enrolled in the three-year catechetical class, and the kneeler was the believer who was in the final stages of instruction before baptism (six weeks before Easter; baptism was on Easter Sunday). But our concern here is with the seeker. Apparently a seeker is someone witnessed to by a neighbor. Showing an interest in the Christian faith, this person is brought to the church for a conference with the leaders of the congregation. The purpose of this conference is to communicate the *demands* the Christian faith makes on its converts (like an education on the cost of discipleship).

What we learn from the comments of Hippolytus is that a person who desires to follow Jesus Christ is confronted with the implications of discipleship before being allowed to enroll in the hearers' class. For example, if a person is engaged in an occupation that involves idol worship or allegiance to the emperor as God, the job must be given up. If a person is involved in practices contrary to the gospel, such as astrology or immorality, it must be given up. In other words, the implications of repentance *(metanoia)* are not only on inner attitudes but on outer actions as well. More than likely many people were turned away from the faith when they discovered the kind of obedience it demanded. Congregations may have been smaller as a result, but the degree of commitment may have been stronger.

But what about the content? What were these people who became hearers, in preparation for baptism and full membership into the church, taught? Fortunately, several early catechetical documents have been discovered which provide insight into the content of evangelism-education. We know from these documents that early Christian instruction centered around orthopraxis (correct living) and orthodoxy (correct doctrine).

Orthopraxis

The earliest catechetical noncanonical document is the *didache*, a short sixteen-chapter document that is dated as early as A.D. 50 and as late as A.D. 130. The *didache* begins "there are two ways, one of life one of death; and between the two ways there is a great difference." The way of life consists of a number of instructions on how to live, drawn mainly from the teachings of Jesus, particularly His Sermon on the Mount. The "way of death," which begins in chapter 5, is a catalog of evils similar to those found in the Epistles. An interesting point about the use of "the two ways" is the thoroughly Jewish nature of the approach. Much of the material included in "the two ways" is found in Leviticus 17–19. Research in the origins of "the two ways," as Lewis Sherrill points out in *The Rise of Christian Education,* suggests with a "high degree of probability, that this part of the *didache* was drawn by the Christian teachers from Jewish material used in the instruction of proselytes to Judaism."[6]

The idea of "the two ways" came into focus as early as the wisdom literature. Proverbs 4:18-19 refers to the "path of the righteous" and "the way of the wicked." Philip Carrington suggests that the two ways are "to be looked on as the catechetical material of the Greek synagogue designed for hearers or catechumens of all kinds, whether children or adult proselytes."[7] We know that the term "way" was used of Christianity in the New Testament as well. In Acts 19:23, the apostle Paul caused much disturbance in Ephesus through his teaching of the "Way." The Gentiles brought into the Christian faith had to be taught the fundamentals of morality and Christian behavior.

To communicate Christian morality the apostles seem to adopt the Jewish method of "the two ways." This seems apparent in Paul's writings. In Galatians 5, Paul lists the sins that characterize those who live "according to the flesh" and the virtues that result from "walking in the spirit." In Colossians 3 he lists what the new man is to "put off" and what he is "to put on." In Romans 6 he urges converts to "yield yourselves to God" and "do not yield your members to sin." This comparison between the way of life and the way of death appears less explicitly, but nevertheless clearly within the practical portions of all the New Testament writings.

It is no wonder then that Christians are instructed to walk in the way of life and to avoid the way of death. This would be particularly true for Gentile converts to the faith who did not have the advantage of the Jewish moral emphasis. The evidence is that Christians coming for baptism had to attest to a good character, that indeed they did live by the way of life. Justin points out that only those who "promise they can live accordingly" are baptized.[8] Hippolytus writes, "they who are to be set apart for baptism shall be chosen after their lives have been examined: whether they have lived soberly, whether they have honoured the widows, whether they have visited the sick, whether they have been active in well-doing."[9] Clearly orthopraxis was as important in the early church as orthodoxy.

Orthodoxy

The second area in which the new convert had to show proof of real conversion before baptism was that of orthodoxy—right belief. Christian faith is not contentless. It has to do with an inward and outward profession of the faith. "The gospel," writes G. R. Beasley-Murray in *Baptism in the New Testament,* "lays a demand on men, to which an obedient response should be given. It calls for a man to cease from himself, to own allegiance to Christ and repose trust in Him . . . all this makes it clear that in the New Testament faith is no mere intellectual acceptance of a set of religious propositions. It has the Lord Christ as its object and calls forth a response of the whole man to Him."[10]

Paul makes the content-orientation of baptism clear in Romans 6 where he indicates that the form of baptism itself speaks to the content of the Christian faith. As Christ died, was buried, and rose from the dead, so the convert who confesses Jesus, confesses these

facts about Him and recognizes his identification in Jesus' act for the
forgiveness of sin by himself symbolizing the death, burial, and
resurrection in baptism. It is clear then, that to confess Christ is to
acknowledge the truth of the gospel about Him. The convert confesses faith in the person, but not apart from who that person is and
what that person has done.

In the previous chapter we saw how the faith, belief, and confession of the early church gradually took shape in a specific form (the
rule of faith) as a means of specifying *exactly* in what the content of
belief in Jesus consists. It was this content that was taught, explained, and expanded for the catechumen. During these three years
of instruction the hearer was given a firm basis in the structure of
Christian orthodoxy over against the teaching and practice of the
heretic. And when the time for baptism came the convert confessed
Christ as he or she had been instructed. According to Hippolytus the
convert "renounced Satan and all his works, then was taken to the
water where the following confession was made along with the
baptism":

> "Dost thou believe in God, the father almighty?" And he who is
> being baptized shall say:
> "I believe."
> then
> holding his hand placed on his head, he shall baptize him once.
> And then he shall say:
> "Dost thou believe in Christ Jesus, the Son of God, who was born of
> the virgin Mary and was crucified under Pontius Pilate, and was dead
> and buried, and rose again the third day, alive from the dead, and
> ascended into heaven and sat at the right hand of the Father, and will
> come to judge the quick and the dead?" And when he says:
> "I believe."
> He is baptized again. And again he shall say:
> "Dost thou believe in (the) Holy Ghost, and the holy church, and
> the resurrection of the flesh?"
> He who is being baptized shall say accordingly:
> "I believe",
> And so is baptized a third time.[11]

During the three years of instruction preceding baptism the convert was trained in the meaning of the creed. This was a "confessional" approach to the Christian faith. The convert understood what
was believed, why it was believed, and how his life was to be
different.

An indication of the actual content of early Christian education has been preserved for us in a number of catechetical lectures. One of the most important of these is *The Catechetical Lectures* of Cyril of Jerusalem (d. 386).

In lectures 1–3 he speaks of the temper of mind necessary for baptism, of sin, the devil, repentance, remission of sin, and the meaning of baptism. In lecture 4 he speaks of the ten Christian dogmas: belief about God; Christ; the virgin birth; Christ's crucifixion and burial; Resurrection; the Second Coming and judgment; the Holy Spirit; the cross; and man's nature and end. He then lectures on the subject of faith, followed by thirteen lessons on the creed. Here, in a most interesting manner is set forth the content of the Christian faith which a convert should know before baptism. We are well justified in concluding that evangelism and education in the early church were regarded in a holistic manner, not as separate functions, but as the mission of the church.

We turn now to the application of early education to evangelical Christianity.

AN AGENDA FOR EVANGELICAL CHRISTIAN EDUCATION

A considerable amount of change has been occurring in evangelical education lately and has been revolving around three movements: 1) education in the context of baptism; 2) education in the context of the church; and 3) education in the context of behavior.

Education in the context of baptism

Since Christian education in the deepest sense of the word means to "live the content," there can be no substitute for a strong content-oriented education. Most churches have some form of instruction prior to baptism, but for the most part it is not thorough enough.

In the first place baptism provides the context in which a person may really come to grips with the Christian faith. The heart of the Christian faith is represented in baptism. To identify with the death, burial, and resurrection of Christ; to be initiated into the power of His resurrection; to be enlisted as a "soldier" in the cosmic battle over evil; to participate in the church, the presence of the kingdom; to become a disciple of Christ; to obey the will of the king; to anticipate the return of Christ—all these images and more are contained within baptism itself.

These images were so important in the early church that they were reenacted only *once* a year, and then on Easter Sunday. This way the early church emphasized the identity of the believer with the death and resurrection through baptism.

In fact, baptism was such an important part of the early Christian community that by the third century the entire local congregation participated with the catechumens in a special six weeks of preparation before Easter. In this way they *repeated* their baptismal vows and renewed their commitment to Jesus Christ. (This may account for the origin of Lent.)

In the third century, the reception of the believers into the church, into the full rights of the body including participation in the Eucharist, was no "side" event. The entire congregation *relived* their own commitment to Christ's body, recalling with the new converts the cycle of repentance, faith, and obedience which they reenacted through meaningful rituals and symbols, which enriched and strengthened the entire community in both orthodoxy and orthopraxis.

There is a desperate need for symbol, for reenactment in our evangelical churches. What better symbol for evangelism and education exists in our midst than baptism (or, also the Lord's Supper). For here, in the physical act, is contained the truth that brings the church together, and sends her forth.

Perhaps the recovery of Christian nurture within the body which is now happening among evangelicals will cause us to restore once again the rightful place of baptism (or confirmation for those baptized as infants) as a means to continually effect the education and evangelism of the whole community.

Education in the context of the church

The most significant development among evangelicals in recent years is the growing awareness that Christian nurture must happen in a dynamic, integral, and transactional way within the church as the body of Christ. In this context orthodoxy and orthopraxis are being brought together in the relational way in which they were originally understood and practiced in the early church.

In *A Theology of Christian Education* Larry Richards recognizes and argues for an education that takes place within the church, based on new life. Richards argues that conversion brings the believer out of death into *new life*. But this new life is not to be thought of individualistically nor in the static sense. It is life *in the body*, and a life of *continual growth*. He writes:

> Christian education then can never deal with individual life alone. Christian education has to concern itself with the processes within the Body which nurture corporate and individual growth in Christ. Any Christian educational approach which focuses on either the individual or the group in exclusion of the other is bound to fall short.[12]

This life orientation of education forces us to recognize the place of the church in the life of the believer. Christians are not an "entity unto themselves." If there is one thing, among others, that the biblical concept of the church teaches us, it is that the church is to be seen whole. To be in Christ means to be in the church. If the whole church is present in every local congregation, then education cannot be divorced from the life of the whole church. The entire congregation together seeks to become Christlike. It is in this context of the goal of the whole body that education must take place.

Furthermore, the discovery that orthodox belief and orthodox living are not to be separated, but constitute the two sides of a single piece, makes it clear that growth in these two aspects can take place only in the church. It is the church which has received from the apostles the faith. The church preserves it and passes it on, not just in creeds but also in living. Consequently, growth takes place in a transactional relationship between persons. The church models the truth, it incarnates the truth, it has "this mind in you which was in Christ Jesus." Therefore, Christians are to be nurtured in the context of the church. The church as a body is to grow, develop, mature, and become more Christlike.

The dynamic which causes this to happen in the church is love. Religious education, both in the Hebrew and Christian past, had to do with life and living; its motivating force then as now is love. As we have seen, both the holiness code and the early catechetical teaching of the church was modeled on love toward God and love toward fellow persons. This brings together both content and action. The content of orthodoxy is "as I have loved you" and the practice of orthopraxis is "so you must love one another" (John 13:35). As the church corporately knows and loves God, so its members corporately know and love one another. In this context education is not mere moralism, a bare fact, or a partial insight, but a holistic experience of learning to know and love God and fellow persons in the context of a loving community. Theory and experience is realized in living!

Education in the context of behavior

The new developments in Christian education pioneered by Ted Ward and Donald Joy, and which are based on the research of Jean Piaget and Lawrence Kohlberg, are making an impact on Christian education in the context of behavior.

Because this is based on a highly complex and detailed view of man which some educators regard as consistent with the biblical view of man as well as the biblical view of growth through nurture, I will concentrate on a summary of its main emphasis.[13] The Piaget-Kohlberg findings as they relate to Christian education may be summarized as follows:

1. A holistic view of man. Because each aspect of the human person is interrelated with the other, facts and feelings are learned together.
2. A positive view of man. Development is a natural process of human persons. Each person has the potential to reach a high level of development. This is true in both the cognitive and moral aspects of persons.
3. Man is active. Human beings are born to mature. Concepts gradually form in the person. When initial immature concepts conflict with other concepts a process of equilibration occurs, and gradually interpretations are formed.
4. Man in transaction. Maturation occurs through transactions with the physical world and social interaction. Through this process persons become increasingly aware of possible interpretations other than his or her own.

These are the four *causes* of development set forth by Piaget. They are, as noted by Stonehouse 1) biogenetic endowment of heredity and maturation; 2) direct experience; 3) social interaction, and 4) equilibration. The research of Kohlberg based on mere notions led to the conclusion that an ordered *pattern of moral development* as well as the cognitive was observable.

5. The pattern of development. Cognitive and moral development takes place according to a universal pattern of sequential stages.

These are predictable stages which each person may follow. Each one leads into the next and none are skipped. Although the rate of development may vary from person to person the order of the stages remains the same. They are: 1) the person looks *within* to determine right and wrong. As development occurs the child recognizes the need for an exterior standard; 2) exterior standards are first found in the actions of persons who are important to the individual. Later it is discovered that there are standards which govern all people; 3) the internalization of the exterior objective standards resulting from an understanding of the reasons for these laws.

6. A comprehensive balance of emphasis. The developmentalist recognizes that both nature and nurture are involved in maturation. In the created order the structure for development already exists. But the *way* in which a person develops, or the level to which the person develops is dependent upon nurture.

The implications of this theory of development appear obvious to evangelism and Christian education. The essence of evangelism and education is to bring a person into the Christian perception of reality, to see growth and maturation within the church as a nurturing community where transactions between growing persons are continually taking place in the context of faith and works.

There are numerous applications of this theory which are now beginning to make their ways known into the teaching curriculum of the churches. Some of the basic applications are:

1. The conviction that the church must be seen as a transactional context in which growth takes place. The impersonal church where people meet once or twice or more a week must give way to the more personal community-centered church. In this context people become caringly involved with each other, experiencing what it means to be the body of Christ.

2. The new convert to Christianity must be brought into the church community immediately. The convert has been born into a new family, and it is in this family that the new Christian is nurtured and brought into a mature Christian faith. In this context three of the four causes for growth occur: 1) direct experience; 2) social interaction; and 3) equilibration. Bumping shoulders with more mature Christians, finding models who provide the example for growth takes place within the context of the church community.

3. Consequently, the church must be accepting of new Christians and provide a context of warmth and love in which the new convert is given the freedom to question, experiment, and grow.

For this reason the church must recognize that there are stages of growth. Not everyone can be at the same stage at the same time. Therefore, the legalistic demand for conformity has no place in the church, neither is there any place for ridicule or a judgmental spirit toward those who don't conform.

4. The church must give primary emphasis to the objective standard of God, to the Ten Commandments and the ethical instruction of the New Testament and to the means by which these standards of true living are internalized. This means that the church community must avoid placing subcultural restraints and standards on the body, allowing a certain freedom in the Spirit to exist among the members of the church.

CONCLUSION

We have argued that Christian education is not a mere memorization of facts, nor a moralization of Scripture. Instead we have set forth the goal of Christian education as the bringing together of orthodoxy and orthopraxis in the life of the church and in the lives of each individual in the church.

Education cannot be divorced from the life context of the church. Evangelism brings us into the church, into Christ's body, where, through our association with Christian truth in the living context of our relationship to other members of Christ's body, we are to grow. Thus the church is the context through which both our understanding and our practice of Christianity is nurtured. Christian education is therefore not the gaining of a mere abstract knowledge, but the assimilation of a new life style, characterized by a new perception of reality and a living which conforms to the values of the Christian community.

Notes

[1] *Evangelism in the Early Church* (Grand Rapids: Eerdmans, 1970), p. 160

[2] See the recent materials of David C. Cook or Gospel Light

[3] (Cambridge University Press, 1940)

[4] (Hamden: Archon Books, 1962), II.17

[5] A possible third reason has been suggested by Jim Hedstrom in a personal letter. "The emerging Christian movement also lost the deeply grounded character of Jewish converts of religion (wherein content from the O.T. was presupposed). Early assemblies contained a deeper grounding in Jewish background, . . . and knowledge of true religion, . . . than later assemblies. Early converts were indeed immediately baptized, but Jesus' three-year ministry, a circulating report of his activities, John's ministry, and *much* diffusion of Jewish religion lay in back of Pentecost and other early 'conversions'. The separation of church from synagogue laid *prime* responsibility for basic orientation in theistic religion in the church, and this was also true of the Gentile mission. One might add this factor to others to better understand early Christianity's quick baptism practices as contrasted to later Christianity's more deliberate attempt to provide initiation orders."

[6] (New York: Macmillan, 1944), p. 149

[7] Carrington, *Primitive Catechism*, p. 13

[8] *Apology*, 61

[9] *Apostolic Tradition*, II., 20

[10] (Grand Rapids: Eerdmans, 1973), pp. 267-268

[11] *Apostolic Tradition*, II., 21

[12] (Grand Rapids: Zondervan, 1975), p. 16

[13] See Catherine Stonehouse, "A Developmental View of Man" *(The Asbury Seminarian)*, April, 1976, pp. 28-33

A note of caution should be exercised here. It is not in the best interests of the Christian faith to closely identify it with a particular philosophy. While the Piaget-Kohlberg model may be useful to Christian educators, it must be remembered that the model for Christian practice is inherent within the Christian message itself and does not need to depend upon a model discovered apart from it. Also, there is a need to inquire about the presuppositions behind the Piaget-Kohlberg model and make a clear distinction between their presuppositions and that of the Christian world-view. I cite this development in Christian Education, then, not for the purposes of supporting the Piaget-Kohlberg model but for the purpose of calling attention to a rapidly growing movement that does give support to the importance of orthopraxis.

Chapter 12

The Mission
of the Church in
Society and Culture

THE PROBLEM

Because the message of the church is concerned with the whole person, the whole of life, and the whole of creation, the mission of the church, which issues from the message, can focus on no less. There are some, however, who ignore the larger mission of the church, treating the relation of the church to society and culture with a degree of indifference.

A basic reason for indifference toward society and culture may be found in the failure to recognize the world-view nature of the Christian faith as well as a minimized view of the battle which the Christian world-view must wage with secular humanism.

For example, the failure to affirm the doctrine of creation results in an inability to come to grips with history and the meaningfulness of life; the privitization of sin results in an ignoring of the permeation of sin in all the structures of society and in the works of culture; the spiritualization of the Incarnation prevents a wrestling with the event of Christ as the inauguration of a new beginning in history; and, an individualized view of the church stands in the way of understanding what it means to be the new creation in the midst of the old.

There are several unfortunate results of this failure to come to grips with a biblical world-view. The first is the split created between the so-called secular and sacred aspects of life: the view that implies that those acts which are spiritual are sacred and those activities which are natural and physical are secular. Consequently it is sacred to pray, read the Bible, witness, and go to church. But work, play, and cultural activities are secular. This dichotomy is an "other-worldly," "this worldly" conflict. It fosters a superspirituality, a private ethic, a Christianity which can successfully withdraw from the conflicts of the world. It causes one to live as though a dichotomy exists between spirit and matter, secular and sacred. It supports loving God with the "heart," but shrinks from loving Him by actions in the social order, or in the public aspects of life.

Piety becomes exclusively private—something practiced at home, in the quiet time, at church, or in the private decisions of life.

The second result of the failure to have a biblical world-view is a retreat from the cosmic battle in which the church is really engaged. Because Christ's death is cosmic—having to do with all the structures of life and the whole of creation—the battle in which the church is now engaged in the period between Pentecost and the Second Coming must be one which *recalls* Christ's victory over sin through the Resurrection and *anticipates* the consummation of His victory over evil in His return. This means that, although secular humanism permeates every area of life, the hope of the church is the reign of Christ in all of life, and the task of the church is to realize that reign in life now—as much as possible. Those who have consciously or unconsciously supported the distinction between the secular and the sacred and have failed to apply Christ's cosmic redemption to every area of life are characterized by an indifference to the Christ and culture issue.

Four kinds of indifference

Georges Florovsky in his work *Christianity and Culture* mentions four approaches to the Christian in culture, which are characterized by indifference.[1]

a. *The devaluation of culture.* The devaluation of culture occurs when those who have met Christ in their personal and private experience believe they need nothing else. The only relation their faith has to culture is to speak a word of condemnation to it. For them, the whole historical process is basically futile and purposeless. The goal of the Christian is to retire from the world, to abstain from involvement in it, to retreat into the closet of a personal and private experience with God.

b. *The role of the Christian in culture is that of service.* In this view culture cannot be renewed, reformed, or redirected. Consequently the role of the Christian is to endure history and culture and to witness here and there, both by word and deed. But this witness to culture is always made with the recognition that this is Satan's world and that culture cannot be changed. Thus the extent of the Christian's role in culture is to improve his or her character, to be honest, kind, and compassionate, and to exemplify all the fruits of the Spirit.

　　c. *The protest against culture.* In this view the Christian stands alone against culture, as a prophet. The believer speaks the Word of God against the predicament of existence, against the atheistic "nothingness" of life. But this witness always stands alone as "nothing" against the power of sin. The word is spoken with no real hope that anything will be changed. It is a word spoken out of duty, not expectancy.

　　d. *The "plain man" approach to culture.* The "plain man" Christian lives in culture, even enjoys it to a certain extent, but wonders what it may have to do with religion. Culture is a vain and perishing thing, a training ground perhaps for souls, but not much more.

　　The obvious weaknesses of these attitudes which are found among many Christians today suggest our need to look more closely at the New Testament and the history of the church. Here we may find a more adequate basis for an evangelical approach to society and culture.

A BIBLICAL AND HISTORICAL VIEW OF THE CHURCH IN SOCIETY AND CULTURE

　　In the history of Christianity churches have disagreed on the exact relationship between Christianity, society, and culture. In particular, three broad models have emerged—the separational, identificational, and transformational.[2] Because each one is built on a selective reading of Scripture and is modeled after a particular theology, each results in a somewhat one-sided emphasis on the role of the Christian in culture. This variety does not need to be a cause for consternation. Recent models in science suggest that no one model contains the whole truth, but only part of the truth. Like science, we need to recognize the validity of looking at a single question from a variety of viewpoints to get at the truth. Through the model approach each observer sees a part of the truth; and through the insights of the many models, he grasps the whole more clearly.

We will now develop these three models. In order to gain a clear description of each, we will go to the Reformation period where the models take on a more distinctive shape than they do in the early church.

The Separational model

The separational model is rooted in those Scriptures which stress the otherworldiness of the Christian life. Their Christ-model is the crucified Lord, the suffering servant, the One whose power is in the weakness of the cross. Their ethos is that of a people who are "strangers and pilgrims in an alien land," a people who believe they are not to "love the world or the things of the world," a people who do good to all men but "especially those who are of the household of faith," a people who firmly believe that it is possible and indeed necessary to live by the Sermon on the Mount. Their patron saint is Peter who reminds them that they are "a chosen race, a royal priesthood, a holy nation, God's own people." And for all this they expect to suffer, to be misunderstood, to be reviled, to be persecuted for righteousness' sake. But that is not of ultimate importance because separationalists look to a city "whose builder and maker is God." Furthermore, seeing that "all these things are to be dissolved" they concern themselves with "what sort of persons they ought to be in lives of holiness and godliness."

One of the earliest Christian thinkers to espouse the *separational model* was Tertullian, the great third-century theologian of North Africa. In this pre-Constantinian world, paganism permeated all of life. Consequently Tertullian admonished Christians to shun much of life; to refrain from involvement in political life, military service, and trade and business. He even regarded literature, theater, and music as ministers of sin.

For our interest, the most important principle to derive from Tertullian is his belief that Christianity is antiestablishment, and that it contains the seeds of a countercultural movement. Every separational model in the history of the church has been, like Tertullian, characterized by these two concerns: a negation of the establishment and an affirmation of a counter culture. These two motifs, with some variation, are evident among Eastern and Western monasticism, the Cathari and Albigensians of the medieval period, the Anabaptists of the sixteenth century, the Quakers and Pietists of the seventeenth century, the Brethren of the nineteenth century, and the so-called young evangelicals of our time.

Nevertheless, the group which has embodied most clearly and forcibly the antiestablishment and countercultural separational model are the Anabaptists.[3] Anabaptists (the word means "rebaptism") emerged in the sixteenth century in what has been dubbed "the left wing of the Reformation." They were persuaded that the reform of Luther in Germany and Zwingli in Zurich had not gone far enough. For them, Luther and Zwingli (and later Calvin) had reformed only the medieval church. They had rid the church of *some* of its false practices and errors but not *all*. Anabaptists sought to restore the church to its original simplicity, poverty, and purity as demonstrated in the New Testament and the pre-Constantinian era.

Anabaptists tend toward the establishment of separatist communities. The community is the pure church, a group of Christians who live their entire lives under the standard of the heavenly kingdom taught by Jesus, particularly in the Sermon on the Mount. This community which represents the kingdom of God on earth is expressed in communities ranging all the way from a very separatistic Hutterite or Amish community to a less separatist Mennonite community, or a group like Reba Place Fellowship in Chicago or other modern communal living centers.

The separationalist is less theological than practical. Their emphasis falls on living in the world rather than theoretical apologetics or system-building. The key idea is *discipleship*, the willingness to take seriously the teachings of Jesus, to follow in life the pattern He set.

For these reasons the separationalist is generally nonmetaphysical. Questions concerning the nature and character of God, His creational activity, and continued relation to creation and history are seldom topics of interest. Similarly their view of Christ emphasizes His teaching and suffering. Rather than dealing with the metaphysical explorations of Christ, they are concerned with an identification with the crucified Lord that issues in a personal piety of discipline, prayer, and discipleship. The tendency is toward an Arminian view of man, accenting the person's ability to follow Christ, to live by the fruit of the Spirit, and to do good works. Redemption is into a community of people, a brotherhood of believers governed by Matthew 18. Here the Christian life of discipleship is taught and lived corporately. Culture and church become one, and both are characterized by purity and simplicity, living in the expectation of the imminent return of Jesus Christ.

Social responsibility among the separationalists is usually very strong. They are characterized by personal austerity, by a concern for the welfare of their immediate brothers, for the general rights of people, and the promotion of peace. (Witness the social concern and pacifism of the Hutterites, Mennonites, Quakers, and Brethren.)

Identificational

The identificationalist stands in the tradition of Scripture which stresses the this-worldliness character of the Christian faith. Their Christ-model is the incarnate Lord, the One who through living in the world can identify with the struggles and tensions of life. Their ethos revolves around the Jesus who ate and drank with the "tax collectors and sinners," with the tension of Paul who, when he wanted to do right found that "evil lies close at hand." Their concern is to affirm the abundant life declared by Jesus and recognized by Paul who insisted that "all things are lawful." They wish to "render unto Caesar those things that are Caesar's," to uphold the state, to pray for kings and emperors, and to admonish slaves and servants to be obedient to their masters.

One of the earliest Christian thinkers to espouse an *identificational* model was Justin Martyr. A major concern of his was to show that God had not left Himself without a witness among the Greeks. Adapting the Greek concept of logos to the Johannine usage of Christ the Logos, Justin argued that all truth and beauty and goodness, etc., reflected in the life either of one person or a whole culture was in fact a revelation of the logos, the Christ-principle of truth and virtue. Consequently the goodness to be found in the Greek culture is a result of the Logos at work in Greek history. And this Logos, Justin argued, manifested Himself in the Incarnation, took on human flesh, and demonstrated before men the life of truth which we all are to emulate.

In our contemporary world an extreme version of the identificational model is espoused in secular theology and its concept of liberation. God, as Tillich describes him, is not a being who acts, but is being itself. This means that God is not a being who loves, who sets men free, who liberates the captives; rather God is love itself, freedom itself, liberation itself. This theology depersonalizes God, puts God within the process of life, and defines Him as life itself. So, wherever liberation—whether personal, political, social, or moral—is taking place, it is not God who is acting in the process to set men free, but it is the process itself that is God. God is love. God is liberation. God is freedom. The advantage of this view is that it compels us to become involved in the liberation of suppressed peoples. The disadvantage is that God ceases to be a real and personal God who acts. Instead He is the action.

Although these two models are widely separated metaphysically, it seems clear that the one controlling principle is the identification of man with the world because God in Christ identified with the world. This identificational model has produced an interesting variety of manifestations such as the icon model of Greek Orthodoxy, the synthesis model of medieval Catholicism, and the Christian realism of Luther. Even those expressions which deny Christian theism such as Gnosticism, Modernism, and so-called Christian secularism may be dubbed identificational. But they arise from completely different presuppositions than the theistic expressions, and in that sense cannot qualify as historically Christian.

For our purposes the Lutheran model is by far the most significant.[4] Mankind, according to Luther, is divided into those who belong to the kingdom of God and those who belong to the kingdom of the world. The *kingdom of this world* is earthy, and its function is to preserve life. It is the rule which God, through creation, has given to man, over everything that is earthly. Man is to function as God's steward over business and secular government, in marriage and the family, in education and art. In other words, man's rule in the kingdom of this world is his function as a creature of God over the total creation of God. On the other hand, *the kingdom of God* is the spiritual kingdom of Christ, His rule in the heart of the man justified by faith, and His rule in the life of the church.

Both of these kingdoms are under the sovereign rule of God. The kingdom of the world is under God by virtue of creation, and is to be ruled by the laws of creation and God's revealed moral law. In this kingdom, man is to rule by justice with retribution and punishment for evil. But the kingdom of God is under God by virtue of redemption. God rules in this kingdom through love and forgiveness mediated by His Spirit. At face value, then, everything in both kingdoms belongs to God. All of life is good and is to be enjoyed because God is the creator. Man is therefore free to enjoy the wealth of creation (not just possessions) because God has declared all things good and lawful for all men.

But Satan is the great spoiler. Because Satan has caused people to sin, people tend to worship the creature (or some aspect of the created order) rather than the Creator. Therefore, people misuse that which is good, and their misuse of that thing (not the thing itself) is evil. Thus wealth or abundance (which is and of itself is good), when made the central desire of a person's life, becomes that person's God and is therefore evil.

The Christian now living in the world finds himself/herself in an awkward tension between the culture of the kingdom of this world (which because of evil misuses God's good creation and mismanages God's government over this world) and the kingdom of God which has different standards such as love, forgiveness, and nonattachment to the goods of this world. Because the Christian has a dual existence, in the world and in Christ, this tension necessarily results in a compromise.

This tradition is, of course, much more metaphysically inclined than the separational. Thus it emphasizes the transcendent God who stands over against culture in judgment. Its view of persons is realistic, being neither pessimistic nor optimistic. A person is in constant tension between what is and what can be through Christ. This lends itself toward a highly individualistic view of the church. The church is made up of people who are struggling to live in the world as sheep among the wolves, participating in the world, yet not of the world. In heaven the believer standing before God is secure, but on earth the Christian is called to live life out in the constant tension of being a citizen of heaven and a citizen of the world. The Christian is both sinner and saint.

The social responsibility which emerges from Luther's view is largely individual. It tends to accept things as they are, to view culture under God's judgment, and to look to the eschatological kingdom as the answer to personal and collective ills.

Transformational

The transformationalist stands in the tradition of those Scriptures which emphasize the power of the gospel to change not only the life of an individual, but also to transform culture. Their Christ-model is the resurrected Christ who reigns in power and glory over the entire cosmos. Their ethos is based on the assertion that God was pleased to dwell in Christ "and through him to reconcile to himself all things, whether on earth or in heaven, making peace by the blood of his cross" (Col. 1:20). Their vision is like that of the prophets who make the demand that "justice roll down like waters, and righteousness like an everflowing stream" (Amos 5:24). Like Isaiah they see that "heaven is my throne and the earth is my footstool; what is the house which you would build for me, and what is the place of my rest? All these things my hand has made, and so all these things are mine, says the LORD" (Isa. 66:1-2). The Christian's responsibility on earth is to transform the world that "thy will be done, on earth as it is in heaven" (Matt. 6:10).

One of the earliest figures to espouse the transformational model was Augustine who, in his vision of society, saw two cities existing side by side, the city of man under a secular rule and the city of God under a sacred rule. Augustine saw Christ as the transformer of culture, as the One who redirects and regenerates the unfolding of culture. Augustine did not accept what is as what ought to be. He saw "what is" as a result of a corrupt and perverse nature. This result of sin was everywhere—in human nature and in the social sinfulness of mankind. But Christ, Augustine argued, had come to convert and redirect humanity, who, in turn, is called into culture to redirect, reshape, and transform the world to the glory of God.

In the modern world this transformational view has been espoused and carried on by the Calvinists,[5] particularly those who stand in the tradition of Kuyper and more recently Herman Dooyeweerd and his school of thought at the University of Amsterdam as well as the Institute for Christian Studies in Toronto.

Calvin, like Augustine, builds on the creation-sin-redemption triad. He goes back to the covenant of works between God and mankind in the garden. In this covenant, Adam and Eve had both a moral and a cultural responsibility. Morally they were to keep God's command not to eat of the tree of knowledge of good and evil. Culturally, they were to dress and keep the Garden, name the animals, and subdue the earth. In other words, they were given a cultural mandate to unfold culture under God. In obedience to God, humanity had the potential to develop a culture that in every way showed forth God's beauty and design in a truly religious civilization.

But because of sin, humanity became morally depraved, disobedient to God's will, and self-centered. Consequently, mankind unfolded culture in keeping with their sinful nature. Civilization was soon full of wickedness and sin, not only in the moral and personal sense, but also in a corporate sense. The order of the world became one of violence, greed, corruption, and injustice. Thus in the world persons hate and cheat each other, kings and governments rule without respect to fairness, equality, and justice. In other words, Satan rules in culture, because he rules in the hearts of people who unfold culture.

But in Jesus Christ a new order has broken into the world. A redemption, a release from the hold that Satan has over the heart has taken place. Satan is no longer Lord and master; Christ is now the Lord over all of life. This lordship of Christ extends over the moral, spiritual, and cultural life of mankind. Believers now have a new awareness of their cultural responsibility; they are to unfold culture according to God's design, which puts them in radical antithesis to the design of Satan. Thus, for Calvinists, they key word describing man's cultural responsibility is *conversion*. The Christian is called under God to convert, to change, to redirect the structures of life according to the design and plan of God.

The transformationalist emphasizes God's transcendence but not without an equal emphasis on His immanence, especially as it is related to His creational and providential activity in nature and history. It stresses the lordship of Christ over the whole universe. Redemption is viewed in its cosmic dimension, having to do not only with the renewal of the individual, but the potential recreation of nature, history, and the whole of humanity as well. Therefore, the Christian is responsible to act in every aspect of life redemptively, that is, bringing to bear on *all* of life the recreating power of the risen and reigning Lord. Redeemed persons are to unfold culture according to the original intent of God, bringing glory to God in every sphere of life. All of life is religious; there is no dichotomy between nature and grace. Thus the transformationalist demands social action as part of the believer's witness to the redemption of the cosmos in Christ. The Christian is the agent of reconciliation, bringing reconciliation to bear on the structures of life which, having been unfolded in the wrong direction (sin), now need to be turned around and restructured in a Godward direction (according to the will of God).

A close examination of each of these models appears to suggest that a particular expression of Christianity in society and culture emerges in relation to culture itself. In other words, we have here a reappearance of the problem of contextualization. For example, the early church was almost exclusively separational in its approach to involvement in the Roman culture. It had to be. Roman culture was rooted in idolatry, and to participate in certain areas of government or trade, a compromise of Christian commitment was inevitable. This is why pre-evangelism in Hippolytus' time screened the *occupations* of the seekers so closely.

But secondly, when Christianity became a legitimate religion and the empire was at least nominally Christian, the church felt free to identify with society and to become a full participant in its administration and activities. However, after the fall of Rome when the barbarians invaded the empire, the motif of conversion became the most pertinent approach for the church to take toward culture.

Today the problem is intensified and made exceedingly complex by the pluralistic situation of society in almost every country of the world. In every city there are Christians who are separatists and witness through their withdrawal from culture; there are identificationalists who feel free to work within society in the "moral man and immoral society" tension, as Reinhold Niebuhr's book by the same title suggests.[6] On the other hand there are those who actively work for the transformation of society, the possession of society for Christ. Who is right? Is it possible that we need all three to show forth a more full and whole witness in today's world? Is it not possible that the approach is somewhat determined by the cultural context? If that is the case, can we then develop a theology of culture which will affirm all three approaches? This question may well define the evangelical agenda for future years.

AN AGENDA FOR AN EVANGELICAL VIEW OF THE CHURCH IN SOCIETY AND CULTURE

The above summary of the three models of Christ-and-culture demonstrate significant differences. Some will despair of this and, suggesting there is no common ground, will insist that each go his own way. Others will want to overlook differences and concentrate on the practical task of accomplishing social action as obedience to the teachings of Jesus. On the other hand, some feel our real task is *to find a common theological ground that will account for all three models of Christ and culture.* The latter option is the most challenging. It demands two things of evangelicals: first, the development of a consensus theological paradigm; second, an examination of the role of the church in the nation. We turn now to both of these issues.

A concensus theological paradigm

The common theological convictions which all evangelicals accept, and which are rooted in the Scriptures, the rule of faith, the Apostles Creed, and affirmed by the Reformational creeds, are creation, sin, and redemption. This is not the place for a full-blown theological treatment. Thus, let it be sufficient to offer the following theological convictions as common to the heritage of the entire church, and as such, the common ground out of which evangelical social concern emerges.

1. Creation
   a. God and creation:
      Rejecting all dualistic, deistic, and pantheistic notions of creation, we affirm creation ex nihilio and the subsequent implications that nature is good, history is guided by the providence of God, and the institutions of family and state as well as moral law are inherent within the structure of creation.
   b. Creation and man.
      Persons are created in the image of God. As rational and moral they are to act as responsible cultural beings. The unfolding of culture which is mankind's responsibility before God is a religious activity. All of life is religious and is to be lived out in obedience to the will of the Creator.
      Persons are also beings-in-history. They are neither a result of a biological accident, or a mere product of environment determined by ironclad rules of economics. Thus they have the responsibility to direct history toward the will of the Creator.
      Persons are also spiritual beings. Life is more than the material. It has a transcendent and ultimate value. Therefore, persons are endowed with a dignity that demands respect and consideration.

    c. Creation and eschatology.

The Scripture speaks of a "new creation," a new heaven and earth. This new creation is the eschatological creation, the kingdom of God where Christ will reign in glory, and will triumph over a creation released from the bondage of sin. History is purposefully moved toward the ultimate fulfillment of God's purposes which because of Christ's cosmic redemption will result in the "new creation."

2. Sin

    a. Sin and creation.

Sin is not something inherent within creation, nor is it the result of a creational activity in competition with God. Instead, evil as the possibility of moving in a direction away from God, is a necessary corrollary of freedom which God has given to His creatures.

    b. Man and sin.

Mankind chose to move in a direction away from God. This choice caused an alienation to occur toward God, in himself, toward nature, and in his relationship to his neighbor.

    c. Sin and culture.

Mankind began to unfold culture in a direction away from God, toward the idols of his own making. Because mankind has worshiped the creature rather than the Creator, God has turned them over to their bent, and they have produced a culture that in every way demonstrates an alienation from God, their neighbor, nature, and themselves.

    d. Sin and eschatology.

The kingdom of God points to a time when humanity will live in a culture where sin has been removed and Christ reigns as Lord over a perfect society.

3. Redemption.

    a. Redemption and creation.

The redemption of Jesus Christ affects the entire cosmos. Christ is not only the Creator and sustainer but also the reconciler of all things. Creation is subject to a new hope. The disintegrating effect of sin is reversed by redemption.

    b. Redemption and man.

Christ the second Adam has reversed the human situation. A healing of mankind's broken relationship with God has been made and a substantial healing of their alienation from themselves, from nature, and from their neighbor is available through faith in action. The Christian lives in *tension* between what is (in Adam) and what ought to be (in Christ).

c. Redemption and the church.

The church, as a redeemed community of people, is called to live now in this world according to kingdom principles. The church lives according to a new set of values under the authority of God's appointed ministers, instructed by the Word, and nourished by prayer and communion.

d. Redemption and the Holy Spirit.

The Holy Spirit who dwells in the believer, and is manifested especially in the church, guides the church in open freedom toward a Christian maturity in the gifts and fruit of the Spirit.

e. Redemption and eschatology.

The church as the redeemed community, points to that eschatological community, the new being of the new heavens and the new earth. As such it acts as the eschaton in the present, in its gifts of love demonstrated through the good works of the kingdom.

The above is an outline for a theology of social responsibility. The Christian as a redeemed cultural being has a reason for and an obligation to the created order. Wherever oppression, war, injustice, hate, greed, and other social and moral ills prevail, the created order still shows signs of its bondage to decay and death because of sin. But the Christian witness is calling to live and act redemptively in all structures of life, to bring to bear the release from sin and its oppressive effects in the totality of the life of man in the created order.

Now the question is whether or not this theology of social responsibility is broad enough to include the three models of Christian cultural consciousness that have emerged in history and are practiced by various evangelical groups. I am convinced that it is.[7]

In the first place, because of its biblically-based theology of creation, it recognizes the necessary *identification* of the Christian with God's world. This is not Satan's world, it is God's and, as such, it is the arena in which the Christian's redemptive activity is to take place. While it recognizes the sinful nature of humanity, it does not commit the error of identifying sin with physical nature or creatureliness. Sin is a matter of direction, unfolding culture in the wrong way. Furthermore, seeing redemption as a restoration of the creature's original direction, this theology realistically presents the Christian as participating in a culture dominated by an evil influence and called to restructure culture according to the kingdom of God. This is both a personal and cultural tension which results in creative social activity.

Secondly, the creation-sin-redemption theology recognizes the necessity of a *separational* stance. Because the Christian is redeemed and is called to live life both personally and communally by a new set of standards, the believer is, insofar as is possible, called to be separate from the gods that rule this world. The gods of materialism, sensualism, greed, war, hate, oppression, and injustice are no longer to rule the Christian. The believer belongs to the new community, and as a new being he is responsible to live by the standards of the kingdom within the old order.

Thirdly, this theology recognizes the validity of the *transformational* view. It affirms the new order in the midst of the old, calling the old into repentance and a turning away from the spirit of the Antichrist toward its renewal affected by the cosmic redemption of Christ. But it does not believe the kingdom comes by the efforts of people. Instead, it recognizes that redeemed persons are to influence culture, and may by their witness cause change in a given historical time and situation. Such a witness may result in more equitable economic patterns, more just laws, less oppression and dehumanization. But it is a *continual* struggle, a fight to the end until Christ comes in final victory over evil to establish His kingdom.

Because the identificational, separational, and transformational ways of being involved in society are all essential aspects of the Christian's total witness, it is necessary for evangelicals who stand in one tradition and not the other, to affirm each approach. We need each other, and the recognition of this fact will go a long way in creating an atmosphere where we can work together for the good of the society in which we are all involved. This argument is certainly illustrated in the current debate of the role of the church in the nation.

The church and the nation

The question of the relationship between church and culture is being raised in particular today in terms of the role of the church in the nation. This problem is especially acute in the Third World where the church exists in the midst of the revolutions of emerging nations. The strong sense of nationalism, the desire to restore authentic historical practices, to affirm selfhood and identity with a past that is being regained, creates an acute situation for the church. What is the relationship of the church to the restoration of primitive cultural practices? This question is such an exercising and difficult one to answer that the 1976 consultation of the theological commission of the World Evangelical Fellowship made it their object of special study in Basel in 1976. In the 1975 meeting Dr. Spurgeon White laid the groundwork for the 1976 conference in his paper "Selfhood and Identity in Relation to Church and Nation."[8] In this paper, he argues for four perspectives on the problem.

1. The authenticity of nationhood. The groupings of peoples into nations with boundaries is not contradictory to the biblical witness. Consequently the church needs to recognize that there is "nothing intrinsically evil" in the desire for selfhood and national identity and that her mission need not be hampered by a strong sense of nationhood.[9]

2. The church *in* the nation. Christians should recognize that they have a real responsibility toward the nation. The church is to render unto Caesar the things that are Caesar's. She is to be subject to the higher powers, both for conscience sake (Rom. 13:5) and for the Lord's sake (1 Peter 2:13).

3. The nation *and* the church. It has to be recognized that the presuppositions from which the state and the church function are opposite. The state generally operates out of some form of humanism, whereas the church is guided by theism and revelation. Therefore a separation between church and state is most desirable. Wherever the church has become involved in the affairs of the state, the "testimony and effectiveness" of the church has been weakened. In countries where the government tries to control the church or its witness "the only Christian option for the church is to continue ministry in obedience to her Lord and to that within the demands of the nation which does not contradict the revealed will of God."[10]

4. The church speaks to the nation. The church's role in the nation is prophetic. It pronounces judgment upon sin and calls the nation to repentance and faith. "While she works, on a human level within the framework of the laws of the nation in which she lives, her primary submission is to the head of the church whom she serves and for whom she speaks. The church speaks to the nations from the position of a servant, but her loyalty is to another king—the King of kings."[11]

The above points indicate that Dr. White recognizes the validity of applying the three models to the role of the church in the nation: That the church is *in* the nation is a recognition of the church's identification with the world; the nation *and* the church recognize that the church and the world function out of two antithetical presuppositions (separational); and the church as it *speaks* to the nation is a recognition of the church's rule in transforming the nation.

CONCLUSION

We have argued that the mission of the church goes beyond evangelism (bringing people into the church), and education (nurturing them in the church), to play a decisive role in the world. The role of the church in the world is first, to be the presence of the new creation and second, to bring about the new creation (insofar as is possible).

The activity of the church toward the world must take into consideration the basic theology of the church—creation, sin, and redemption. The church, then, acting according to the principle of the Incarnation, must be identified with the world, yet separate from her ideologies, always acting redemptively in the structure of life, bringing the world into closer conformity to the standards of God, the will of the Creator.

Notes

[1](Belmont: Nordland, 1974)

[2]See H. Richard Niebuhr, *Christ and Culture* (New York: Harper & Row, 1956). My classifications are a simplification of Niebuhr's models.

[3]For a brief introduction to the Anabaptist view see Robert Friedmann, *The Theology of the Anabaptists* (Scottdale: Herald Press, 1973), pp. 36 ff.; in addition see John Howard Yoder, *The Politics of Jesus* (Grand Rapids: Eerdmans, 1972) and Vernard Eller, *The Simple Life* (Grand Rapids: Eerdmans, 1973)

[4]See J. M. Porter (ed.), *Luther: Selected Political Writings* (Philadelphia: Fortress, 1974). See also Gerhard Ebeling, *Luther: An Introduction to His Thought* (Philadelphia: Fortress, 1972), ch. 11 & 12; and Paul Althaus, *The Ethics of Martin Luther* (Philadelphia: Fortress, 1972)

[5]See Henry Van Til, *The Calvinistic Concept of Culture* (Philadelphia: The Presbyterian & Reformed Publishing Co., 1959)

[6](New York: Scribners, 1932)

[7]See especially Lane T. Dennis, *A Reason for Hope* (Old Tappan: Revell, 1976). Dennis brings these three concerns together in a modern evangelical approach to the problem.

[8]See *Defending and Confirming the Gospel:* The Report of the 1975 Consultation of the Theological Commission of the World Evangelical Fellowship (New Delhi, India: WEF Theological Commission, 1975), pp. 50 ff.

[9]Ibid., p. 52

[10]Ibid., p. 54

[11]Ibid., p. 50

Section V
Bibliography for Further Reading

More has been written in the area of the mission of the church by modern evangelists than in any other area discussed in this book. What we will do therefore, is pick out the books which seem to be the most helpful. This approach runs the danger, of course, of bypassing some excellent books.

First for the issue of the relationship between evangelism and education read Robert C. Worley, *Preaching and Teaching in the Early Church* (Philadelphia: Westminster Press, 1967). He summarizes the material of Dodd as well as that of those who have taken issue with Dodd. As far as evangelism itself is concerned, nothing among evangelicals is more authoritative on current evangelical thought than the proceedings of the Lausanne International Congress on World Evangelism. These reports, papers, and addresses are all contained in *Let the Earth Hear His Voice*, edited by J. D. Douglas (Minneapolis: World Wide Publications, 1975). In addition read Michael Green, *Evangelism in the Early Church* (Grand Rapids: Eerdmans, 1970). This is a thorough work covering everything in quite some depth in a readable and most interesting style. A very helpful work for evangelism in the local church is *What's Gone Wrong with the Harvest?* by James F. Engel and H. Wilbert Norton (Grand Rapids: Zondervan, 1975). Another work which raises some critical questions is Peter Beyerhaus, *Missions: Which Way?* (Grand Rapids: Zondervan, 1971).

As far as education in the church is concerned read Gerard S. Slogan, *Shaping the Christian Message* (New York: Macmillan, 1958); for a good historical overview for New Testament education read *The Primitive Christian Catechism* by Philip Carrington (Cambridge: University Press, 1940). For an example of early church catechesis read volume 4 in the Library of Christian Classics, *Cyril of Jerusalem and Nemesuis of Emesa* edited by William Telfer (Philadelphia: Westminster Press, 1960). For a modern evangelical writer read Lawrence Richards, *A Theology of Christian Education* (Grand Rapids: Zondervan, 1975). For further reading in human development read Jean Piaget, *The Moral Judgment of the Child* (New York: Macmillan, 1965). For the application of these ideas to Christian education write to Dr. Donald M. Joy, Asbury Theological Seminary, SPO 004, Wilmore, Kentucky 40390. He has published a number of articles on the subject and has made them available in printed brochures.

There are numerous books on missions. You will want to read the material that deals with crosscultural communication. In addition to the material in *Let the Earth Hear His Voice*, there is Marvin Mayers, *Christian Confronts Culture* (Grand Rapids: Zondervan, 1974) and *Crucial Issues in Missions Tomorrow* by Donald McGavern (Chicago: Moody, 1972). You will also want to read the *Evangelical Missions Quarterly* and *Missiology*, both of which contain articles of continuing importance. Also, the articles in *Defending and Confirming the Gospel*, the report of the 1975 consultation of the theological commission of the World Evangelical Fellowship edited by Bruce J. Nicholls.

For the mission of the church in the world see Orlando E. Costas, *The Church and Its Mission: A Shattering Critique from the Third World* (Wheaton: Tyndale House, 1974). For the church in society, see Georges Florovsky, *Christianity and Culture* (Belmont: Nordland, 1974) as well as Richard Niebuhr's classic work *Christ and Culture* (New York: Harper & Row, 1951). *The Social Conscience of the Evangelical* by Sherwood Wirt (New York: Harper & Row, 1968) is helpful. Also, Richard Pierard, *The Unequal Yoke* (Philadelphia: Lippincott, 1970); Vernon Grounds, *Revolution and the Christian Faith* (Philadelphia: Lippincott, 1971); David Moberg, *The Great Reversal* (Philadelphia: Lippincott, 1972), and Francis Schaeffer, *The God Who is There* (Downers Grove: InterVarsity Press, 1968) are all very helpful.

SECTION VI

AN AGENDA
FOR SPIRITUALITY

Chapter 13

The Restoration
of Historic Spirituality

WHAT IS SPIRITUALITY?

For most people spirituality is a very personal thing, not to be judged by others. A meddler in such affairs is usually considered unspiritual, or at best lacking in the grace of common sense. Nevertheless, a few critical statements about our spirituality, or the lack of it, are in order as a means of becoming more spiritually sensitive to God's presence and His demands upon our lives.

There are two ways in which spiritual failure is evidenced. First, in what we sometimes *negate* and second, in what we sometimes *affirm*. The failure in negation occurs when the church, culture, and the mind are rejected; the failure of affirmation occurs when we insist on conformity to subcultural standards, overemphasize familiarity with God, and preach a success-oriented spirituality.

Failure of negation

One of the most crucial ways in which the Protestant break with the past is evidenced is through the loss of much of the spiritual resources of the church. For fifteen centuries prior to the Reformation a vast reservoir of spirituality had developed within the church. Hours of prayer, exercises of devotion, personal and corporate discipline, communal values and harmony with nature, were introduced to say nothing of schools of spirituality such as the monastic movements. These movements, which produced leaders like Bernard of Clairvaux (1090–1153) and Francis of Assisi (1182–1226), and the mystical movements which produced such figures as John Tauler

(1300–1361), John of Ruysbroeck (1293–1381) and Thomas a Kempis (1380-1471), were largely lost to the Protestant church. Unfortunately, when the Reformers attempted to rid the church of her bad habits of devotion such as the excessive emphasis on Mary, a preoccupation with the saints, the worship of relics, and devotion to the host, she failed to retain other positive approaches to spirituality which had always characterized the church.

In the second place, the gradual secularization of culture along with the retreat of Christianity from culture resulted in a spirituality of the closet. God was "up there" and "out there," a kind of causation figure. His relationship to the world was seen almost exclusively in terms of the "spiritual" as over against the "secular." God was to be found in church, in the Bible, in prayer, but not in the field, in the steel mill, in nature, or in history. Consequently, spirituality was gradually reduced to something that runs alongside of life, no longer the central dynamic force of life itself. For some, the spiritual life lost its connection to the activities of the day, to the values by which decisions are made in business and politics and became instead the "hour with God," a matter of the closet, shut away from life.

In the third place, in the last several hundred years Christianity has gradually retreated from the intellect into the heart. In the past the Revelation of God in Scripture has commanded the minds of His followers. Most of the great Christian thinkers never capitulated to the notion that the Christian faith was a matter only of the heart. But recently science and reason, philosophy and psychology, sociology and anthropology, based on a humanistic and not a theistic world view has taken over the minds of many people, even Christians. This has resulted in the creation of a cadre of Christians who live "with two caps." The one cap is worn in church or in the doing of "religious" things, the other in thinking or living in the world. Consequently, spirituality no longer connected to "thinking" has become for some an indefinable and contentless matter of the "heart," an experiential, emotional, and all too often romantic feeling.

Failure of affirmation

The second error of contemporary spirituality is expressed in what is often unthinkingly affirmed. First, there is the insistence on conformity to subcultural standards. The danger here is that spirituality, instead of being free to affirm what the Bible teaches and what the church has always affirmed, is reduced to legalism. The insistence that spirituality be measured by external standards reduces spirituality to a few easy rules. It's easy not to wear jewelry, to refrain from tobacco and alcohol, and to separate from definable "worldly" practices. While these rules may produce a well-trained "spiritual army," they often fail to bring a person into a deeper internalization of the spiritual life. Equally, such an externalization fails to help a person grow into a more holistic and integral relationship with all of life. If anything, legalistic spirituality tends to make a person fearful of these people who are not part of the subculture, it produces negative attitudes toward the world, and a lack of personal confidence in what is believed. In short, it reduces spiritual responsibility to readily defined limits, both in terms of what a person may do, and with whom a person may associate. This, in turn, helps to create an individualistic, personalistic spirituality which cannot come to grips with the expanded spiritual responsibilities of the Christian to culture and to thought.

Second, there is a spirituality which emphasizes an overfamiliarity with God. The recent emphasis on sensitivity, community, and getting to know each other, which certainly has its good qualities if developed within the limits of reason and common sense, has been carried too far in defining the Christian's relation to God. Suddenly, God is no longer "The Holy One of Israel"; He's just "of Israel." He is no longer the God of wrath and judgment, just our buddy, our pal, our friend. When you need "somebody to love you"—He's there. When lonely and down—He's there. If you need a friend, Jesus is always available. These notions, while they contain some truth, have been so overworked and oversentimentalized in evangelical music, poetry, and publications that they border on blasphemy. When a group of singers can gyrate all over the stage and croon sentimental mush about God the Father, God the Son, and God the Holy Spirit, and people clap and shout and stomp their feet, then surely our religion has been reduced to the lowest level of commercial entertainment. There is no majesty nor dignity left in our relationship to God. He is no longer the King before whom we bow, but the teenager we placate with vulgar language and cheap symbols. The end result of this kind of familiarity is not relevance, but a loss of the awe and respect due God.

Finally, a new success-oriented spirituality has recently entered front and center. It is now the age of "God likes to do things big and beautiful." "If you follow God," our religious hucksters tell us, "He'll make you healthy, wealthy, and wise." God is now the great psychiatrist who can cure every ill; the financial wizard who can bring money in for big churches. While God can do these things, the overemphasis on this "possibility thinking" may in some ways be a reflection of the "American dream" mentality. The emphasis, both in terms of an individual, and in a church, may fall on bigness, beauty, success. Spirituality then can be measured by beautiful buildings, large crowds, or 300 dollar suits, Cadillacs, and a beautiful home in the suburbs. "God does not want you to be poor, or weak, or sad; God wants you to be rich, strong, and happy." The danger is that of measuring spirituality in terms of the quantity of wealth, power, beauty, popularity, and acceptance. Consequently, Christianity is made attractive; it's the "in thing." The result may be an exchange of the true quality of spirituality as a life of humble service, which affirms real Christian values, for Western values dressed up to look Christian.

In summary, the root of the problem may be found in the failure to understand the implications of the Incarnation for spirituality. In Christ, both the divine and the human have come together affirming both the transcendence and immanence of God. He is "the Holy One of Israel." When His humanity is overemphasized a spirituality that concentrates almost exclusively on the Christian's relationship to the world emerges. When His divinity is overemphasized a spirituality which concentrates on the "other-worldly" develops. Surely, the point at which we must begin in restructuring a visible spirituality is with the Incarnation and the implications that "God made flesh" has on the spiritual life.

An incarnational understanding of spirituality

In the first place, an incarnational understanding of spirituality affirms that Christ is our spirituality. It is His life, death, and resurrection that makes us acceptable to God. We cannot love God with our whole heart, soul, and mind. But Christ can and has. We cannot love our neighbor as ourselves. But Christ can and has. It is Christ therefore who presents us to the Father, and it is because of Him and through Him and in Him that we are spiritual. But like the church, the Christian is *simul justus et peccator*. The Christian is a saint because Christ has done everything needed to be done to make the sinner acceptable to God. But the Christian is a sinner because God's work of grace in the sinner is not yet complete. The sinner must struggle with what it means to be in Christ and in the world. Thus, the Christian, even though redeemed, is subject to the limitations of creaturehood. Our best efforts to discipline ourselves toward response to Christ and maturity in the spirit are always thwarted and incomplete because we are incapable of Christian maturity in the fullest sense of the word until God's work of redemption has been fulfilled in the second coming of Christ. God is both beyond our grasp so that Paul can speak of "the glass darkly," and yet within our reach so that we can know "the fellowship of his sufferings." For this reason spirituality is something seldom "attained," but that which is always "sought for."

Secondly, the Incarnation compels us to recognize the fact that spirituality is a response to God in the church.

The church is His body, an essential dimension of His existence, the continuation of the Incarnation, the locale where the "other" is made "near." And here, in the church, are the visible and tangible communicators of His presence. For He is present to us in the ministry, in the Scriptures, in prayer, in preaching, in the sacraments, and in Christian living. This means that spirituality may take the specific form of a response to God through His presence in the church. Spirituality may take place through the loving work of service, the devotion of prayer, the attentive hearing and studying of the Word, the reaffirmation of baptismal vows, frequent participation in the communion, confession, unction for the sick, a Christian marriage and home, and virtuous living. It also means that spirituality is not merely the response of the individual, but that of the whole church. No one person (other than Christ) can fulfill all that it would take to "love God with our whole heart, soul and mind, and our neighbors as ourselves." But the whole church, of which we are a part, fulfills this more perfectly than any person, or subculture, or emphasis, or approach.

Third, the Incarnation clearly points to spirituality as a response to God in the world. Christianity affirms that the created order is dependent upon God for its existence. It rejects the deistic notion that God is absent from His creation; the Manichean notion that this world is not good; and the pantheistic notion that God is the world,

Instead, the Christian doctrines of creation and incarnation affirm that God is immanent within His world.

Spirituality, however, recognizes that there are two powers at work in history: the power of Satan and the power of Christ. It recognizes in the words of the Lausanne Covenant "that we are engaged in constant spiritual warfare with the principalities and powers of evil, who are seeking to overthrow the church and frustrate its task."[1] For this reason spirituality may take shape in the world. It may be expressed by the attempt to establish justice, feed the hungry, clothe the naked, heal the sick. It may concern itself with the disastrous effects of sin in the world, attempt to restore the ecological balance, resist war, fight greed, distribute the wealth, or bring reconciliation between people. In this struggle spirituality recognizes that it is not thereby bringing in the kingdom, but instead is acting out of love and obedience to Jesus Christ, caring for His creation, anticipating the return of Christ when the words of the disciples' prayer "thy kingdom come, they will be done on *earth* as it is in heaven," will become a reality.

I believe we have defined spirituality in a way that is consistent with the teaching of the Bible and the faith of the church. This view sets forth the basis from which a wide variety of approaches to spirituality have developed in the church. It is a perspective that allows us to be inclusive in our attitude toward the many responses God's people have made toward Him, and thus to learn and benefit from the struggle of the entire church to offer not only the "praise of her lips," but also the "praise of her deeds." We turn now to a brief examination of spirituality in the church.

SPIRITUALITY IN THE HISTORY OF THE CHURCH

The most striking feature of New Testament spirituality is its variety. While the response is always to Christ and in Christ, the shape of this response, or the way in which it is expressed, appears to vary from author to author. In general, two strands or broad emphases of spirituality appear to emerge—one stresses detachment from the world, the other stresses involvement in the world. These are not contradictory however, for no one writer stresses one to the exclusion of the other. Nevertheless the emphasis as a *distinctive* is clearly there. Two examples will suffice: Paul and Matthew.

First, Paul's central emphasis is around the death and resurrection of Christ. In this event something new happened. And Paul describes this in words that convey a contrast between the "old" and the "new" using such opposites as: flesh and spirit; law and grace; the present age and the age to come; but above all, the contrast between Adam and Christ. We were "in Adam," and we participated in the old man in the old humanity, in the old order. But now, because of faith in Christ, we are "in Christ"; we participate in a new humanity, in a new order. This new man has been "clothed with Christ," "walks in the Spirit," has Christ living "in" him, lives in the "body" of Christ, and is "adopted" into the family of God, to use only a few of the famous Pauline metaphors. Consequently this new person is no longer to be a "slave of sin" but a "slave of righteousness," a person who "puts off the old" and "puts on the new." These motifs lie at the heart of Pauline spirituality. They indicate the transfer of loyalty from one master to the other—complete and full identity that can be described in terms of death to the one and life to the other: "You have died, and your life is hid with Christ in God . . . Put to death therefore what is earthly in you . . . put on the new nature" (Col. 3:3,5,10).

It is not unfair to Paul to conclude that in his writings there is a strong emphasis on the "other worldly." This is not to say that Paul rejects the body or humanity or creation. It simply recognizes that Paul definitely leans toward spirituality as the denial of self, a mystical union with Christ, an ascetic approach to life.

Second, Matthew's spirituality is rooted in the Sermon on the Mount. Here is the "new" law, the one that fulfills and completes the old. It calls, as did the Old Testament law, for poverty of spirit, for mercy, for a desire for justice that *practices* the holiness of God. It is this spirit, this action, this approach to life that will issue forth in the knowledge of God and "peace." The active aspect of spirituality is clearly indicated in the sermon which takes up the commandments one after the other and stresses the necessity to go beyond a mere external act to the affirmation of a positive and active love—one that forgives and gives. The three essential practices of Jewish piety— almsgiving, prayer, and fasting—are urged on the believer. They are to be acts which come from the heart, not mere external acts done for show. Next, the trust in the providential care of God emphasizes the fact that trust in God, which begins in the inner self, must actualize itself in an exterior manner in every aspect of life. Unless it does, it is faith built on sand, not on the rock. Consequently, there are two ways between which we must choose. The one is easy, the other is hard and rugged and demanding. If we commit ourselves to the ascent, then everything must be left behind.

The clear and unmistakable emphasis of the Sermon on the Mount is an *active* spirituality—a spirituality that reflects the Jewish past, especially the emphasis of the prophets for creative love, for justice, and mercy.

Interestingly, in the history of the church the two differing emphases of Paul and Matthew have emerged in the *via negativa* (way of negation) and the *via positiva* (way of affirmation).

The *via negativa* has always affirmed the knowledge of God through some form of direct experience. Historically the way of negation has received more attention than the way of affirmation, partly because it provides a stark contrast to the ordinary way of life, and partly because it uses biblical language, especially that of Paul's to describe the experience. It is a way of knowing God that has always been impressed with the transcendence of God, His "otherness," His "hiddenness." For this reason it always emphasizes the need for an experience that is supranatural, an experience that transcends the mundane, the business as usual, the humdrum. Sometimes, in its most extreme forms, it is an experience that can be realized only through the annihilation of self or the rejection of reason . . . and that is its greatest danger.

On the other hand, the *via positiva* has always affirmed the knowledge and experience of God through an indirect means. Historically the way of affirmation has been less popular than the way of negation, partly because it demands greater attention to the spiritual significance of the mundane, the earthy, the usual, and partly because it requires action within the structures of life which is in many cases more difficult and more demanding than the more passive approach of negation.

The way of affirmation has always been impressed with the doctrine of creation and subsequent emphasis on the immanence of God in the existing order of creation as well as the ongoing creative activity of God in history. For this reason it has always emphasized the "form" of things, the "imagery" of God in creation. It is the way of the artist, the poet, the social, moral, and political activist. It affirms humanity, the structures of life, history, and beauty. It calls for an affirmation of God within life and looks for God in the here and now. For this reason, it has, in its most extreme forms, failed to recognize the biblical difference between God and creation. A good example being the current emphasis on ecumenical theology to identify the process of liberation as God Himself.

Putting aside the extremes, however, the church has always recognized the need for both affirmation and negation in the spiritual life of the individual as well as in the life of the church. No one has more adequately commented on the need for both than Charles Williams in *The Descent of the Dove:*

> Both methods, the affirmative way and the negative way, were to co-exist; one might almost say, to co-inhere, since each was to be the key of the other: in intellect as in emotions, in morals as in doctrine . . . no affirmation could be so complete as not to need definition, discipline, and refusal; no rejection so absolute as not to leave necessary (literally and metaphorically) beans and a wild beast's skin and a little water.[2]

In order to understand these two sides of spirituality more fully, we turn to some of the ways in which these approaches to spirituality evidenced themselves in the life of the church.

We gain an insight into the negative and the positive approach to spirituality in the early church in respect to preparation for baptism. The person is to "fast" and "renounce the devil and all his works" before entering into the waters. The way of affirmation is clearly seen in the testing of the new convert by the criterion of good works, "whether they have lived soberly, whether they have honoured the widows, whether they have visited the sick, whether they have been active in well-doing."[3] For the most part the early church maintained a good balance between a passive and active spirituality.

The first movement toward a strong emphasis on negation came from the neo-Platonic emphasis of the Alexandrian school, beginning in the third century. Here, the hermeneutic principle that Scripture reveals a "spiritual" sense, beyond its literal meaning, laid the foundation for viewing the literal and physical as less important than the mystical and spiritual. This resulted in an emphasis on the cultivation of the spiritual which found its way into Eastern monasticism seen particularly in the Anchorites, led by Anthony (250–356), who emphasized an individual asceticism; and the Cenobites, led by Pachomius (292–346) and St. Basil (330–379), who emphasized a communal monasticism.

The main emphasis of these monastics was to carry on an important tradition within the religious community that goes back into Judaism. Theirs was a *desert* spirituality. It was a movement into the most desolate and forsaken part of God's creation, where, in solitude, they entered into an intense battle with God's enemy, Satan. It was in the *desert* that Moses, Jeremiah, John the Baptist, and Jesus wrestled with temptation and were instructed by God. In a sense it is in the desert where one goes, not to flee the world, but to go into its very heart, where, in its center a victory over evil may be experienced. "The desert is," as John Meyendorff suggests in *St. Gregory Palamas and Orthodox Spirituality*, "the archetypal symbol of the world that is hostile to God, subject to Satan, the dead world to which the Messiah brought new life. And as his first coming was proclaimed by John the Baptist in the desert, so the Christian monks felt that their flight to the desert was an assault on the power of the Evil One, heralding the second coming."[4]

This is not to say that there were no excesses by the desert monks. In spending so much time alone, they failed to participate directly in the "building up of the body of Christ" in the world. They paid little attention to the mission of the church. They were not active in evangelism, teaching, or reshaping the foundations of culture. Instead, they were involved in prayer, continual and fervent prayer on behalf of the church.

In the meantime, after the legitimation of the Christian faith by Constantine, other Christians began to assume a role of public responsibility which they had previously shunned because of the emperor worship it required. Now their attention was drawn toward an effort to master the world, to bring into focus a spirituality which emphasized involvement in the structures of life and in the institutions of man. Augustine's *City of God*, which posited two cities, the city of God and the city of man existing side by side, set forth an affirmative spirituality in terms of the *creator* who by His providence controls history and moves it toward its end, according to His purposes. The struggle between these two cities is interpreted in view of the struggle between good and evil.

Ultimately the church was to view its task in the world as a call to convert the world, to realize the city of God here on earth. Spirituality therefore, extended to the activities of the believer in church, society, and culture. Every aspect of life belongs to God the creator, and is His by right of redemption as well. Therefore the church is called to redeem the structures of life, to Christianize the social order, to produce a culture which bears the stamp of its creator. But this approach to spirituality also carried its dangers. The temptation was to synthesize with culture, to accommodate to worldly materialistic goals, to lose sight of spiritual values, to fail to negate or confront the secularization of the church. As a result the late medieval church became a bureaucracy, burdened with the management of land, susceptible to corruption, hungry for power and wealth. She lost a sense of her spiritual mission and stood in drastic need of reform and renewal.

Protest movements grew up within the church to bear witness against a worldly and secular church. The monastic movements, particularly those inspired by the rule of Benedict, emphasized prayer and work. Here was a synthesis of humanity, discipline, and religion. Here was a movement that was both passive and active. They observed the hours of prayer, contemplation, meditation, and Scripture study, yet they were involved in the fields, in education, in preaching, and in works of charity. As David Knowles writes in *Christian Monasticism:*

> The monastic life is therefore, in the first place, an explicit and visible assertion of a way (not the only way) of moving towards a total acceptance of Christ's call, and as this requires a more than ordinary disentanglement from the attractions, distractions, desires and cares of this world in the scriptural sense of merely earthly considerations, the element of withdrawal and solitude is essential . . . St. Benedict saw the monastic life as others have seen the Christian life, as a warfare: "soldiering under a rule and an abbot," and this must be, normally, a lifelong service, with others, who in a special way, as brothers of a single family, are the "neighbors" towards whom the second commandment is directed.[5]

Monasticism sought for a balance between negation and affirmation and became a key factor not only in the reform of the church, but also in transmitting education, culture, and works of charity.

Mysticism emerged as another protest movement against a worldly church. It stands in the tradition of negation emphasizing the cultivation of an individual relation to God. It calls for an abandonment of self and a purging of sin and selfishness, as a means to probe through "the Divine Dark" to enter into an ecstatic union with the transcendent deity where a feeling and knowing of God takes place.

Mystical experience cannot be confined to the Medieval period, or to one or two writers, or to a single movement. It spans time and includes Augustine as well as Bernard, St. Francis, Meister Eckhart, John Tauler, and a number of Protestants since the Reformation. Mystical movements vary greatly depending on their orientation. Donald Bloesch in *The Crisis of Piety*[6] distinguishes between those mystics who go so far as to appropriate insights from Hinduism, Buddhism, and other oriental religions, and those who draw on the biblical tradition. Biblical mysticism is based on the doctrine of justification by free grace as opposed to those mysticisms which are based on the negation of self as a way of works-righteousness. At any rate, the significance of mystical movements in the church is that they often point to the need for a *personal* relationship to God. The way of affirmation sometimes stresses the "love of neighbor" to the neglect of the "love of God." While mysticism may often turn this around and overemphasize the "love of God," it is nevertheless an often-needed corrective in the church.

The Protestant reform movements were also involved in an attempt to bring a corrective into the spiritual life of the church. The popular piety of the late medieval church had corrupted true spirituality. It was characterized by the superstitious adoration of the host, the witch hunting of the Inquisition, the superficiality of visions, ignorant beliefs about the Bible, the materialism of relics, the subjectivism of devotion to the Sacred Heart, and moralistic and emotionalistic preaching which produced fear and anxiety.

In this context Luther, Calvin, and the Anabaptists stressed the need for individual faith, for confidence in the Bible, for a direct approach to God through Christ. But even among these leaders, there was a strong difference of opinion on how the spiritual life was actually fleshed out. All three groups affirmed the necessity of personal faith and trust in Christ. Both Luther and Calvin stressed the need for involvement in the world, but the Anabaptists stressed the negation of the world through communal withdrawal, refusal to participate in state functions, pacifism, and rigorous personal moral and spiritual discipline.

Again, Protestants in the seventeenth century became too "this worldly," too involved in the affairs of the state, too dependent on mere external forms, on rational and objective religion. In response, Spener and Francke spawned the Pietist movement which stressed the need to have a personal religion of the "heart," a religion of experience combined with good works. Again, in the eighteenth century in England, Wesley began a preaching movement to counteract the deadness of the Anglican church. This movement awakened faith in the hearts of thousands of people, restoring both an inner experience of the reality of God and the outward demonstration of good works in society and culture. Don Dayton in *Discovering an Evangelical Heritage*[7] and Earle Cairns in *Saints and Society*[8] have shown us that this evangelical movement produced a balanced spiritual emphasis, providing the world with Christians who brought together biblical negation and affirmation. The evangelicals of the nineteenth century had a strong and lively sense of being "in" Christ coupled with a fervent desire to act in the world as agents of reconciliation in the social order. They seemed to have a better grip on the relationship between creation and redemption, conversion and action, than popular evangelical Christianity of the twentieth century.

It is, of course, the regaining of this balanced sense of spirituality which is the agenda for evangelical spirituality. The recovery of both the negative and the affirmative, the transcendent and the immanent will come only as we regain a truly incarnational understanding of the faith not only in our perception of the church, in our worship, in our theology, in our mission, but also in our personal and collective spirituality. We turn now to the task of developing what is involved in the recovery of an incarnational spirituality.

AN AGENDA FOR EVANGELICAL SPIRITUALITY

Spirituality begins, not with experience nor with social action, but in Christ. In Him and in His death and resurrection offered up for the life of the world is the key to spirituality. Here transcendence and immanence are brought together. But we fail to grasp the total meaning of the Incarnation if we see it as the only means by which God's transcendence and immanence are made visible. The Incarnation is the *crucial* point in history in which all other realities of life find their true ground, meaning, and significance. A significance of the Incarnation is that, as the unique entrance of God into history, it serves as the focal point through which a holistic and sacred view of life is recognized.

The Incarnation breaks down those false distinctions between the spiritual and the material, the sacred and profane, the supernatural and the natural. Jesus Christ is both God *and* man in the fullest sense of the words, and when the totality of the church's christological creed is denied, we fall into the error of affirming the divine to the neglect of the human or the human to the neglect of the divine. The consequence is the failure to affirm, in a balanced way, the juxtaposition of the human and divine elements in our own quest to be spiritual people. We need to face these dangers as the negative element of an agenda for spirituality before we set forth some positive steps to take toward spirituality. We may call this failure forms of spirituality which deny the full implications of the Incarnation.

FORMS OF SPIRITUALITY WHICH DENY THE FULL IMPLICATIONS OF THE INCARNATION

There are four forms of spirituality which tend to deny the full implications of the Incarnation: 1) the offices and the spirit; 2) mysticism and reason; 3) dualism; and 4) monism.

The first problem may be defined as the spirit without the offices or the offices without the spirit. The problem of the spirit without the office is similar to the problem encountered by Paul in the Corinthian church. It is an emphasis on the spiritual gifts as though they exist apart from the appointed offices of ministry in the body. It arises out of the strong desire to affirm the mystical experience with Christ through ecstatic spontaneity, raptures, and sometimes abnormal demonstrations. In this sense it tends to deny the ministry structure of the church as the visible and tangible means through which, in an orderly way, the divine is communicated to man. On the other hand, the opposite extreme occurs when the institutional structures of the church are made ends in themselves, as though there is no need for the power of the Spirit to work through them.

Genuine spirituality in the church develops through the affirmation of both spirit and office. In the continued affirmation of the two, God is made real. Even as the Incarnation took place in human form, so the forms of apostles, prophets, teachers, workers of miracles, healers, helpers, administrators, speakers in various tongues (1 Cor. 12:28) are the visible and tangible means through which "all things

[are] done for edification" and all things are done "decently and in order" (1 Cor. 14:26,40). We need both form and freedom—*all* the forms of the New Testament, and *all* the freedom of the Spirit which is realized through those forms.

The second problem is the experience of mysticism without reason or an emphasis on reason without the presence of mystery. New Testament spirituality is beyond full comprehension and therefore mystical, but also within the realm of understanding and therefore reasonable. In the history of Christian spiritual experience one or the other of these elements often has been denied. This error may be seen today. The current experience-oriented approach practices a mystical approach to interpreting the Scripture. The "what does it say to you" approach can scarcely be corrected by informed and knowledgeable insights based on the grammatical-historical-theological method of interpretation without running headlong into the accusation of being "unspiritual." Often the interpretations of well-meant personal insights have to be regarded as sacrosanct simply because "it makes me feel good" or "it gives me a lift." Such a perversion of scriptural interpretation is a docetic hermeneutic which desperately needs the correction of the human insight of reason. God has endowed us with minds and given us the tools of reason. The rejection of the mind, whether it be by the layman in a home study-circle or a preacher in the pulpit, is a blasphemy against creation, a denial of the human in the Incarnation.

But the rejection of the mystical by those who overemphasize reason is equally blasphemous and irreverent to the Incarnation. Once Christian truth is grasped, the intellectual apprehension of it becomes personal only as we act on it and live by it. Furthermore, intellectuals need to be characterized by a humility which recognizes that what is known is not *fully* known. Paul knows the limitation of reason, the frailty of the human, and can speak therefore of seeing "through a glass darkly." We hold these truths in earthen vessels, and the failure to forget that is a denial of what it means to be human, to recognize the mysterious nature of even that which is known.

The third problem is dualism. The problem of dualism is expressed through the separation between the human and divine, the supernatural and the natural. In Christology this took the form of Nestorianism, where the two natures in Christ were so separated that it became necessary to speak almost in terms of the two persons of Jesus Christ. But the Chalcedonian definition insisted on *two* natures, *one* person. In spirituality, dualism emerges in the failure to keep body and soul together in our understanding of persons. Evangelism, as well as the approach taken toward growth in Christ, all too often cultivates the "soul" or the "spiritual" aspect of man. A truly biblical spirituality modeled on the Incarnation treats the whole person.

Spiritual growth is not divorced from ethics. Human values are spiritual values. All growth in love, justice, honesty, morality, wisdom, and knowledge is spiritual growth. Conversely the goals of wealth, power, autonomy, and recognition are the marks of an unspiritual person as much as immorality, impurity, evil desires, greed, anger, wrath, malice, slander, abusive speech, and lying. True spirituality does not cultivate habits of prayer, Bible reading, and witness, and at the same time disregard time, money, or neighbor. There is only one person—body and soul—and the refusal to regard persons as whole is a failure to recognize the full implication of Jesus Christ as fully God and fully man.

The fourth way the full implication of the Incarnation is denied is in monism. Monism is the Eutychian heresy. It refuses, like Eutychius, to recognize that there are *two* natures in the one person, and instead makes the mistake of affirming *one* nature, the divine. Eutychian spirituality makes the human divine. It fails to recognize the separation that is there between transcendence and immanence. To argue, for example, as do the Christian secularists, that history is God, and that the struggle for liberation is the process of God in history, is to fall into a Eutychian spirituality. It is the spirituality that says "my spirituality is expressed exclusively through setting the captives free, righting the wrongs of human society, establishing justice and equality." Such an attitude fails to recognize the difference between the human and divine.

The only hope for a truly biblical and historic evangelical spirituality is that we affirm the whole Christ, the whole incarnation, the human and the divine in our spirituality. We turn now to suggest some positive ways in which this can be accomplished.

POSITIVE STEPS TOWARD AN INCARNATIONAL SPIRITUALITY

First, spirituality cannot be divorced from the church, worship, theology, and mission. This may seem like a strange course to take toward spirituality, but in essence, what this means is that we cannot divorce spirituality from our life in the body of Christ. And since our life in the body includes being the church, participating in worship, thinking about truth, doing God's work, and living in the world, then everything discussed in this book belongs to spirituality.

One can hardly be spiritual if an involvement with the presence of Christ in the world through the church is neglected. We cannot negate the church as though it exists only in the mind of God, and we cannot affirm it as though the sum and substance is the local building or proper structure. Our spirituality will have to be fleshed out in that constant tension of being the church in mystical union with its head, Jesus Christ, and being the church in the humanity of her offices and in her structure of community. We can no longer say, "I don't need the church."

To be spiritual also means that we are to be involved in worship. Worship is the rehearsal of our relationship to God. It is that point in time when through the preaching of the Word and through the administration of the sacrament God makes Himself uniquely present in the body of Christ. Worship is not entertainment. We must restore the incarnational understanding of worship, i.e., that in worship the divine meets the human. God speaks to us in His Word. He comes to us in the sacrament. We respond in faith and go out to act on it!

Furthermore, to be spiritual means that we are to be involved in theology—not as theologians—but as Christians who are willing to *think* about truth. The incarnational approach to truth affirms that truth is beyond our comprehension, but within our grasp. To assume we know it all is not spiritual. To assume we know nothing is not spiritual. If we would be spiritual, we must learn to care about truth. We must learn to test our ideas and subjective notions by good exegesis and the traditions of the church.

In addition, to be spiritual means that we are to be involved in the mission of the church. All Christians are called to proclaim and to live by the gospel. To proclaim it is to stress the divine side; to live it is to stress the human side. True spirituality seeks to do both; it is not content to serve God only by the lips, but also to serve Him by deed.

By affirming that our whole life in the world belongs to God in and through the church, worship, theology, and mission is to recognize the total claim of Christ over our lives. It is to enter into His kingdom and to live under His reign.

Second, we should recognize that spiritual imbalance in one area sometimes necessitates a strong counteremphasis to provide a corrective. An examination of the current spiritual movements suggests that imbalance in the past necessitated the emergence of the charismatic movement as well as the emphasis on social involvement. For example, J. Rodman Williams, a well-known charismatic leader, in his work, *The Era of the Spirit*, says "He (God) may have seemed absent, distant, even non-existent to many of us before, but now His presence is vividly manifest. Suddenly, God is here not in the sense of a vague omnipresence but of a compelling presence."[9] Likewise Jim Wallis in *Agenda for Biblical People*, after describing his conversion experience, adds, "the call to costly discipleship wasn't raised that night, nor would I ever hear it sounded in the churches as I was growing up . . . the church people didn't care to do anything but justify themselves and the country they loved, the country that seemed uglier and uglier to me."[10] Both of these writers point to a lack which they and others felt in the spiritual life of the church. Their way of correcting the situation may be regarded by some as extreme, but it has had the advantage of calling attention to the need for the Spirit and the need for social action. And in doing so, these movements are making an impact on the church, awakening many to spiritual growth through the recovery of the Spirit and the place of social outreach in the church.

In history the church has seldom, if ever, achieved the desired balance. God has, for that reason, raised up movements to stress what is lacking in the church. The implication of this, we dare not deny, is that the whole church belongs to God, and not just part of it. We need to see the particular emphasis of our own subculture as well as that of others as a necessary and vital part of the whole. True spirituality is inclusive, not exclusive.

Third, we should draw on the spiritual resources of the entire Christian community. The primary source of spiritual reading is the Bible. But we must not in our love of Scripture avoid the mystics and the activists. Exposure to the great devotional literature of the church is essential. We can grow out of our ghetto mentality by reading the great works of the mystics. Consider such works as Augustine's *Confessions*, Bernard of Clairvaux's *The Steps of Humility*, the anonymous *Theologia Germanica, The Cloud of Unknowing*, as well as *The Imitation of Christ* by Thomas á Kempis, the writings of Meister Eckhart and John Tauler, the works of the Spanish mystics such as Teresa of Avila and John of the Cross, the writings of Protestant mystics like George Fox or William Law, the Russian spiritual literature of St. Theodosius, St. Sergius, and *The Way of a Pilgrim*, and the contemporary writings of Thomas Merton or Dag Hammarskjöld. All these writings and more belong to the church. To immerse ourselves in these works is to allow ourselves to be expanded by the great treasury of spirituality in the church.

We should likewise draw on the less abundant but equally important social writings of the church: Augustine's *City of God*, Thomas Aquinas' writings on church and society contained in his *Summa*, the *Social Gospel* by Rauschenbusch as well as *Moral Man and Immoral Society* by Reinhold Niebuhr, and *Christ and Culture* by his brother Richard Niebuhr are all enriching. These works belong to the church. We may not agree with everything in them, for, like works on theology, they were written for a special time and place. Nevertheless their value to the ongoing life of the church in the world is indispensable. Those who neglect these works do so to their own harm, and those who read them do so to their own inspiration and spiritual growth.

Fourth, we should cultivate the art of meditation. Meditation is not a contentless wandering of the mind, but a fixed attention on the object of faith, Jesus Christ, which increases our awareness of Him and His work for us. In turn this awareness creates an identification with Christ, a love for Him, and a desire to serve Him. The early church adopted the practice of Judaism: prayer three times a day at the third, the sixth, and the ninth hour. The prototype is Daniel. Of him we read, "and he got down upon his knees three times a day and prayed and gave thanks before his god" (Dan. 6:10).

Hippolytus in his work *The Apostolic Tradition*, provides a detailed picture of personal meditative prayer in the early church. It was the custom of Christians throughout the day to meditate on the successive phases of Christ's passion. At the third hour, Christians meditated on the suffering of Christ for "at that hour Christ was nailed to the tree."[11] Hippolytus compares Christ to the shewbread of the old covenant which was to be offered at the third hour and to the lamb that was slain. Christ, by contrast, is the living bread, and the Good Shepherd who gave His life for the sheep. At noonday, or the sixth hour, the Christian is to meditate on the last moments of Christ's life. *The Apostolic Tradition* has this to say:

> At the sixth hour likewise pray also, for, after Christ was nailed to the wood of the cross, the day was divided and there was a great darkness; wherefore let (the faithful) pray at that hour with an effectual prayer, likening themselves to the voice of him who prayed (and) caused all creation to become dark for the unbelieving Jew.[12]

The ninth hour is the moment of Christ's death. At this time the Christian is to make a "great thanksgiving" for His death marks the beginning of the Resurrection:

> At that hour therefore, Christ poured forth from His pierced side water and blood, and brought the rest of time of that day with light to the evening; so, when He fell asleep, by making the beginning of another day He completed the pattern of His resurrection.[13]

That a mere formal repetition of daily prayer may have little meaning is not disputable. On the other hand, a regular habit of prayer throughout the day (even it it is only in the mind owing to circumstances preventing a person from being alone) is a means for continual spiritual nourishment. Alexander Schmemann, commenting on the Christian approach to time which sees every hour of the day in respect to Jesus' death and resurrection, has this to say:

> And thus through that one day all days, all time were transformed into times of *remembrance* and expectation . . . all days, all hours were now referred to this *end* of all "natural" life, to the *beginning* of the new life.[14]

Fifth, there is a need to return to the practice of spiritual directors. The office of a spiritual director emerged within monasticism in the early church among the monks who needed the direction of a wise and mature person. The principle is already laid down in the personal relationship that existed between Paul and Timothy in New Testament times. Theologically the idea is grounded in the New Testament notion that the church is the body of Christ, that Christians are "members" of each other. It asserts that no one is a Christian alone. The church is a community of people committed to Christ and each other. And in this context growth occurs.

The office of a spiritual director is not an actual church office but a function in the body. A mature Christian assumes responsibility toward one or more other Christians and guides them through regular counsel into a disciplined growth in Christ. The ultimate task of a spiritual director is to help younger Christians find the will of God. In the process, the director may help the person develop disciplined habits of prayer and spiritual reading, may listen to the confession of sin, and may encourage and counsel the growing Christian in many areas of life and conduct.

CONCLUSION

We have argued for an incarnational view of spirituality which recognizes the validity of the divine and the human in our struggle to be a spiritual people. There is both a negative and a positive side to spirituality. Through the negative, we assert the necessity of rising above life to reach God through self-abandonment and quiet. In the positive, we meet God in the responsibility of life, in the process of history, in the issues of the day. One without the other is incomplete, although at times an individual or the church is called to lay greater stress on one than on the other.

We must learn, then, not to *have* a spirituality, something we turn on at a particular place or time, but to *be* spiritual, as a habit of life, a continuous state of being. It is to this end that we seek after God in the stillness and the hubbub of life, but always and everywhere in and through the church, where Christ is made present to us and, through us, to the world.

Notes

[1]See J. D. Douglas (ed.), *Let the Earth Hear His Voice* (Minneapolis: World Wide Publications, 1975), p. 7 (Art. 12)

[2](Grand Rapids: Eerdmans, 1965), p. 57

[3]See Burton Scott Easton, *The Apostolic Tradition of Hippolytus* (Hamden: Archon Books, 1962), p. 20

[4](St. Vladimir's Press, 1974), p. 14

[5](New York: McGraw, 1969), p. 229

[6](Grand Rapids: Eerdmans, 1968)

[7](New York: Harper & Row, 1976)

[8](Chicago: Moody, 1960)

[9](Plainfield: Logos, 1971), p. 10

[10](New York: Harper & Row, 1976), IX

[11]Hippolytus, *Apostolic Tradition*, p. 55 (IV, 36:3)

[12]Ibid. (IV, 36:4)

[13]Ibid. (IV, 36:6)

[14]*An Introduction to Liturgical Theology* (Crestwood: St. Vladimir's Press, 1966)

Section VI
Bibliography for Further Reading

For an introduction to spirituality I suggest Donald G. Bloesch, *The Crisis of Piety* (Grand Rapids: Eerdmans, 1968). Bloesch approaches the subject from a firm evangelical commitment and an excellent understanding and appreciation of the history of spirituality. An extraordinary work written by a thoroughly evangelical orthodox is *For the Life of the World* by Alexander Schmemann (St. Vladimir's Press, 1973). The work is the clearest application of an incarnation spirituality to the life of the church and the world that I have come across. And then, of course, A. W. Tozer, *The Divine Conquest* (New York: Revell, 1950), continues to be a favorite and a very helpful book written by an evangelical.

For the early church I suggest Louis Bouyer, *The Spirituality of the New Testament and the Fathers* (London: Burns and Oates, 1960). For the issue of the way of negation and the way of affirmation in the history of the church I suggest *The Descent of the Dove* by Charles Williams (Grand Rapids: Eerdmans, 1965). This terse book offers a masterful interpretation of history. A helpful guide to Williams' view of negation and affirmation is Mary McDermott Shideler's work, *The Theology of Romantic Love* (Grand Rapids: Eerdmans, 1962).

If you are interested in a general introduction to spiritual literature you will find Georgia Harkness, *Mysticism: Its Meaning and Message* (New York: Abingdon, 1973) to be particularly helpful. The same is true of Evelyn Underhill, *The Mystics of the Church* (New York: Schocken Books, 1964). Both books provide excellent surveys into mystical movements and the major writings. For a more detailed study I suggest George Fedotov, *A Treasury of Russian Spirituality* (Belmont: Nordland, 1975). An interpretive work of orthodox spirituality is John Meyendorff, *St. Gregory Palamas and Orthodox Spirituality* (St. Vladimir's Press, 1974).

For an activist spirituality I suggest the writings of contemporary evangelicals in this area. You will find Vernard Eller's work, *The Simple Life* (Grand Rapids: Eerdmans, 1973) to be particularly helpful in setting forth the general biblical idea of simplicity. Dave and Neta Jackson, *Living Together in a World Falling Apart* (Carol Stream: Creation House, 1974) tell you how it's done from a practical point of view. A strong creational approach is found in *Pro-Existence* by Udo Middelmann (Downers Grove: InterVarsity Press, 1974). Another work on the Christian in culture is Lane T. Dennis, *A Reason for Hope*

(Old Tappan: Revell, 1976). This work combines the practical and the theoretical in a historical perspective that is rarely found in evangelical works.

SECTION VII

CONCLUSION

Chapter 14

A Call for Christian Maturity:
A Summary of the Principles

What we have been urging in the call for Christian maturity is indeed far reaching and all-pervasive. It touches on the whole of evangelical existence in the world and reaches out for a thorough-going renewal in the life of the entire community.

It would be a mistake, however, to assume that these changes can occur only as the result of traditional exterior practices. To think, for example, that we only need to be more ecumenical, or restore a more frequent use of the sacrament, or recognize theology as human thinking about truth, or practice a more world-oriented mission, or restore spiritual readings from the fathers, would be misleading indeed. For, what we are calling for is not only the restoration of external observance, but a recovery of the *inner spirit* which gave rise to the beliefs and practices which exteriorized the inner reality. We are arguing the fact that there is a correspondence between the experience of the church and the exterior shape which is given to that experience.

Our concern has been to recover the interior reality of the spirit which gave shape to the forms of early Christianity. The basis of that interior reality, as we have seen, is the incarnation—God in Christ . . . Christ in the church. The church, in her worship, her theology, her mission, and her spirituality, is to incarnate Jesus Christ in visible form. The question then is: "What kind of Christ have we incarnated?" When an outsider looks at the life of our church, or our own life for that matter, what image of Christ do we bear? What is seen behind the external form?

The call, then, for popular evangelicalism, is to recover the biblical Christ in all His fullness. For He is the One who, having been internalized by the early church, gave an incarnate shape to the external form of the early church, to her worship, to her theology, to her mission, and to her spirituality. It is with this in mind that we offer the following summary of the principles of a call for Christian maturity:

1. Evangelical Christianity has much in common with historic Christianity. Nevertheless some of the beliefs and practices of popular evangelicalism represent a movement away from the reformational heritage and a digression from the historic Christian faith. Therefore if evangelicalism as a movement is going to be more representative of the historic faith, it must become more conscious not only of the cultural shape of certain aspects of its own faith, but also by way of contrast, to the aspects of the historic faith which it has forgotten. Examples of this problem may be drawn from popular evangelical views of the church, worship, theology, mission, and spirituality.

THE CHURCH

2. As we learn to take the broader view of the church implicit in the image "the people of God in Christ" more seriously, we will gradually see the barriers of our exclusivism break down. We will learn that God's people are found in every cultural expression of His church. And, in proportion to our more inclusive appreciation of the church, we will become increasingly interested in the pilgrimage of God's people in history.

3. When we learn more fully what it means to be the "new creation" we will become increasingly aware of the church as the visible society of God's people who are called to act as the presence of the future, the eschatological community of the world made new through Christ.

4. The new creation is concretized in the "fellowship in faith." The immediate focus of community for each Christian is the local body of believers. Beyond that, we must face the implications of our fellowship with the global community in faith, as well as to the church throughout history, and the departed saints who are now with Christ. In a mystical way we are members of the whole church, the living and the dead who

constitute the fellowship in faith.

5. Paul's reference to the church as "the body of Christ" is not a mere metaphor containing social and psychological value, but a statement about the humanity of that relationship which exists between Christ and the redeemed. From an incarnational perspective, the church is not a human organization, but a divine creation which, in a mystical, yet real way, co-inheres with the Son who is made present in and through her.

6. The church is one. Oneness belongs to her essence. Consequently there is a need to envision a unity which accepts pluriformity as a historical reality, one which seeks for unity in the midst of diversity.

7. The church is holy. Holiness belongs to Christ and is the eschatological goal of the church. Thus the church, like the sinner, is *simul justus et peccator*. The church is sinless before God, but sinful in the world. The church is divine, but also quite human.

8. The church is catholic. Catholic means to possess the whole truth, to stand continuous with the past to reject the spirit of sectarianism. The full catholicity of the church is shown more through the totality of her life, than in any particular cultural manifestation. Thus, we need to affirm our identity with the whole church, both past and present.

9. The church is apostolic. The apostolic witness is the constitutive basis of the church. Thus apostolic precedent is to be taken seriously, for the church is to be tested by it. The church, to be apostolic, ought to have within it all the charismatic gifts which were present in the primitive church, practiced within the body, as well as the spirit and practice of submission and service to each other in the body of Christ.

THE WORSHIP OF THE CHURCH

10. Primitive Christian worship, drawing from the Hebraic past, was oriented around the Word and the sacrament. Worship was a celebration, not only of the spoken word, but also the Word which had come in the flesh. Thus, liturgical action was shaped around the central conviction of the Christian faith and was a reenactment of the faith in which the entire congregation participated. We need to go beyond our program/audience ap-

proach to recapture the true meaning of worship as rehearsal in Word *and* sacrament.

11. Because early Christianity affirmed a holistic concept of reality, it continued to stand in the Hebraic conviction that we can see God through the material world, that material things may be signs and symbols of sacred realities. There is a need to recapture the aesthetic sense of worship in our buildings, in our forms, our music, and through other tangible means of communicating eternal realities, especially the sensible signs of bread and wine as body and blood.

12. There is a need to restore the Christian concept of time, especially as it relates to the restitution of the church year. Worshiping in respect to the Christian seasons (Advent, Epiphany, Lent, Easter, and Pentecost) will help us break down the unhealthy distinctions we have made between the secular and the sacred, and cause us to realize that all time belongs to the Lord who has created it, redeemed it, and will consummate it in His coming.

THE THEOLOGY OF THE CHURCH

13. In theology, we must learn to separate what the church believes, teaches, and confesses from the human systems of theology which persons have developed. The fact that these can be two very different things, and that contemporary evangelicals sometimes confuse their theology with what the church has always taught, underscores the necessity to recover the historic theology of the church.

14. The authoritative basis for Christian truth does not rest on a doctrine of verbal inerrancy, but apostolic tradition. The apostles received their knowledge from Christ and transmitted it to the church for safekeeping. This knowledge came first by way of oral tradition and was later committed to writing. Thus the apostolic witness represents the authoritative source of Christian teaching. For this reason the church has always had a high view of Scripture.

15. There is within Scripture an authoritative substance of Christian truth. This substance consists of the basic outline of the Christian message found in the early creeds, especially the "rule of faith," the baptismal creeds such as the old Roman

symbol, and the Apostles Creed. It derives from the preaching
and teaching of the apostles and has received universal acceptance in the church. It is the key to the interpretation of
Scripture.

16. We should come to grips with the fact that the Scriptures
belong to the church. The living church receives, guards,
passes on, and interprets the Scripture. Consequently the
modern individualistic approach to the interpretation of Scripture should give way to the authority of what the church has
always believed, taught, and passed down in history.

17. Theological interpretations of the truth are conditioned by
time, location, and culture. The interpretation of truth therefore is the ongoing activity of the church. The church is to be
always at work formulating her faith in such a way that she
remains faithful to the original deposit, yet communicates
within her own generation, geographical place, and cultural
condition.

THE MISSION OF THE CHURCH

18. The tendency to separate evangelism and education has had
disastrous effects on the mission of the church. Whenever
Christianity is preached without its historical content, it is
reduced to a social or psychological panacea, or worse yet, a
mere manipulation of the feelings, moving the individual into
contentless response. On the other hand, whenever the content
of Christianity is presented as factual or intellectual data without the accompanying call to commitment and change of life,
Christian education loses its power to form character in the
convert. Clearly evangelism and education must stand together. There must be content in preaching and proclamation
in teaching.

19. The evangelical understanding of mission is limited by the
failure to have a truly biblical understanding of history. This
failure is grounded in a simplistic theology which does not seem
to grasp the implication of creation, incarnation, and redemption to the mission of the church. Creation affirms that God not
only called the world into being, but that He is active in it
purposefully moving it toward a final destination. Incarnation
affirms that God entered into human history, became a part of

the struggle of life, and shared in what it means to be fully human. Redemption affirms that Christ died, not only for men, but also for the world. Consequently his death affects history, for it inaugurates a new humanity (the church), which, as a historical people, has a responsibility to the ongoing process of God in history through which, by God's providence, the world is being directed toward its final consummation in the second coming of Christ. The Creator has entered His creation to redeem it. Thus, the mission of the church is to participate redemptively in the process of history.

THE SPIRITUALITY OF THE CHURCH

20. Spirituality begins and ends in Christ. The incarnation of Christ constitutes the crucial point in history in which all other realities of life find their true ground, meaning, and significance. The significance of the incarnation is that, as the unique entrance of God into history, it serves as the focal point through which a holistic and sacred view of life is recognized. Jesus Christ is both God *and* man in the fullest sense of the words, and when the totality of the church's christological creed is denied, we fall into the error of affirming the divine to the neglect of the human or the human to the neglect of the divine. The consequence is the failure to affirm, in a balanced way, the juxtaposition of the human and divine elements in our own quest to be spiritual people.

CONCLUSION

21. What is needed now, is a theological corrective of such a nature that the evangelical church will be shed of her social, political, and cultural identification. We need a corrective which will allow Christ to emerge through the church's worship, theology, mission, and spirituality as the hope of the world.

APPENDIX

The Chicago Call

"The Chicago Call: An Appeal to Evangelicals" is a document that was put together by a representative group of evangelical leaders in May of 1977. It is included in this book for two reasons. First, the document was written after the manuscript for this book was complete, making it impossible to go back and insert sections of the document at places where it would have been appropriate. And second, because the document so clearly speaks to the same issues raised in *Common Roots*, it shows that there are many other evangelicals who share the same concerns about the need for content and substance in evangelical Christianity.

My thanks are due to the planning committee for allowing me to include "The Chicago Call" in this work.[1]

PROLOGUE:

In every age the Holy Spirit calls the church to examine its faithfulness to God's revelation in Scripture. We recognize with gratitude God's blessing through the evangelical resurgence in the church. Yet at such a time of growth we need to be especially sensitive to our weaknesses. We believe that today evangelicals are hindered from achieving full maturity by a reduction of the historic faith. There is, therefore, a pressing need to reflect upon the substance of the biblical and historic faith and to recover the fullness of

[1]For further expansion of the contents of "The Chicago Call," see Robert Webber and Donald Bloesch, *The Orthodox Evangelicals* (Nashville: Thomas Nelson Inc., 1978).

251

this heritage. Without presuming to address all our needs, we have identified eight of the themes to which we as evangelical Christians must give careful theological consideration.

A CALL TO HISTORIC ROOTS AND CONTINUITY:

We confess that we have often lost the fullness of our Christian heritage, too readily assuming that the Scriptures and the Spirit make us independent of the past. In so doing, we have become theologically shallow, spiritually weak, blind to the work of God in others and married to our cultures.

Therefore we call for a recovery of our full Christian heritage. Throughout the church's history there has existed an evangelical impulse to proclaim the saving, unmerited grace of Christ, and to reform the church according to the Scriptures. This impulse appears in the doctrines of the ecumenical councils, the piety of the early fathers, the Augustinian theology of grace, the zeal of the monastic reformers, the devotion of the practical mystics and the scholarly integrity of the Christian humanists. It flowers in the biblical fidelity of the Protestant Reformers and the ethical earnestness of the Radical Reformation. It continues in the efforts of the Puritans and Pietists to complete and perfect the Reformation. It is reaffirmed in the awakening movements of the 18th and 19th centuries which joined Lutheran, Reformed, Wesleyan and other evangelicals in an ecumenical effort to renew the church and to extend its mission in the proclamation and social demonstration of the Gospel. It is present at every point in the history of Christianity where the Gospel has come to expression through the operation of the Holy Spirit: in some of the strivings toward renewal in Eastern Orthodoxy and Roman Catholicism and in biblical insights in forms of Protestantism differing from our own. We dare not move beyond the biblical limits of the Gospel; but we cannot be fully evangelical without recognizing our need to learn from other times and movements concerning the whole meaning of that Gospel.

A CALL TO BIBLICAL FIDELITY:

We deplore our tendency toward individualistic interpretation of Scripture. This undercuts the objective character of biblical truth, and denies the guidance of the Holy Spirit among his people through the ages.

Therefore we affirm that the Bible is to be interpreted in keeping with the best insights of historical and literary study, under the guidance of the Holy Spirit, with respect for the historic understanding of the church.

We affirm that the Scriptures, as the infallible Word of God, are the basis of authority in the church. We acknowledge that God uses the Scriptures to judge and to purify his Body. The church, illumined and guided by the Holy Spirit, must in every age interpret, proclaim and live out the Scriptures.

A CALL TO CREEDAL IDENTITY:

We deplore two opposite excesses: a creedal church that merely recites a faith inherited from the past, and a creedless church that languishes in a doctrinal vacuum. We confess that as evangelicals we are not immune from these defects.

Therefore we affirm the need in our time for a confessing church that will boldly witness to its faith before the world, even under threat of persecution. In every age the church must state its faith over against heresy and paganism. What is needed is a vibrant confession that excludes as well as includes, and thereby aims to purify faith and practice. Confessional authority is limited by and derived from the authority of Scripture, which alone remains ultimately and permanently normative. Nevertheless, as the common insight of those who have been illumined by the Holy Spirit and seek to be the voice of the "holy catholic church," a confession should serve as a guide for the interpretation of Scripture.

We affirm the abiding value of the great ecumenical creeds and the Reformation confessions. Since such statements are historically and culturally conditioned, however, the church today needs to express its faith afresh, without defecting from the truths apprehended in the past. We need to articulate our witness against the idolatries and false ideologies of our day.

A CALL TO HOLISTIC SALVATION:

We deplore the tendency of evangelicals to understand salvation solely as an individual, spiritual and otherworldly matter to the neglect of the corporate, physical and this-worldly implication of God's saving activity.

Therefore we urge evangelicals to recapture a holistic view of salvation. The witness of Scripture is that because of sin our relationships with God, ourselves, others, and creation are broken. Through the atoning work of Christ on the cross, healing is possible for these broken relationships.

Wherever the church has been faithful to its calling, it has proclaimed personal salvation; it has been a channel of God's healing to those in physical and emotional need; it has sought justice for the oppressed and disinherited; and it has been a good steward of the natural world.

As evangelicals we acknowledge our frequent failure to reflect this holistic view of salvation. We therefore call the church to participate fully in God's saving activity through work and prayer, and to strive for justice and liberation for the oppressed, looking forward to the culmination of salvation in the new heaven and new earth to come.

A CALL TO SACRAMENTAL INTEGRITY:

We decry the poverty of sacramental understanding among evangelicals. This is largely due to the loss of our continuity with the teaching of many of the Fathers and Reformers and results in the deterioration of sacramental life in our churches. Also, the failure to appreciate the sacramental nature of God's activity in the world often leads us to disregard the sacredness of daily living.

Therefore we call evangelicals to awaken to the sacramental implications of creation and incarnation. For in these doctrines the historic church has affirmed that God's activity is manifested in a material way. We need to recognize that the grace of God is mediated through faith by the operation of the Holy Spirit in a notable way in the sacraments of baptism and the Lord's Supper. Here the church proclaims, celebrates and participates in the death and resurrection of Christ in such a way as to nourish her members throughout their lives in anticipation of the consummation of the kingdom. Also, we should remember our biblical designation as "living epistles," for here the sacramental character of the Christian's daily life is expressed.

A CALL TO SPIRITUALITY:

We suffer from a neglect of authentic spirituality on the one hand, and an excess of undisciplined spirituality on the other hand. We have too often pursued a superhuman religiosity rather than the biblical model of a true humanity released from bondage to sin and renewed by the Holy Spirit.

Therefore we call for a spirituality which grasps by faith the full content of Christ's redemptive work: freedom from the guilt and power of sin, and newness of life through the indwelling and outpouring of his Spirit. We affirm the centrality of the preaching of the Word of God as a primary means by which his Spirit works to renew the church in its corporate life as well as in the individual lives of believers. A true spirituality will call for identification with the suffering of the world as well as the cultivation of personal piety.

We need to rediscover the devotional resources of the whole church, including the evangelical traditions of Pietism and Puritanism. We call for an exploration of devotional practice in all traditions within the church in order to deepen our relationship both with Christ and with other Christians. Among these resources are such spiritual disciplines as prayer, meditation, silence, fasting, Bible study and spiritual diaries.

A CALL TO CHURCH AUTHORITY:

We deplore our disobedience to the Lordship of Christ as expressed through authority in his church. This has promoted a spirit of autonomy in persons and groups resulting in isolationism and competitiveness, even anarchy, within the body of Christ. We regret that in the absence of godly authority, there have arisen legalistic, domineering leaders on the one hand and indifference to church discipline on the other.

Therefore we affirm that all Christians are to be in practical submission to one another and to designated leaders in a church under the Lordship of Christ. The church, as the people of God, is called to be the visible presence of Christ in the world. Every Christian is called to active priesthood in worship and service through exercising spiritual gifts and ministries. In the church we are in vital union both with Christ and with one another. This calls for community with deep involvement and mutual commitment of time, energy and possessions. Further, church discipline, biblically based and under the direction of the Holy Spirit, is essential to the well-being and ministry of God's people. Moreover, we encourage all Christian organizations to conduct their activities with genuine accountability to the whole church.

A CALL TO CHURCH UNITY:

We deplore the scandalous isolation and separation of Christians from one another. We believe such division is contrary to Christ's explicit desire for unity among his people and impedes the witness of the church in the world. Evangelicalism is too frequently characterized by an ahistorical, sectarian mentality. We fail to appropriate the catholicity of historic Christianity, as well as the breadth of the biblical revelation.

Therefore we call evangelicals to return to the ecumenical concern of the Reformers and the later movements of evangelical renewal. We must humbly and critically scrutinize our respective traditions, renounce sacred shibboleths, and recognize that God works within diverse historical streams. We must resist efforts promoting church union-at-any-cost, but we must also avoid mere spiritualized concepts of church unity. We are convinced that unity in Christ requires visible and concrete expressions. In this belief, we welcome the development of encounter and cooperation within Christ's church. While we seek to avoid doctrinal indifferentism and a false irenicism, we encourage evangelicals to cultivate increased discussion and cooperation, both within and without their respective traditions, earnestly seeking common areas of agreement and understanding.

LINCOLN CHRISTIAN COLLEGE AND SEMINARY

64984

269.2
W373

3 4711 00187 0791